TRANSITIONING STUDENTS INTO HIGHER EDUCATION

CW01563805

Transitioning Students into Higher Education focuses on the relationship between philosophy, pedagogy, and practice when designing programs, units or courses for transitioning students to new educational spaces in the university environment. The term 'transition' is used to describe the academic as well as social movement and acculturation of students into new higher educational spaces.

This book offers both theoretical perspectives and real-world practical examples that reveal the successes and challenges of implementing philosophically driven pedagogies with diverse transitioning cohorts. Drawing on examples from Australia, New Zealand, US, and Canada, it writes through the relationship between philosophy, pedagogy, and how it can effectively shape the practice of transition and develop the flourishing student. This book is split into three main subthemes: Flourishing in Transition, Engaging Diverse Cohorts and Challenges for Educators, and sits at the intersections between philosophy and pedagogy in the practice of effectively engaging and transitioning different enabling groups.

This book will be of great interest to researchers and educators working with culturally diverse cohorts in the fields of enabling or bridging education, higher education and distance learning.

Dr Angela Jones is a lecturer in Access Pathways at Murdoch University, Western Australia. She is the chief curriculum designer and unit coordinator of the FlexiTrack pre-university enabling program. Her current research projects focus on enabling education, learning communities and popular culture. She is a self-confessed EduPunk.

Anita Olds is a lecturer and coordinator of the FlexiTrack High pre-university enabling program at Murdoch University, Western Australia. She brings to the enabling space 17 years of diverse teaching experience. Her research focus is on authentic and engaging enabling programs, holistic curriculum design and the emotional labour demands on enabling educators.

Dr Joanne G. Lisciandro is a lecturer and coordinator of the OnTrack pre-university enabling program at Murdoch University, Western Australia. Her current research interests focus on best practice in enabling education, and understanding the mechanisms that support retention, success and achievement of non-traditional students in their transition to university.

TRANSITIONING STUDENTS INTO HIGHER EDUCATION

Philosophy, Pedagogy and Practice

Edited by Angela Jones, Anita Olds and Joanne G. Lisciandro

Routledge
Taylor & Francis Group

LONDON AND NEW YORK

First published 2020
by Routledge
2 Park Square, Milton Park, Abingdon, Oxon OX14 4RN

and by Routledge
52 Vanderbilt Avenue, New York, NY 10017

Routledge is an imprint of the Taylor & Francis Group, an informa business

British Library Cataloguing-in-Publication Data
A catalogue record for this book is available from the British Library

Library of Congress Cataloging-in-Publication Data
A catalog record has been requested for this book

ISBN: 978-0-367-23337-2 (hbk)
ISBN: 978-0-367-23341-9 (pbk)
ISBN: 978-0-429-27935-5 (ebk)

Typeset in Bembo
by Taylor & Francis Books

Printed in the United Kingdom
by Henry Ling Limited

CONTENTS

ILLUSTRATIONS

Figures

Tables

FOREWORD

I am delighted to write the foreword for this manuscript, which is a carefully and thoughtfully curated collection of purposeful research-informed ideas and evidence-based practice. Personally, I am pleased to contribute these words because I believe deeply in and have experienced the transformative power of higher education, which is the collective thesis of the editors and authors of this book and their contributions.

Many years ago, I was someone who was academically capable, but not from the social group that defined my university-bound peers. As this book attests and has as its mission to address, powerful messages sent by dominant social and cultural groups have real and sustained negative effects on who participates in higher education. Sadly, and unfairly for some, this impact can extend to successive generations. More than a decade passed before I gained the confidence to believe that 'people like me' could attend university. Others could see this, but it was some time before I really understood that I was as capable of success at university as those around me. Ultimately, however, my experiences of not-going and then going and being successful, has been a beacon for my academic career. Bookending my early experiences, during the last decade and more, I have been fortunate to have been able to harness my lived experiences and knowledge to establish conditions in which marginalised and non-dominant 'others' are provided with the best opportunity to succeed; the beacon shines brightly for them.

Emeritus Professor Denise Bradley and her colleagues seemed to be speaking about my experiences when they emphatically and so eloquently stated:

> Higher education can transform the lives of individuals and through them their communities and the nation by engendering a love of learning for its own sake and a passion for intellectual discovery.[1]

If transforming lives, empowering communities, embracing learning and valuing intellectual effort, is the real purpose of a higher education, and I firmly believe it is, then the philosophies, pedagogies and practices set out in this book provide the theoretical underpinnings, insights and practical examples for shaping how we transition diverse cohorts into higher education for the future benefit of us all, our families, communities and countries. The authors have worked hard to bring this collection of writing together in an elegant and coherent way that contains actionable insights.

The philosophies of social justice, emancipation, and flourishing explored in one of the early chapters provides a useful foundation, not only for enabling education pedagogies and practice but for framing learning, teaching, and the student experience in higher education more broadly. These philosophies are exemplified in the chapters that follow, which dive more deeply into the enabling effects of reflective practice and active learning. These chapters follow a well-informed narrative by one of the greatest champions of inclusive practice in post-secondary education, the estimable Professor Emeritus, Vincent Tinto. I've had the pleasure of conferring with Professor Tinto several times and as always, he provides some very reassuring arguments in his chapter. Demonstrating his well-honed communication skills and with great humility, he compellingly argues that universities are responsible for creating the conditions that promote students' motivation to learn, or in the language of the chapter that follows, that allow students to flourish. These environments promote confidence (self-efficacy) and competence (skills), engagement, relatedness, and belonging, and the relevance (value) of the curriculum. All students, irrespective of their backgrounds, would be well served by our institutions universally embracing his advice and implementing these conditions.

Following this theme, it is of great concern to me and many others, that students from non-western backgrounds not only remain under-represented in our western higher education systems, but they have poorer outcomes. As Gale[2] contends, Raewyn Connell "draws attention to the fact that the majority of social theory that informs higher education is from the perspective of the Eurocentric global north and fails to account for voices and knowledge from non-dominant peoples". Gale goes on to explain that "the term 'Southern Theory' represents Connell's attempt to acknowledge that a variety of knowledges and ways of knowing have been denied a voice in social theory and that they have their own contributions to make."

I am in no doubt that we need to increase our attention to these injustices, albeit of the past, and perpetuated to this day. The philosophies, pedagogies, and practices that are part of non-western knowledge systems need to be privileged in genuine ways, so that diverse knowledge systems are inculcated into western curriculum (and vice versa) to build understanding, cultural capability, and, importantly, respect for other (non-western) ways of knowing. Thus, I was heartened that the second section of this book contains a collection of works by Indigenous and non-Indigenous colleagues who have woven traditional knowledge systems into and around the western academy, and have provided examples of practice that seek novel ways to build the conditions that foster success for Tinto's "under-served" cohorts.

However, theorising alone or exploring what works in discrete examples of good practice in isolated subjects or courses of study, while informative, will not engender the scale of attitudinal or cultural change required; we need to influence the broad academy of teachers and teaching. The final section of this book begins to grapple with these topics and explores the pedagogies and practices that university teachers can deploy to militate against the structural conditions, dominant culture and political influences that prevent diverse cohorts of students accessing, engaging, succeeding and completing their higher education.

For all people to live fulfilling and prosperous lives as active and contributing members of civil society, there is much we can do from positions of influence to reach the ideal promoted by recognitive social justice. Together, we must consciously address the structural impediments that sustain a privileged status for those who are already north of Connell's Southern Theory. I look forward to a truly committed democratic society where all members are empowered through education to be self-determining. This book, like my beacon, paves the way. I commend it to you.

Professor Karen Nelson
Deputy Vice-Chancellor Academic
University of Southern Queensland

Notes

1 Bradley, D., Noonan, P., Nugent, H., & Scales, B. (2008). *Review of Australian Higher Education: Final Report*. Canberra: Australian Government
2 Gale, Trevor. (2009). Towards a southern theory of higher education. In *Preparing for tomorrow today: the first year experience as foundation*. Paper presented at First Year in Higher Education Conference 2009, Townsville, Queensland (pp.1–15). Brisbane, Qld: Queensland University of Technology.

PREFACE

This book was born from the editors' desires to deeply understand the connection between philosophy and pedagogy in their own practice. We wanted to share our understandings, and bring together other educators' experiences of transitional education to articulate the nuanced relationship between philosophy, pedagogy, and practice, and the richness of educational experiences when these three elements are rigorously aligned. With the ebbs and flows of the higher education sector, and as increasing proportions of non-traditional students arrive via alternative pathways, the time is ripe for a text such as this to be written.

ACKNOWLEDGEMENTS

We would like to acknowledge all of the authors that contributed to this manuscript, as well as our families, friends, and colleagues who supported us throughout this journey.

CONTRIBUTORS

Associate Professor Kathie Ardzejewska is the manager of the Learning and Teaching Office (LTO) at the University of Notre Dame Australia. She is currently presenting and writing about leadership in higher education's assessment and transition; and the intersection of social determinants and how these play out in the success and wellbeing for people on the margins.

Dr Fiona Beals currently works in a strategic position across two community polytechnics in New Zealand advising on delivery of programmes within industry and community. Outside of this role she leads a variety of programmes in social services including youth development. When she has the opportunity she is involved in teaching and research in critical youth studies.

Dr Rebecca Bennett is currently working in the Kulbardi Aboriginal Centre at Murdoch University. Her research in the Scholarship of Teaching and Learning (SoTL) is informed by her Cultural Studies disciplinary background. Current projects focus on social justice in higher education, including critical ethnographic studies of non-traditional student and academic experiences, inclusive pedagogies and innovative curriculum design.

Sian Bennett works at the Kulbardi Aboriginal Centre at Murdoch University, in a pre-university course for Indigenous students. Sian is enrolled in a PhD addressing issues of wellbeing for educationally disadvantaged students transitioning into university, drawing on her extensive experiences providing academic and pastoral support for Aboriginal and Equity students in tertiary education.

Dr Rosalie J. Bunn was an enabling educator for 21 years, teaching and coordinating Social Enquiry at the University of Newcastle, Australia. She has published on many aspects of enabling pedagogy and the effectiveness of non-traditional tertiary education. Her interest in social justice and equity has been a feature of her career and she continues to champion the cause of enabling students.

Dr Nicole Crawford is a lecturer in Pre-degree Programs at the University of Tasmania. She is passionate about inclusive teaching, learning and support. She has received several national research grants, and her interests include enabling education; student and staff mental wellbeing; and equity and inclusion in higher education.

Joanne Forrest has contributed in local, national and international contexts, specifically in the Indigenous education, EAL/D and English literacy fields. As a lecturer at Batchelor Institute of Indigenous Education since 2012, Joanne is constantly re-shaping a Both-Ways strength-based approach to teaching and learning, to prepare Indigenous learners for higher education studies.

Dr Peter Geerlings is a lecturer at Murdoch University, Western Australia. He grew up in a working-class suburb, was the first in his family to attend university, and has worked for several years as a consultant in student support and in interdisciplinary enabling programs for secondary school students, school-leavers and mature-age students.

Dr Michelle Gorzanelli is an academic developer in the Learning and Teaching Office (LTO) at the University of Notre Dame Australia. She is also a fellow of the Higher Education Academy and her research interests continue to focus on first-year experience, and the pedagogy of pre-service teacher education and schools in relation to Personal Development, Health, and Physical Education.

Dr Emma Hamilton is the convenor of the Open Foundation Online program and acting deputy director (domestic programs) of the English Language and Foundation Studies Centre at the University of Newcastle, Australia. Her current research projects concern online enabling education, widening higher education participation amongst adult learners living in rural and regional communities throughout Australia, and history-specific projects.

Dr Sarah Hattam, PhD, is a program director and lecturer at UniSA College. Sarah supports and leads a team of teaching focused academics to adopt and embrace enabling pedagogies. Sarah has extensive experience at teaching and curriculum development within the higher education sector and currently teaches courses on critical thinking and global sociology.

Dr Michelle M. Hogue is an Associate Professor and Coordinator of the First Nations' Transition Program (FNTP), at the University of Lethbridge. Her teaching and research focus on building bridges between Indigenous and Western ways of knowing and learning using culturally relevant, innovative methodological approaches that enable success with a focus on STEM.

Evonne Irwin is an associate lecturer: Humanities and Online Enabling Education and Acting Deputy Program Convenor of the Open Foundation Online program of the English Language and Foundation Studies Centre at the University of Newcastle, Australia. She is currently undertaking PhD research examining 'third space' professionals in higher education with a focus on the 'hidden' work of online learning and teaching.

Dr Lynn Jarvis has previously been the manager of Pre-degree Programs at the University of Tasmania. Her research interests include enabling education; the negotiation of risk; and equity and inclusion in higher education.

Dr Angela Jones is a lecturer in Access Pathways at Murdoch University, Western Australia. She is the chief curriculum designer and unit coordinator of the FlexiTrack pre-university enabling program. Her current research projects focus on enabling education, learning communities and popular culture. She is a self-confessed EduPunk.

Professor Sally Kift PFHEA FAAL is President, Australian Learning & Teaching Fellows. Until 2017, she was DVC (Academic) at James Cook University. Sally is a national Teaching Awardee, Senior Teaching Fellow and Discipline Scholar, Law. In 2017, she received an Australian University Career Achievement Award for her contribution to higher education.

Dr Joanne G. Lisciandro is a lecturer and coordinator of the OnTrack pre-university enabling program at Murdoch University in Western Australia. Her current research interests focus on best practice in enabling education, and an understanding of the mechanisms that support retention, success and achievement of non-traditional students in their transition to university.

Debra Monteith is an early career academic, working for social equity in education for 30 years. Her holistic, student-centred philosophy of education has continued to be informed and grow as a teacher, principal and as a staff member at Murdoch University where she currently works as a lecturer in Access Pathways.

Anita Olds is a lecturer in Access Pathways at Murdoch University, Western Australia. She brings to the enabling space 17 years of diverse teaching experience. Her research focus is on authentic and engaging enabling programs, holistic curriculum design and the emotional labour demands on enabling educators.

Arden Perrot is the personal development manager for the Hurricanes. Previously he was a senior academic at Wellington Institute of Technology, New Zealand. His research interests are Pasifika and Maori education, leadership, mentoring, coaching and youth development.

Jennifer Stokes is an award-winning educator, who specialises in digital media and enabling pedagogy. She coordinates courses in digital and information literacy at UniSA College (University of South Australia). Her doctorate explores enabling pedagogy, and she received a 2018 Australian Award for University Teaching citation for leadership in this area.

Emeritus Professor Vincent Tinto, a Distinguished University Professor at Syracuse University, has carried out research and has written extensively on student success in higher education. Dr Tinto received his BS from Fordham in Physics and Philosophy, his MS from Rensselaer Polytechnic Institute in Physics and Mathematics, and his PhD from the University of Chicago in Education and Sociology.

Dr Thomas Wanner is senior lecturer in the department of Anthropology and Development Studies at the University of Adelaide, South Australia. His research and teaching interests concentrate on the political economy of environment and development issues with a particular focus on international environmental governance, gender and development, and climate change adaptation.

Dr Sarah Wanner is senior lecturer in the Department of Transport, Emergency and Safety Science at the University of Central Queensland, South Australia. Her research and teaching interests concentrate on accident prevention and the use of accident models to determine failure; and the impact of aviation on environmental sustainability with a particular focus on biofuels and carbon offsets.

Dr Julie Willans is a senior lecturer in the School of Access Education at CQ University Australia. Her research background focuses on transformative learning theory and enabling education, strategies to enhance retention in enabling education, and the use of the Hero's Journey framework as a metaphor for learning.

1

PHILOSOPHY, PEDAGOGY AND PRACTICE IN TRANSITIONAL EDUCATION

An introduction

Dr Joanne G. Lisciandro, Anita Olds and Dr Angela Jones

John Dewey is considered a godfather of twentieth-century educational philosophy, and his musings remain relevant and applicable in the flux of today's global higher education economy. A firm believer in growth, Dewey's pedagogies were deeply rooted in philosophies that recognised the impact of culture on humans, especially in the realm of education. His work inspired contemporary understandings of social constructivism, student-centred and problem-based learning, all of which acknowledge the role of culture within them. Let's pause for a moment and reflect on Dewey's impact on historical and contemporary education; what would have happened if Dewey had not acknowledged the philosophical foundations for his pedagogies? And what if he had never shared them? As Garrison, Neubert, and Reich (2012) articulate:

> In the field of education, there is a tendency to think one can get by with a little theory and perhaps no philosophy of education at all. However, we all have a tacit theory of teaching and learning as well as a philosophy of education, whether or not we ever articulate it to others or ourselves.
>
> *(p. X)*

When we read Dewey and his contemporaries' work, it is explicit. It moves the theoretical into the practical and provides the reader with a rationale for their practice. However, these texts tend to focus on K to 12 education or higher education, and in the emerging field of transition education, examples are lacking. As more and more generations of non-traditional students hit physical and digital campuses, understanding the 'back story' of educational practice within the space of transition is paramount.

Intention and purpose

This monograph focuses on the relationship between philosophy, pedagogy, and practice when designing programs/units/courses for transitioning students to *new* spaces in higher education. It offers both theoretical perspectives and case studies that reveal the successes and challenges of using philosophically driven pedagogies with diverse transitioning cohorts. The explicit goal of this book is to encourage educator reflection on the philosophies that influence pedagogy and practice, to improve education in transitioning spaces, and to provide practical examples of how to make it happen. While other manuscripts have offered insight into the transitional space, such perspectives have been predominantly macro, focussed on implementation or changing of educational policy. This book journeys the reader into the minds and classrooms of educators as they theorise the space of transition across Australia, New Zealand, United States of America and Canada. Drawing on these examples, this manuscript writes through the relationship between philosophy (including the programs' philosophies, educators' philosophies, and cultural beliefs), pedagogy and how it can effectively shape practice in transitional education. While these chapters mainly focus on transition of domestic students to undergraduate or Bachelor level studies, it is worth noting that many of the principles explored and tips offered are transferrable to a wide range of other educational contexts including those that engage postgraduate and/or international students in transition.

A little context ...

The term 'transition' in the context of higher education is used to describe the academic as well as social movement and acculturation of students into new educational spaces. The process of transition to higher education begins in the pre-university educational context (for example, in high school, college, vocational education, sub-bachelor or alternative access pathways) with the building of aspiration and expectations for university study, and continues into the first months or even year(s) of university, with the development of a learner identity and acquisition of the capacity to "act autonomously as a university student" (Briggs, Clark, & Hall, 2012, p. 6). This liminal space is the bridge into higher education and "support is needed on both sides of the transition bridge to enable students to adjust to university" (Briggs et al., 2012, p. 6). Research shows that the transitional period is the time when the highest attrition and academic failure rates are recorded (Mills, Heyworth, Rosenwax, Carr, & Rosenberg, 2009). However, once progressing into second year, students are more likely to continue to completion (Hillman, 2005; Marks, 2007; McInnis, Hartley, Polesel, & Teese, 2000). Therefore, if we want to ensure positive outcomes for our students, we need to examine closely and critically the transitional education space and our influence over it as educators. As Tinto and Engstrom (2008) put it, "access without support is not opportunity".

Part of this is understanding the context in which universities operate, which is constantly evolving under the influence of political, economical, educational, and institutional processes (Bradley, Noonan, Nugent & Scales, 2008). Universities are no longer simply spaces for learning, they have also become businesses offering education as a commodity in a global marketplace; and students are not just learners they are now also clients. "Globally, neoliberalism in higher education policy reforms has been characteristic of capitalist societies, including Australia, since the 1980s" (Zajda, 2013, p. 234). Alongside government policies aligned with "market-oriented ideologies" (Zajda, 2013, p. 246) and designed to bolster the knowledge economy across developed countries, national policies with widening participation agendas that aim to create "*a fair chance for all*" have also emerged (DEET, 1990). In Australia, recent transformation and massification of higher education was prompted by the 2008 *Review of Higher Education* (Bradley et al., 2008) which set in motion targets for increasing and widening participation, particularly for under-represented groups. Following this review, a demand-driven system for government funding of university places was introduced, and substantial investments made to support identified equity groups including provision of alternative pathways to access university (Harvey, Burnheim, & Brett, 2016). Similar trends and policy reforms have also emerged across Northern America, the United Kingdom, Europe, and Oceania (Brett & Pitman, 2018). This has led to enhanced uptake by students and a diversifying demographic profile of incoming cohorts. More students from disadvantaged, low socioeconomic and/or first-in-family backgrounds are coming to university than ever before. Importantly, the nature and needs of these incoming cohorts are not necessarily the same as the traditional, middle-class student typical of the former elite system of higher education (Trow, 2007) who had always envisioned university as a part of their future. Moreover, access to university is simply not enough to ensure successful participation and completion. An understanding of the factors within our control for delivering the best possible outcomes for these diverse transitioning cohorts, within the current neoliberal climate, is of paramount importance to educators, universities, and governments alike.

A major emphasis of this monograph is on transition in the context of alternative access or pathway programs. As localised responses to contextual factors and global trends shaping higher education, these pre-degree programs have become a key widening participation and university recruitment strategy across many English-speaking countries (Agosti & Bernat, 2018; Brett & Pitman, 2018). In Australia, these are generally known as enabling programs (NAEEA, 2019), and defined by the government as "a course of instruction provided to a person for the purpose of enabling the person to undertake a course leading to a higher education award" (DotAG, 2003, p. 302). Apart from the rare long-running enabling program such as that offered by the University of Newcastle, enabling education has had a short history of rapid expansion in Australia following the 2008 Bradley Review. In 2017, the number of students commencing enabling courses nationally was 23,933 compared with only 7796 in 2007 (Australian Government, 2018). Further, national audits identified that across 27 Australian universities, there were 35 enabling programs offered in 2013 (Hodges et al., 2013), with that number rising to at least 48 more recently (McKay et al., 2018). An equity strategy turned mainstream marketing strategy, there is no doubt that enabling programs are becoming less 'alternative' or 'non-traditional' and more normalised as a "legitimate pathway" to university in Australia (Hodges et al., 2013).

Enabling programs in Australia share many similarities with 'access programmes'[1] in the United Kingdom, which have had a longer and more established history, and differ in that they tend to lead to a qualification in their own right (QAA, 2019; SWAP, 2019). 'Bridging or foundation programmes' in New Zealand (Trewartha, 2008), and 'developmental education' in the United States (NCDE, 2019), are also similar to Australia's enabling education sector, but delivered through different types of institution. In "nations with a colonial past such as Canada and New Zealand", pathway programs are considered of particular importance for servicing students "from First Nation or Indigenous populations" (Brett & Pitman, 2018, pp. 39–40). Notably, while the overarching goals are generically similar in aiming to "prepare students for the rigours of university" (Taylor, van Eyk, & Syme, 2018), differences exist in university pathway program offerings both within and between these countries in the duration, content, structure, modes of delivery, and types of institutions that deliver them, as they attempt to meet the specific needs of the local communities in which they serve (Agosti & Bernat, 2018).

Philosophy, pedagogy and practice

The philosophy of education is a highly complex and contested (Davids, 2018) area of research. Volumes have been written on the topic and further work on this topic alone would likely not end the contention. Bailey (2010) argues that the very meaning of philosophy is not agreed upon. Educational philosophy offers an attempt to capture the "unique purposes, concepts, learner roles and instructional methods" (Coello & Casanas, 2004, p. 385), and can describe many aspects of the teaching (Lal & Ebrary, 2006). Most poignantly educational philosophies provide "a holistic conception of people making and world-making" (Freeman-Moir, 2014, p. 118). It is recognised that the authors in this book possess different knowledges and come from a range of disciplines, and that this tints the individual interpretations of "philosophy" and indeed the particular approaches to each chapter. Some chapters in this book refer in more depth to particular educational philosophies. For example, emancipatory philosophies and philosophies of flourishing are reoccurring themes in this space, possibly because they are so well aligned with the purposes of widening participation. Upon encountering any educational philosophies that resound, we encourage the reader to explore beyond our conceptualisations. For the context of this book, however, we ask that the word philosophy be understood in a broader sense, as an attitude that acts as a guiding principle for behaviour, or as a form of intellectual inquiry (Carr, 2004). Here we invite a philosophical imagination (Carr, 2004) to guide reflection.

There is much to be gained from making explicit the philosophies and pedagogies that drive our practice. Our own beliefs surrounding the purpose of education can greatly shape not only our curriculum design but the way in which we relate to students. Reflecting on educational philosophies allows one to examine which educational values are promoted and which are marginalised (Carr, 2004).

Furthermore, Carr (2004) argues that there are those that focus on educational philosophy, yet fail to let it influence practice, and on the opposing side, those that focus on practice yet lack philosophical rigour. Articulating and making explicit these values and beliefs, and how they influence our choice of pedagogy and in turn practice, can guide more conscious choices when creating appropriate learning experiences for students in transition.

Yet, how can we make these sometimes covert parts of our work more overt? We offer an iceberg analogy for seeing the interconnectedness. The tip of the iceberg, seen above the water, is practice, the daily activities an educator engages in to enhance learning. During our development as educators we receive training and accumulate theoretical concepts that guide us in choosing these learning activities. This accumulation, located just beneath the surface of an iceberg, can be conceived of as pedagogy. The deeply submerged parts of an iceberg, formed not only through educational training but also from life experience, are our beliefs, values, and attitudes *about* education. These can be considered our underpinning philosophies. It is this third layer that truly influences practice. Zinn (2004) similarly asserts that our life beliefs lay the foundation of our educational philosophies. It is our philosophical lens that leads us to either claim or discard certain pedagogies. For example, if I believe my job as an educator is to impart only academic skills, then I will ignore any pedagogy the extols the virtue of holistic education and will likely focus only on activities that build academic literacies. We will struggle to implement anything that is in discord to our educational philosophies.

The term pedagogy is often associated with ideas of training and discipline (Hinchliffe, 2000) and provides justification for the inclusion for certain learning activities. It refers to the contents of teaching through a human-specific social learning system (Gergely, Egyed, & Király, 2007). In this context, we offer that pedagogy be understood as a set of theories that guide practice, and practice is understood as the series of processes and activities implemented in a learning environment. It is useful to mention that a number of teaching and learning pedagogies specific to undergraduate transitional spaces have been recognised in the field for their merit and influence on practice. Kift, Nelson, and Clarke (2010) proposed that an institutional wide pedagogical approach was necessary to facilitate effective student transition. In their "third generation approach" to the first-year experience, they argued that certain curriculum principles must be cross-institutional in order to achieve a holistic, student focused education experience. We further adapted the third-generation model into an enabling transition pedagogy specifically for enabling students (Jones, Olds, & Lisciandro, 2016). Lane and Sharp (2014) further offered that specific pedagogies need to be employed to enable students to enter first year with confidence. These pedagogies were not just centred on academic learning principles such as explicit instruction but also considered student supports such as counselling and mentoring. They further argued that implementing these pedagogies required significant contribution from leadership, but also from the teaching and learning staff, the community and the students themselves. Students required a "student-centred philosophy with an emphasis on principles and practices that help build a sense of belonging and community" (Lane & Sharp, 2014, p. 70). Finally, the University of

Newcastle published a report that detailed the ethos, values, and practices that constituted enabling pedagogies in their own enabling programs and proposed that enabling pedagogies are necessary across all areas of higher education. They further emphasised the importance of dialogical learning, pedagogies of care and valuing the existing knowledges of students (Bennett et al., 2017). The chapters within this book provides examples of how these recommended pedagogies are enacted in a range of higher education settings.

The journey starts here ...

Each chapter offers the reader a philosophical lens with which to view a snapshot of the transitional education paradigm. This text is split into three main themes that explore the intersections between philosophy and pedagogy in this sector, an innovative approach within the discussion of transition to higher education, especially in a time where widening participation is an international focus. This three-part journey commences by pondering what flourishing looks like in the transitional space. We continue this discussion by turning our attention to diversity – diverse cohorts, diverse curriculum and diverse practice – highlighting the rich pedagogical tapestry found within enabling education. The final destination of this book is to locate the reader in the present and share the very real political, cultural and social challenges faced by educators. This is not only in terms of macro pressures such as neoliberalism and widening participation but also the micro pressures that challenge academic and student identity. The ultimate goal of these pages is to reveal that when pedagogy is visioned through a philosophical lens it can shapeshift, challenge and ignite the transitional educational space, giving deeply transformative experiences to students and the educator.

Note

1   The spelling of the word "programmes" is interchanged with "programs" throughout this monograph, in order to accurately represent the correct spelling of branded or trademarked names of educational programs and/or to reflect convention in different locales/contexts.

References

Agosti, C. I., & Bernat, E. (2018). *University pathway programs: Local responses within a growing global trend*. Switzerland: Springer.

Australian Government. (2018). *Higher education statistics. Department of Education and Training*. Retrieved from https://www.education.gov.au/higher-education-statistics.

Bailey, R. (2010). *The philosophy of education: An introduction*. London: Bloomsbury Publishing.

Bennett, A., Motta, S., Hamilton, E., Burgess, C., Relf, B., Gray, K., ... Albright, J. (2017). *Enabling pedagogies: A participatory conceptual mapping of practices at the University of Newcastle, Australia*. Centre of Excellence for Equity in Higher Education. Retrieved from https://www.newcastle.edu.au/__data/assets/pdf_file/0005/462272/Enabling-Pedagogies-Research-Report.pdf.

Bradley, D., Noonan, P., Nugent, H., & Scales, B. (2008). *Review of higher education in Australia, final report*. Canberra: Australian Government.

Brett, M., & Pitman, T. (2018). Positioning pathways provision within global and national contexts. In C. I. Agosti & E. Bernat (Eds), *University pathway programs: Local responses within a growing global trend* (pp. 27–42). Switzerland: Springer.

Briggs, A. R. J., Clark, J., & Hall, I. (2012). Building bridges: Understanding student transition to university. *Quality in Higher Education*, 18(1), 3–21. doi:10.1080/13538322.2011.614468

Carr, W. (2004). Philosophy and education. *Journal of Philosophy of Education*, 38(1), 55–73. doi:10.1111/j.0309–8249.2004.00363.x.

Coello, H. M., & Casanas, J. A. (2004). Educational philosophies. *Radiologic Technology*, 75(5), 385–392.

Davids, N. (2018). Voices from the past and present. In P. Smeyers (Ed.), *International handbook of philosophy of education* (1st ed., pp. 11–15). New York: Springer.

DEET (1990). *A fair chance for all: National and institutional planning for equity in higher education*. Canberra: Department of Education Employment and Training (DEET), Australian Government Publishing Service.

DotAG (2003). *Higher Education Support Act*. Australia: Department of the Attorney General. Retrieved from https://www.legislation.gov.au/Details/C2017C00003.

Freeman-Moir, J. (2014). A context for educational philosophy. *Knowledge Cultures*, 2(2), 118–124.

Garrison, J., Neubert, S., & Reich, K. (2012). *John Dewey's philosophy of education: An introduction and recontextualization for our times*. New York: Springer.

Gergely, G., Egyed, K., & Király, I. (2007). On pedagogy. *Developmental Science*, 10(y), 139–146. doi:10.1111/j.1467–7687.2007.00576.x.

Harvey, A., Burnheim, C., & Brett, M. (2016). Towards a fairer chance for all: Revising the Australian student equity framework. In A. Harvey, C. Burnheim, & M. Brett (Eds), *Student equity in Australian Higher Education: Twenty-five years of A Fair Chance for All* (pp. 3–20). Singapore: Springer Singapore.

Hillman, K. (2005). *The first year experience: The transition from secondary school to university and TAFE in Australia*. LSAY Research Reports. Australian Council for Educational Research. Retrieved from https://research.acer.edu.au/lsay_research/44.

Hinchliffe, G. (2000). Education or pedagogy? *Journal of Philosophy of Education*, 35(1), 31–45. doi:10.1111/1467–9752.00208.

Hodges, B., Bedford, T., Hartley, J., Klinger, C., Murray, N., O'Rourke, J., & Schofield, N. (2013). *Enabling retention: Processes and strategies for improving student retention in university-based enabling programs*. Sydney, Australia: Australian Government Office for Learning and Teaching. Retrieved from https://eprints.usq.edu.au/26824/.

Jones, A., Olds, A., & Lisciandro, J. (2016). Understanding the learner: Effective course design in the changing higher education space. *International Studies in Widening Participation*, 3(1), 19–35.

Kift, S. M., Nelson, K. J., & Clarke, J. A. (2010). Transition pedagogy: A third generation approach to FYE: A case study of policy and practice for the higher education sector. *TheInternational Journal of the First Year in Higher Education*, 1(1), 1–20. doi:10.5204/intjfyhe.v1i1.13.

Lal, B. M., & Ebrary, I. (2006). *Educational philosophy*. New Delhi: Pragun Publications.

Lane, J., & Sharp, S. (2014). Pathways to success: Evaluating the use of "enabling pedagogies" in a University Transition Course. *Journal on Education*, 2(1), 66–73.

Marks, G. (2007). *Completing university: Characteristics and outcomes of completing and non-completing students*. LSAY Research Reports. Victoria, Australia: Australian Council for Educational Research. Retrieved from https://research.acer.edu.au/lsay_research/55/.

McInnis, C., Hartley, R., Polesel, J., & Teese, R. (2000). *Non-completion in vocational education and training in higher education. A literature review commissioned by the Department of Education, Training and Youth Affairs. A literature review commissioned by the Department of Education, Training and Youth Affairs*. Melbourne: Centre for the Study of Higher Education.

McKay, J., Pitman, T., Devlin, M., Trinidad, S., Harvey, A., & Brett, M. (2018). The use of enabling programs as a pathway to higher education by disadvantaged students in Australia. In C. I. Agosti & E. Bernat (Eds), *University pathway programs: Local responses within a growing global trend* (pp. 45–66). Switzerland: Springer.

Mills, C., Heyworth, J., Rosenwax, L., Carr, S., & Rosenberg, M. (2009). Factors associated with the academic success of first year Health Science students. *Advances in Health Sciences Education*, 14(2), 205–217.

NAEEA. (2019). National Association of Enabling Educators of Australia. Retrieved from http://enablingeducators.org/.

NCDE. (2019). The National Center for Developmental Education: Improving the quality of practice in postsecondary developmental education. Retrieved from https://ncde.appstate.edu/

QAA. (2019). Access to higher education. Retrieved from https://www.accesstohe.ac.uk/Pages/Default.aspx.

SWAP. (2019). Scottish Wider Access Programme. Retrieved from https://www.scottishwideraccess.org/.

Taylor, J. A., van Eyk, T., & Syme, S. (2018). Enabling success at university: The impact of an Australian programme to provide access to university. *Journal of Further and Higher Education*, 1–14. doi:10.1080/0309877X.2018.1504011.

Tinto, V., & Engstrom, C. (2008). Access without support is not opportunity. *Inside Higher Ed*, 9, 8–18.

Trewartha, R. (2008). Innovations in bridging and foundation education in a tertiary institution. *Australian Journal of Adult Learning*, 48(1), 30–49.

Trow, M. (2007). Reflections on the transition from elite to mass to universal access: Forms and phases of higher education in modern societies since WWII. In *International handbook of higher eEducation* (pp. 243–280). Dordrecht: Springer.

Zajda, J. (2013). Globalization and neo-liberalism as educational policy in Australia. In H. Yolcu & D. Turner (Eds), *Neoliberal educational reforms: A global analysis* (pp. 182–201). New York: Routledge.

Zinn, L. M. (2004). Exploring your philosophical orientation. In M. W. Galbraith (Ed.), *Adult learning methods: A guide for effective instruction* (3rd ed., pp. 39–56).Malabar, FL: Krieger Publishing.

PART I
Flourishing in transition

INTRODUCTION

Anita Olds

Flourishing is often a topical word when describing the ultimate goal of education. In its broadest sense, flourishing can be synonymous with growth or development, or a realising of full potential. I find the definition offered by Nussbaum (2000) most useful. They suggest that a flourishing life is multifaceted; it is a healthy and lengthy life with many forms of freedom, freedom to use all of our senses, freedom to express our creativity and our emotions, and freedom to exercise our reason. A flourishing life knows the dance of respect, is well acquainted with the glow of relatedness and belonging, has the opportunity to play, and a chance to exercise control over our environments. Educators committed to such Aristotelian ideals understand that carefully crafted learning environments play a vital role in enabling students to lead fuller and more competent lives. Kristjansson eloquently suggests that an education experience grounded in a philosophy of flourishing, can give students an opportunity to explore "the good, the true and the beautiful" (2016, p. 712). Such educational ideals defiantly stand in stark contrast to neoliberal attempts to provide an education that is grounded simply in employability (Grant, 2012).

Educational philosophies of flourishing can be evident in many transitional tertiary spaces. Most authors in this book regard flourishing as an important outcome of transitional education. It is important to note that the idea of emancipation is also raised here on multiple occasion, for the kinds of education found within transitional spaces as described in this book offers students opportunities for liberation. The inclusion of critical pedagogies in enabling curriculums for example, provides students freedom to exercise reason. Grant (2012) argues that social justice education is essential for flourishing lives. We, as educators in this space, entertain the notion that our learning environs sponsor flourishing lives in such ways.

The first part of this book begins with a reflection on the critical role of learning communities for building student motivation and self-efficacy, something Tinto argues is crucial for students to grow and flourish as they settle into university culture.

Olds, Jones and Lisciandro makes explicit the flourishing philosophies that can underpin enabling programs and the certain ingredients needed to ensure the ideal is enacted effectively. Drawing on superhero metaphors, Chapter 3 describes how a shared devotion to the philosophy of flourishing can lay the foundation for new and effective pedagogies that can engage learners. Willans argues that reflexivity, when nurtured through learning activities that foster greater insights into self, can sponsor flourishing. In the final chapter of this section, Hattam and Stokes extend the discussion of emancipatory education and stress the importance of critical pedagogies for teaching students how to strengthen their critical consciousness and exercise their reasoning for more autonomous lives. Together the chapters provide multiple approaches to flourishing. At the conclusion of this section you will find some top tips for fostering such flourishing in transitional tertiary spaces.

References

Grant, C. A. (2012). Cultivating flourishing lives: A robust social justice vision of education. *American Educational Research Journal*, 49(5), 910–934. doi:10.3102/0002831212447977

Kristjansson, K. (2016). Flourishing as the aim of education: Towards an extended, "enchanted" Aristotelian account. *Oxford Review of Education*, 42(6), 707–720. doi:10.1080/03054985.2016.1226791.

Nussbaum, M. C. (2000). Women's capabilities and social justice. *Journal of Human Development*, 1(2), 219–247. doi:10.1080/14649880020008749.

2

LEARNING BETTER TOGETHER

Emeritus Professor Vincent Tinto

In Australia, as in many other countries such as Denmark and the United States, there is growing concern about the extent and quality of student learning in higher education (Arum & Roksa, 2011; Lacy, Croucher, Brettand, & Mueller, 2017). Universities and colleges alike are asking themselves how can they get students to spend more time on their studies and improve their learning especially during the critical first year of university study; a period of transition during which students need to acquire the orientations, skills, and habits of mind that are the foundation upon which learning is built.

Let me suggest that an answer to that question lies in asking a different question; namely how should universities act to lead students to want to spend more time on their studies and learn? When one strips away the many layers of theory that seek to explain how institutional and student actions influence learning, one is left with one simple conclusion; students who want to learn are more likely to learn. Simply put, motivation drives learning.

The question then is what influences student motivation to learn and what, in turn, can universities reasonably do during the first year of university study to promote student learning. It is to these questions that we now turn.[1]

Student motivation to learn

While there are a number of different theories of motivation, this chapter draws primarily from self-determination theory [SDT] (Deci & Ryan, 1985, 2000, 2002; Ryan & Deci, 2000) and Keller's model of motivation that emphasises the role of attention, relevance, confidence and satisfaction in promoting and enhancing motivation in the learning process [ARCS] (Keller & Kopp, 1987). From the former theory we draw upon the important distinctions between intrinsic and extrinsic of motivation and the basic needs of students whose fulfilment shape motivation, namely competence, autonomy, and relatedness (Deci & Ryan, 2002, p. 7).[2] From the latter we draw upon the focus on the academic and social environment in which learners find themselves and the need for those environments to address issues of attention, relevance, confidence, and satisfaction. In this instance, as our concern is what an understanding of student motivation to learn suggests about university practice, we will focus on issues of confidence/competence, relatedness, and relevance, and indirectly with students' need for autonomy and having some control over their learning.[3] In doing so we make the assumption that students possess the motivational resources to constructively engage themselves in learning; that most students are inherently motivated to learn. Furthermore, we take the position that the academic and social environment of the classroom can support or thwart student motivation to do so (Reeve, 2002, 2012; Reeve & Lee, 2014).

Confidence and competence

Confidence, or what is commonly referred to as self-efficacy, refers to a person's belief in their ability to organise and execute a course of action to produce a given outcome, to be able to succeed at a particular task or in a specific situation (Bandura, 1998). That belief is learned, not inherited. It is the result of past experiences and interactions with others, of past successes and failures, that lead a person to believe they can succeed in the future and have some degree of control over the outcome of their actions. It is not generalisable to all tasks or situations. It can vary according to the task or situation at hand. That one believes in being able to succeed at one task or in one situation does not imply that one also believes in being able to succeed at a different task or in a different situation (Bandura, 1994).

Self-efficacy affects not only what goals or tasks a person chooses to accomplish, but also how they are addressed as challenges arise. As regards student self-efficacy, a strong sense of self-efficacy promotes learning while a weak one undermines it. Students with high self-efficacy will more readily engage in a learning task, invest more effort and persist longer in its completion even when faced with challenges, whereas students with low self-efficacy will often become discouraged and withdraw when challenges arise (Bong, 2001; Bodkin-Andrews, O'Rourke, Dillon, Craven, & Yeung, 2012; Chemers, Hu, & Garcia, 2001; Vuong, Brown-Welty, & Tracz, 2010). For this reason self-efficacy is seen as the bedrock upon which student learning is built. Students need to believe they can succeed. If not, there is little reason for them to continue trying to do so.

Self-efficacy is not fixed. It can change. It is influenced by a range of student experiences within the university in ways that can enhance or diminish it. This is especially true of the classrooms of the first year as students try to adjust to the increased demands of university study. Even those who begin their studies confident in their ability to succeed may encounter challenges that weaken their self-efficacy. Conversely students who begin unsure of their ability to succeed may discover they can succeed, if not flourish, in the university. It is telling that self-efficacy assessed at entry to the university is less predictive of students' academic success in the first year than when it is assessed near the end of the first year

(Gore, Jr, 2006). What matters is less a function of students' perceptions of their ability when they enter the university as it is that they come to believe or continue to believe they can succeed as a result of their experiences in the first year. The messages they derive from those experiences impact their self-efficacy and in turn their performance in the first year and beyond (Owens & Massey, 2011). New students, especially but not only those who are first in their family to attend university and those from culturally different backgrounds, are particularly sensitive to those messages because they often encounter messages from a variety of sources that they are unlikely to succeed; that they are unfit for university studies.

Of the many experiences students have in the first year that influence their self-efficacy, none are more important than those in the classroom. This is especially true of the actions of instructors whose expectations of students and the messages their behaviours convey influence student's sense of their own abilities to learn and succeed. Rarely are faculty expectations of the ability of their students to succeed in their courses uniform. They reflect a range of forces and past experiences as well as their perception of students' behaviours in class. Importantly, they also mirror faculty views of student development, in particular, whether faculty believe all students can flourish in the appropriate environment or whether some are more limited in their capacity to grow. This may sometimes take the form of stereotypes some faculty have as to the ability of some students to succeed in class or in a particular subject. Take, for instance, the view held by some faculty that women are not cut out for science or that some students from different cultural backgrounds may be less likely to succeed than other students (Steele, 1997; Dandy, Durkin, Barber & Houghton, 2015). This does not mean that student academic ability does not matter. Rather it argues that there are expectational forces at play that can also influence students' perceptions of their ability to learn and flourish in the university.

Nevertheless, more than a few students begin their studies without the requisite academic skills for university study. Many will struggle during the first year. But even among those who are skilled, some will also have difficulty adjusting to the academic demands of the first year. They, too, will struggle. This is why it is important that all students are able to obtain the academic support they need when they encounter difficulties. To be effective, support needs to be early before unaddressed student struggles undermine motivation. The challenge for universities is knowing when support is needed. To determine when it is, universities have employed a variety of early warning systems that identify students who are struggling during the first year and beyond.[4] In some instances, these are based on first-year course performance and/or class attendance. In others cases, they are the outcome of predictive analytic systems that monitor a range of student attributes, behaviours, and course grades to calculate the likelihood of course success (National Forum on Education Statistics, 2018).[5]

Support must not only be timely, it must also be proactive and structured to enhance student utilisation of support.[6] Otherwise student uptake of support is spotty at best. That this is the case reflects a variety of student beliefs about academic struggles in the first year. Some students think they are the only ones in class who are struggling, while others blame themselves for their struggles. At the same time, more than a few students maintain the erroneous view that help-seeking behaviour is an admission that they are not cut out for university. To counter such feelings and improve student utilisation of support, it is important that universities 'normalise' first-year academic struggles by making it clear that such struggles are the norm, not the exception, among first year students, that they are typical of the transition students have to make during that year. But even then, students frequently access support too late in the semester to improve their grades. In response, an increasing number of universities have come to the view that it is better to bring support to the students rather than wait for them to access it. This is why more universities are embedding support in the courses that comprise the first-year curriculum.[7] In so doing, universities are not leaving student access of support to chance, it becomes part and parcel of their course experience.

It should be noted that student motivation to learn is also influenced by the expectations for learning the university and faculty establishes for students. This applies generally and specifically in individual courses. The latter are particularly important because they influence students' expectations for their learning in the course and in turn what would be required of them to meet those expectations. Unfortunately, not all instructors make clear what learning outcomes are expected of students or develop ways of assessing those outcomes so that students are able to adjust their behaviours during the course. Even then, not all course learning goals are sufficiently interesting or challenging to warrant students' attention. Little wonder then that so many students put only enough effort into their classroom learning to ensure a passing grade.

Engagement, relatedness, and belonging

While believing in one's ability to succeed in the classroom and having the competence to do so are essential to learning, they do not ensure it. What is also required is that students become engaged with others and come to see themselves as a member of an academic community whose members, faculty, staff, and students, value their participation; that they matter and belong (Bean & Eaton, 2001; Stebleton, Soria, Huesman, & Torres, 2014; Strayhorn, 2012). The result is a relatedness or better yet a sense of belonging that serves to bind the individual to the group or community even when challenges arise.

This is especially important during the first year and the classrooms of that year. Students whose engagement leads them to perceive themselves as belonging in class are more likely to learn not only because it enhances student motivation to learn, but also because it results in students' willingness to invest greater effort in pursuit of their learning (Strayhorn, 2012; Trujillo & Tanner, 2014; Zubrunn, McKim, Buhs, & Hawley, 2014). At the same time, a sense of belonging leads to subsequent forms of engagement with others that further promotes learning. This is especially true for those forms of engagement that call for students to be actively engaged with other students in learning activities. By contrast a student's sense of not belonging, of being out of place in the learning environment of the classroom, leads to withdrawal from engagement and undermines motivation to learn (Walton & Cohen, 2007).

It is important to note that it is not engagement per se that matters, though some engagement is certainly better than none, as it is students' perceptions of their engagements and the meaning they derive from them (Hurtado & Carter, 1996). This is particularly true of the classroom whose culture influences not only students' self-efficacy, but also their sense of academic belonging and mattering (Freeman, Anderman, & Jensen, 2010). Engagements that are seen as supportive and inclusive lead to a sense of belonging that further promotes learning (Zubrunn et al., 2014). It is in such environments that students flourish and where learning is richest as it arises from the shared learning of other students with whom the student is meaningfully engaged. On the other hand, engagements that are seen as not supportive nor inclusive typically lead students to withdraw from learning activities thereby undermining their learning (Walton & Cohen, 2007).

Student perceptions of mattering and belonging can vary greatly, reflecting differences not only in student backgrounds and prior experiences, but also in the value-laden situations students encounter on campus. Universities are rarely homogeneous. They typically consist of multiple academic and social communities that may have quite different value orientations and embedded cultures. It is entirely possible for students to feel they matter and belong in one setting but not in another. But to the degree that a university has a dominant culture, so too does its actions as a university influence student behaviour.

Relevance

Students' motivation is also affected by their perception of the relevance of what they are asked to learn. Though there is considerable debate as to what constitutes relevance, what is not in debate is that students need to perceive the content of their courses to be of sufficient quality and relevance to warrant their attention, time, and effort (Frick, Chadha, Watson, Wang, & Green, 2009). Only then will they be willing to engage with their courses in ways that promote deeper, not purely instrumental, learning (Kahu, Nelson, & Picton, 2017; Keller & Kopp, 1987). Curriculum and teaching practices that are seen as irrelevant or of low quality will lead to inattention and minimal, if any, serious engagement in learning activities (Lizzio, Wilson, & Simons, 2002). This is especially true for students whose motivation is driven by the intrinsic rewards of university participation such as learning and personal growth.

Perceptions of the relevance reflect a complex interplay among a variety of issues, institutional and personal. As regards the university, it is shaped, among other things, by student perceptions of institutional quality, faculty teaching methods, and the degree to which the material to be learned is seen to apply to meaningful situations or problems. It also mirrors a range of individual attributes, in particular student learning style preferences and values. This is the case because the curriculum is more than a collection of facts and modes of analysis. It also contains, at least implicitly, the values of faculty that in large measure determine which facts and concepts are judged worthy of being presented and which perspectives are deemed appropriate to the analysis of those facts (Zepke, 2015). Too often education is as much socialisation into a particular way of understanding as it is empowering the exploration of alternative ways of making sense of the world around us.

Before turning to a discussion of implications for practice, it bears repeating that the current conversation is not meant to deal with all aspects of motivation to learn but those that are within the institution's capacity to reasonably influence. Its focus is as much on institutional practice as it is theory. Nor is it concerned with student experiences beyond campus that may also influence motivation. For instance, it is entirely possible that even the most motivated students may be forced by external events to withdraw from university study. By contrast, it is possible that some students may acquire knowledge even when there is little sense of belonging or perceived relevance of the curriculum as may be the case for students who are primarily concerned with the perceived extrinsic benefits of earning a university degree.

Learning communities and student learning

The question remains as to what universities can do to enhance student motivation to learn and improve student learning, especially during the first year of transition to university study. Let me suggest that learning communities, when properly implemented, are one especially powerful way of doing so.

It is important to understand what learning communities are and are not. Unfortunately, too many programs that are described as learning communities are little more than two or sometimes three courses in which students enrol that have little or no connection. While learning communities require that students co-enrol in several courses, co-enrolment is only one of the requirements of a learning community. What is also required is that the courses in which students co-enrol are linked by an issue, problem or project that connects the courses and provides a way of connecting what is learned in one course with what is being learned in the other(s). Doing so provides the mechanisms for the development of an interdisciplinary environment that structures student experiences in ways that enable students to see the same issue, problem or project through multiple disciplinary lenses.

Not the least of these experiences are those in which students work together in collaborative groups as equal members. In doing so they form smaller academic and social communities of learning within the learning community in which students find meaning and belonging. The most powerful of these experiences are those which require students to assert control over the analysis and proposed solution to a problem or project. Having to apply what they are learning to a meaningful problem or project gives rise not only to deeper learning but also to the development of critical skills that enable them to effectively address other problems or projects in the future. At the same time, students have to become interdependent learners who understand the need to balance their need for autonomy with the need for autonomy of their peers in order to arrive at a shared solution that draws upon the talents of each member of the group; that each student's voice matters. This is especially important because of the need to ensure that learning communities are inclusive not only of multiple disciplines but of the diverse voices of students from different backgrounds and cultural orientations.

To develop such learning communities instructors who teach in the learning community have to work together to link their individual courses and modes of teaching or better yet develop a common pedagogical and curriculum framework for the learning community that specifies a set of learning outcomes for the linked courses and a coherent and scaffolded series of shared educational experiences that enable students to attain those outcomes. In effect, faculty have to form a learning community of their own in which they learn from each other and develop not only a shared curriculum that lays out the knowledge students need acquire and experiences that would give rise to those learning outcomes but also a shared philosophy of student learning that recognises the potential for all students to flourish and learn. When implemented in this fashion, learning communities have been shown to have a number of positive impacts on students which, in turn, influence not only what they learn but also how they learn (Tinto, Goodsell-Love, & Russo, 1994; Tinto, 1995, 1996). Not the least of these have to do with the support students find within the learning community that enable them to overcome the social and academic challenges first-year students frequently encounter trying to adapt to the new demands of university study.

Read here a quote from a first-year student from a disadvantaged background we interviewed about her experiences in a learning community and how it enabled her to learn and continue in the face of often turbulent conditions.

> In the cluster we knew each other, we were friends, we discussed everything from all the classes. We knew things very, very well because we discussed it all so much. We had discussions about everything … it was like a raft running the rapids of my life.

For her and other students in the learning community, academic and social support arose from the collaborative learning activities of the community. She speaks of learning things "very, very well" while gaining support to continue in the face of sometimes turbulent conditions; support that is often difficult of any staff member to provide. Such support also helped her and many of her classmates manage the stress of the transition to university.[8]

Beyond providing the support so many students need to pursue their studies, learning communities also provide a social context within which learning arises and is enhanced. Another student described his experience in the learning community in the following manner.

> You know, the more I talk to other people about our class stuff, the homework, the tests, the more I'm actually learning … and the more I learn not only about other people, but also about the subject because my brain is getting more, because I'm getting more involved with the other students in the class. I'm getting more involved with the class even after class.

His comment speaks to how social affiliations within the learning community lead students to spend more time in learning activities. They do so in part because they can make friends and learn at the same time. One drives the other. More importantly, students in the learning community typically continued working on their shared assignments even after class ends. That is what the student meant by "class after class". For him and others, class was not defined by a set time but by their engagement with their peers in learning activities. Little wonder then that such learning communities enhance student learning.

But they do more. When learning communities adopt applied learning strategies such as problem or project-based learning, students gain a sense of autonomy; that they have to become responsible for their own learning. Within a supportive structured setting, students are empowered to freely pursue learning (Alfieri, Brooks, Aldrich, & Tannenbaum, 2011). But as noted above, they also need to learn to balance their need for autonomy with those of other students in the community. In other words, they need to come to understand that their learning is enriched when the learning of others members of the community is also enriched. As one student put it "We all learn better when we all learn together".

More importantly, when learning communities are inclusive of students of diverse backgrounds, student learning is enriched in ways not possible in less diverse settings. The quote below speaks for itself.

> I think more people should be educated in this form of education. I mean because it's good. We learn not only how to interact with ourselves, but with other people of different races, different sizes, different colors, different everything. I mean it just makes it better. Not only do you learn more, you learn better.

For this student and many of his classmates, the diverse learning community enabled them to hear the voices of students that they might not otherwise hear and learn how they made sense of an issue, problem or project being addressed in the learning community. More importantly, they came to understand how their learning was enriched by the inclusion of the voices of others. They all learn better together when all voices are included in the dialogue of learning. It is an understanding that all of our students need as we seek to build more inclusive and just societies.

Closing thoughts

Though we have treated the issue of motivation to learn as largely an academic matter, one that is shaped by the academic environment of the classroom, learning is necessarily social in character. The classroom exists in a larger social and cultural setting of the university and is shaped by the values that are embedded in that culture (Zepke 2015). It follows that substantial improvements in students' learning cannot occur without a rethinking of the cultural norms that frame how we think about the character of the academic setting of the classroom, indeed of the university, and our view of the capacity of all students, not just some, to flourish.

This is but one reason why learning communities, when properly implemented, offer the promise of significant improvement in both the quantity and quality of student learning. But implementing communities that offer a different vision of how to construct the learning setting requires that our existing view of faculty work and curricular structure change. For the curriculum, it calls for a view of knowledge that recognises the interdependent nature of learning and the need for more inter-disciplinary curricular structures; one which also recognises the role of values and cultural orientation in our judgments about which knowledge is worthy of con-sideration. For the faculty, it calls for a rethinking of their work that would emphasis on one hand, the need to employ problem and project-based learning strategies that requires students to gain some degree of autonomy over their learning, and on the other, the need for them, like their students, to become more interdependent lear-ners. Rather than sit in their own knowledge fiefdoms, they too would form learn-ing communities in which they learn from the voices of their colleagues in different fields and disciplines they typically do not hear; that they too learn better together. The university, for its part, has to rethink how it organises itself. Rather than main-tain the current structure that separates knowledge into separate organisational units, a structure that has persisted for hundreds of years, it needs to find a way of pro-moting interdisciplinary centres that bring together students and faculty from dif-ferent fields of knowledge to address pressing societal issues so that they too learn better together. And it must do so at the very start of university during the critical period of transition to university study; a period of becoming during which the foundations for student learning are established.[9]

Notes

1 For a fuller exposition see Tinto (2015).
2 Self-determination theory assumes that humans are inherently interested in learning about their environment and gaining some mastery over it. Moreover, it argues that such intrinsic motivation to learn is more powerful than that which is driven by extrinsic needs (Ryan & Deci, 2000, p. 69).
3 For the purpose of the present discussion, we will assume that students' motivation is largely intrinsic. Students whose attendance is primarily driven by their concern with the extrinsic benefits of university study, such as its perceived role in occupational and income attainment, are less likely to be influenced by university practice. Their approach to learning may be more instrumental in nature.
4 The use of early warning systems is not without pitfalls, not the least of which is that its uncritical use can lead institutions to prematurely label students as unlikely to succeed when the issue is primarily one of adjustment rather than lack of ability. Nevertheless, it is apparent that many universities have implemented such systems, some with considerable success.
5 Predictive analytic systems are part of the wider movement to employ 'Big Data' to improve university decision-making (Earls, 2019, May 6). But while a number of universities have successfully implemented predictive analytic systems to improve student retention and com-pletion (e.g. Georgia State University), using student and institutional data to predict future student behaviour is no easy feat (Ekowo & Palmer, 2016, October 24). Of special concern is not only the need to protect individual privacy, but also thorny issues of how far should institutions go to track students (Blumenstyk, 2018, July 31).

6 Peer mentoring can also play an important role in supporting student success (Leidenfrost, Strassing, Schütz, Carbon, & Schabmann, 2014). For students who are first in their family to attend university, who are from different cultural and racial backgrounds as well as those from low-income families, having a peer mentor of similar attributes can be instrumental in their success. This is the case because that mentor can provide insights into how to manage the challenges of university studies that only the mentor knows having already managed them in their journey through the university.

7 One way of doing so is through the contextualisation of support to individual courses as is the case in Supplemental Instruction (Stone & Jacobs, 2008). Another is where academic support is embedded in the course as is the case in the I-Best model first used in the state of Washington (Washington State Board for Community and Technical Colleges, 2005).

8 Evidence abounds that stress among first-year university students is increasing (Hibbs & Rostain, 2019). The effects of such stress are many not the least of which are diminished academic performance, increased likelihood of withdrawal from university studies and, in some cases, increased risk of suicide (Garett & Young, 2017). Beyond the need for individual counselling, it is important that universities make clear that stress during the first year is typical of the challenges students face in making the transition to university. While not diminishing the need for students to seek assistance, universities should seek, within reason, to normalise stress in the same way they do academic struggles in the first year. Otherwise, students tend to blame themselves for their struggles and further isolate themselves from others and the help they can provide thereby exacerbating stress. At the same time they should further the use of collaborative learning strategies and learning communities that when properly implemented provide, as noted above, support that is otherwise difficult to obtain.

9 There are a number of projects underway in the United States whose goal it is to redesign the first year of university. The most notable of these is a project of the American Association of State Colleges and Universities (AASC&U) entitled *Re-Imagining the First Year of College* involving 44 universities and colleges working together to develop comprehensive, institutional transformation that redesigns the first year of university and creates sustainable change for student success with the goal of dramatically improving the quality of learning and student experience in the first year, increase retention rates, and improve long-term student success.

References

Alfieri, L., Brooks, P., Aldrich, N., & Tannenbaum, H. (2011). Does discovery-based instruction enhance learning? *Journal of Educational Psychology*, 103(1),1–18.

Arum, R., & Roksa, J. (2011). *Academically adrift: Limited learning on college campuses.* Chicago, IL: The University of Chicago Press.

Bandura, A. (1994). Self-efficacy. In V. S. Ramachaudran (Ed.), *Encyclopedia of human behavior* (Vol. 4, pp.71–81). New York, NY: Academic Press.

Bandura, A. (1998). Health promotion from the perspective of social cognitive theory. *Psychology and Health*, 13(4), 623–649.

Bean, J., & Eaton, S. (2001). The psychology underlying successful retention practices. *Journal of College Student Retention*, 3(1), 73–89.

Blumenstyk, G. (2018, July 31). Big data is getting bigger. So are the privacy and ethical questions. *The Chronicle of Higher Education.* Retrieved from https://www.chronicle.com/article/Big-Data-Is-Getting-Bigger-So/244099.

Bong, M. (2001). Role of self-efficacy and task-value in predicting college students' course performance and future enrollment intentions. *Contemporary Educational Psychology*, 26(4), 553–570.

Bodkin-Andrews, G. H., O'Rourke, V., Dillon, A., Craven, R., & Yeung, A. (2012). Engaging the disengaged? A longitudinal analysis of the relations between indigenous and non-indigenous Australian students' academic self-concept and disengagement. *Journal of Cognitive Education and Psychology*, 11(2), 179–195.

Chemers, M., Hu, L., & Garcia, B. (2001). Academic self-efficacy and first-year college student performance and adjustment. *Journal of Educational Psychology*, 93(1), 55–64.

Dandy, J., Durkin, K., Barber, B., & Houghton, S. (2015). Academic expectations of Australian students from Aboriginal, Asian and Anglo backgrounds: Perspectives of teachers, trainee-teachers and students. *International Journal of Disability, Development and Education*, 62(1), 60–82.

Deci, E. L., & Ryan, R. M. (1985). *Intrinsic motivation and self-determination in human behavior.* New York, NY: Plenum.

Deci, E. L., & Ryan, R. M. (2000). The "what" and "why" of goal pursuits: Human needs and the self-determination of behavior. *Psychological Inquiry*, 11(4), 227–268.

Deci, E. L., & Ryan, R. M. (2002). An overview of self-determination theory. In E. L. Deci and R. Ryan (Eds), *Handbook of Self-Determination Research* (pp. 3–33). Rochester, NY: University of Rochester Press.

Earls, C. (2019, May 6). Big data science: Establishing data-driven institutions through advanced analytics. *Educause Review*, Retrieved from https://er.educause.edu/articles/2019/5/big-data -science-establishing-data-driven-institutions-through-advanced-analytics.

Ekowo, M., & Palmer, I. (2016, October 24). The promise and peril of predictive analytics in higher education: A landscape analysis. *New America*. Retrieved from https://na-pro duction.s3.amazonaws.com/documents/Promise-and-Peril_4.pdf.

Freeman, T., Anderman, L., & Jensen, J. (2010). Sense of belonging in college freshman at the classroom and campus levels. *The Journal of Experimental Education*, 75(3), 203–220.

Frick, T., Chadha, R., Watson, C., Wang, Y., & Green, P. (2009). College student perceptions of teaching and learning quality. *Association for Educational Communities and Technology*, 57(5), 705–720.

Gore Jr., P. (2006). Academic self-efficacy as a predictor of college outcomes: Two incremental validity studies. *Journal of Career Assessment*, 14(1), 92–111.

Garett, B., & Young, S. (2017). A longitudinal analysis of stress among incoming college freshman. *Journal of American College Health*, 65(2), 228–331.

Hibbs, B. J., & Rostain, A. (2019). *The stressed years of their lives. Helping you kid survive and thrive during the college years.* New York, NY: St Martin's Press.

Hurtado, S., & Carter, D. (1996). Latino students' sense of belonging in the college community: Rethinking the concept of integration on campus. In F. K. Stage, G. L. Anaya, J. P. Bean, D. Hossler & G. Kuh (Eds), *College students: Evolving nature of research* (pp. 123–136).Needham Heights, MA:Simon & Schuster Custom Publishing.

Keller, J., & Kopp, T. (1987). An application of the ARCS model of motivational design. In C. Reigeluth (Ed.), *Instructional design theories and models* (pp. 289–320). Hillsdale, NJ: Erlbaum.

Kahu, E., Nelson, N., & Picton, C. (2017). Student interest as a key driver of engagement for first year students. *Student Success*, 8(2),55–66.

Lacy, W. B., Croucher, G., Brettand, A., & Mueller, R. (2017). *Australian universities at a crossroads: Insights from their leaders and implications for the future.* Melbourne: Melbourne Centre for the Study of Higher Education.

Leidenfrost, B., Strassing, B., Schütz, M., Carbon, C., & Schabmann, A. (2014). The impact of peer mentoring on mentee academic performance. *International Journal of Teaching and Learning in Higher Education*, 26(1), 102–111.

Lizzio, A., Wilson, K., & Simons, R. (2002). University students' perceptions of the learning environment and academic outcomes: Implications for theory and practice. *Studies in Higher Education*, 27(1), 27–52.

National Forum on Education Statistics. (2018). *Forum guide to early warning systems (NFES2019035).* US Department of Education. Washington, DC: National Center for Educational Statistics.

Owens, J., & Massey, D. S. (2011). Stereotype threat and college academic performance: A latent variable approach. *Social Science Research*, 40(1), 150–166.

Reeve, J. (2002). Self-determination theory applied to educational settings. In E. L. Deci and R. M. Ryan (Eds), *Handbook of self-determination research* (pp. 183–203). Rochester NY: University of Rochester Press.

Reeve, J. (2012). A self-determination theory perspective on student engagement. In S. L. Christenson, et al. (Eds), *Handbook of research on student engagement* (pp. 149–172). New York, NY: Springer Science + Business Media.

Reeve, J., & Lee, W. (2014). Students' classroom engagement produces longitudinal gains in classroom motivation. *Journal of Educational Psychology*, 102(2), 527–540.

Ryan, R. M., & Deci, E. L. (2000). Self-determination theory and the facilitation of intrinsic motivation, social development, and well-being. *American Psychologist*, 55(1),68–78.

Stebleton, M., Soria, K., Huesman Jr., R., & Torres, V. (2014). Recent immigrant students at research universities: The relationship between campus climate and sense of belonging. *Journal of College Student Development*, 55(2), 196–202.

Steele, C. (1997). A threat in the air: How stereotypes shape the intellectual identities and performance of women and African-Americans. *American Psychologist*, 52(6), 613–629.

Stone, M. E., & Jacobs, G. (Eds). (2008). *Supplemental instruction: Improving first-year student success in high-risk courses* (Monograph No. 7, 3rd ed.). Columbia, SC: University of South Carolina, National Resource Center for The First-Year Experience and Students in Transition.

Strayhorn, T. (2012). *College students' sense of belonging*. New York, NY: Routledge.

Tinto, V., Goodsell-Love, A., & Russo, P. (1994). *Building learning communities for new college students*. A publication of the National Center on Postsecondary Teaching, Learning, and Assessment, Pennsylvania State University.

Tinto, V. (1995). Learning communities, collaborative learning, and the pedagogy of educational citizenship. *AAHE Bulletin*, 47(7), 11–13.

Tinto, V. (1996). Learning communities and the reconstruction of the first year of college. *Planning for Higher Education*, 25(1), 1–7.

Tinto, V. (2015). Through the eyes of students. *Journal of College Student Retention: Research, Theory & Practice*, 19(3), 254–269.

Trujillo, G., & Tanner, K. (2014). Considering the role of affect in learning. *CBE Life Science Education*, 13(1),6–15.

Vuong, M., Brown-Welty, S., & Tracz, S. (2010). The effects of self-efficacy on academic success of first-generation college sophomore students. *Journal of College Student Development*, 51(1),50–64.

Walton, G., & Cohen, G. (2007). A question of belonging: Race, social fit, and achievement. *Journal of Personality and Social Psychology*, 92(1), 82–96.

Washington State Board for Community and Technical Colleges. (2005). *A program integrating adult basic education and workforce training*. Olympia, WA: Washington State Board for Community and Technical Colleges, Research Report No. 05–2.

Zepke, N. (2015). Student engagement research: Thinking beyond the mainstream. *Higher Education Research and Development*, 3(6), 1311–1323.

Zubrunn, S., McKim, C., Buhs, E., & Hawley, L. R. (2014). Support, belonging, motivation, and engagement in the college classroom: A mixed method study. *Instructional Science*, 42(5), 661–684.

3

THE SOCIAL JUSTICE LEAGUE

Philosophies of flourishing and emancipation in enabling education

Anita Olds, Dr Angela Jones and Dr Joanne G. Lisciandro

> Education is a social process; education is growth; education is not preparation for life but is life itself.
>
> *John Dewey*

Introduction

Transitional education is a unique space that often places academics in a pedagogical pastiche that layers multiple disciplinary knowledge with academic skills development, and elements of pastoral care. The array of disciplinary perspectives can lend itself to conflict, but so too can it sponsor rigorous conceptual debate and foster innovative pedagogical strategies. One way to unify a disciplinary diverse group is to uncover the team's shared set of educational philosophies – to make the unconscious, conscious. We, the authors of this chapter, are trained in three different disciplines, yet through the discovery of a shared set of beliefs, a wonderful collaboration has been made possible. The roots of our synergy were not well understood when we met, but after reflecting on our collaborative practice through discussions held over years, we have come to appreciate it is possible because of a unified ethos. Our shared ideological position is that pedagogies underpinned by philosophies of social justice and flourishing can emancipate enabling students from any limiting self-beliefs, and build their academic skills and self-efficacy, so that they can flourish in their transition to higher education. This shared ethos concerning the transformative role of education ultimately drove our curriculum design, problem solving and processes.

In this chapter, we distil our shared beliefs, or rather, our foundational philosophies, by describing how they inform the pedagogical approaches and in turn the practices in enabling education at Murdoch University in Western Australia (WA). As suggested by Coello and Casanas (2004, p. 385), "educators can benefit from defining and clarifying their own educational philosophies, which in turn can help them establish learning activities and evaluate learning outcomes". Hence, we argue that explicit reflection on philosophies aids in the generation of new and effective pedagogies and ultimately practice. It is our belief that collaborative and intentional educatory practice contributes to student flourishing and emancipation. In the following pages we set the scene of enabling education within the WA higher education landscape, and situate the role of "chimaera" enabling academics within it. Through this discussion we ponder our collaboration as an evolutionary process, where philosophies of flourishing and social justice emerged as the grounding ideologies that shaped our pedagogical strategies. We also extract the three pedagogic strategies of *engagement, belonging* and *learning* from our enabling transition pedagogy model and demonstrate how, when underpinned by philosophies of social justice and flourishing, these can be unleashed as an almighty pedagogical trident. We provide the Engagement Zone as an example of a pedagogical trident and unpack how this three-pronged approach is enacted in Murdoch University's OnTrack and OnTrack Sprint enabling programs. These paragraphs are peppered with the philosophical – cultural, political, and mythological – ideals that are often possessed by that of superheroes, like DC Comics' Justice League. The Justice League is a dream team of superheroes, including (but not limited to) Batman, Wonder Woman, Superman, Cyborg and Aquaman, who join forces and combine powers in their fight against injustice, for freedom and to help people thrive. While we do not conceive of ourselves as actual superheroes (if we were, we would obviously be Marvel characters, not DC), the strength and evolution of our collaboration is analogous to that of a group of philosophically driven Lycra-clad misfits.

The prequel to this story

A scientist, a teacher and a popular culture academic walk into a bar ... or in this case, an enabling classroom. Our educational backgrounds and individual journeys to the transitional space of enabling education are nuanced. The scientist completed her PhD before commencing as an enabling program tutor. Headhunted to redevelop the science component of the program, she progressed into unit coordination and curriculum design roles. The teacher, with a background in English and teaching in international baccalaureate schools, also began as an enabling tutor. Promotion into the role of program designer and unit coordinator soon followed. The pop culture academic began her life as a tutor, unit coordinator, and curriculum designer of foundational Arts and Humanities units, and was poached by the Access Pathways team to design and coordinate enabling programs. All three coordinators work across a suite of access programs. While we all have different backgrounds, we were headhunted to lead curriculum design in the enabling space. We were recognised for our different disciplinary and design expertise and yet, all deeply held a belief that past educational disadvantage should not close the door on future educational opportunities. Over time, through many round table discussions and co-created curriculum, we explicated the submergent philosophies that ultimately drive our practice. Social justice, a growth mindset, and transformative learning were noted as vital to our practice. When whittled down further, a team ethos centred around flourishing and social justice education, with particular attention to Freire's (1973) concept of emancipation, became our philosophical identity.

The scene – not quite Gotham City

Enabling programs are no longer operating on the fringe of higher education, but instead have become a key part of tertiary access strategy for Australian universities and prospective students alike. This is due to key contextual factors such as a review of higher education in Australia (Bradley, Noonan, Nugent, & Scales, 2008), which set targets for widening participation, and the introduction of a demand-driven system for the government funding of student places in 2012. Bachelor degree enrolments became largely uncapped in many courses at most public universities. Traditional pathways to access university based on high-stakes testing in high school and a tertiary entrance ranking[1] of students have proved inadequate for meeting these objectives (Blyth, 2014). This remains particularly the case in WA, and even more so in regional and remote areas of the state, where opportunities for obtaining a tertiary entrance rank are limited or unequal due to school and socioeconomic factors (Blyth, 2014; Vernon, Watson, Moore, & Seddon, 2018). In order for universities to capture students who are capable but lack opportunity for access, non-traditional pathways such as pre-university enabling programs have become increasingly offered by universities and increasingly selected by students "as a legitimate pathway for Higher Education" (Hodges et al., 2013). Indeed, enrolments in enabling programs also known as "bridging courses, university preparation courses, foundation courses and pathway courses" (Hodges et al., 2013) have expanded rapidly at our university, throughout the state and across the country over the last decade (Australian Government, 2018; Lisciandro & Gibbs, 2016).

As contemporary Australian academics, we find ourselves stretched globally and domestically, stuck between tensions of neoliberalism, bureaucracy, widening participation, technological determinism, and a user pays system. The commodification of the tertiary learning experience has created a "tendency to centralise, standardise and rationalise" (Hanley, 2011, p. 10). Not only is it suggested that neoliberalism corrodes learning, rendering it as a transaction (Naidoo & Jamieson, 2005) but contemporary university marketing campaigns have reduced "decades of high-level inquiry and life changing innovation to slogans like 'awesome'" (Rea, 2016, p. 14). This corporate approach, while encouraging freedom through access to education, is some distance from Freire's (1973) emancipatory conceptualisation of education. The goal of transition education in the realm of enabling education has economic, political and social justice agendas.

As enabling academics in Western Australia, we find ourselves in a unique position in the higher education space. We are "chimaera" academics (Bennett et al., 2016) dancing between our academic disciplines and the emerging space of enabling education. As both cultural insiders and outsiders – or institutional fringe dwellers – our job is to weave our non-traditional students into the traditional tapestry of the 'university culture'. Our role requires us to have knowledge of the contemporary university structure that remains deeply rooted in traditional understandings of what knowledge is, as well as have specific disciplinary expertise in an area of study. However, the nature of the 'enabling academic' as an acculturator of non-traditional students, is underpinned by beliefs that challenge many historical conceptions. Our pedagogies and practice must do more than develop academic literacies, as we are building 'cultural capital' (Bourdieu, 1984), and addressing the holistic needs of the learner at the same time. Therefore, this role requires an understanding of *how* to demystify and acculturate non-traditional students into this new world, while not devaluing these students' knowledges outside of the university structure.

Our mission: Social justice and the flourishing way

Of central concern to us, as designers and coordinators of enabling programs, is the creation of a learning environment that enables students to flourish in the university setting and beyond. Whilst on one level we aim to strengthen our students' academic literacies, it is also understood that the holistic needs of the learner must be considered in order to support the emergence of higher order skills. We are unified in our belief in the role of enabling education in uncovering students' potential and unlocking their agency. Though space within this chapter limits the discussion on how these beliefs fit into the larger scheme of our educational philosophy, we offer the following.

Social justice

Our philosophical approach could be considered emancipatory. At the macro level we seek to emancipate our students from stigmatisation (Freire, 1973), to close the division between cultural insiders and cultural outsiders, to share the insiders 'playbook' per se. Staff in our team – aka Social Justice League – acknowledge the importance of empowering our students and offer a curriculum that lays bare the power structures that influence our lives. Students are developed into critical thinkers capable of challenging limiting ideologies, including those that have impacted their own lives and identity. Freire (1973) argues that to overcome oppression, the oppressed must first have a critically awareness of the causes. This challenge lends itself to social justice educational philosophies, wherein the goals are to create an awareness of the systems that oppress, and to empower individuals to challenge these systems (Bell, 2016).

The flourishing way

On the micro level one of our endeavours is to emancipate our students from any limiting beliefs about self and their learning. Phrases such as "foster autonomy" and a "promote a new consciousness" are used when describing the implicit outcomes of our courses. In our programs the students are encouraged to embrace their agency and to explore how their thinking influences their functioning and life circumstances (Bandura, 2006). This shared devotion to the actualising of individual human potential or as Freire (1973, p. 44) offered, the "vocation of becoming more fully human", can be described as a commitment to the philosophy of flourishing. Deeply rooted in Aristotelian philosophy and self-determination theory, often referred to as eudaimonia, flourishing can be appreciated as "a practice of human improvement" (Cohen, 1988, p. 55). An education grounded in the idea of flourishing aims to develop virtues, provide a regulative ideal to structure development (Wolbert, De Ruyter, & Schinkel, 2015) and foster such capacities as autonomy, competence, and relatedness (Deci & Ryan, 2000). We are not alone in perceiving flourishing as an overarching aim of education (Brighouse, 2006; Kristjansson, 2016; Wolbert et al., 2015). Policy makers and organisations see the merit in fostering flourishing: it's good for the economy and is positively correlated to wellbeing and prosocial behaviour (DeHaan, Hirai, & Ryan, 2016).

Unleashing the power of the pedagogical trident – a three-pronged approach

Our shared philosophies create a filter for selecting pedagogies, therefore shaping the curriculum design and the scaffolding activities we choose. Activities in our program are chosen for their ability to foster the many implicit and explicit outcomes such as academic skills development, self-efficacy, flourishing, and transition. Our enabling transition pedagogy (Jones, Olds, & Lisciandro, 2016) model is an adapted version of the Nelson, Creagh, Kift, and Clarke (2014) first year transition pedagogy model. It contains a set of interconnected curriculum principles that form a holistic framework underpinning the academic, social and support facets of the student transition experience. It also specifies three key enabling pedagogical (EP) strategies for enacting these curriculum principles that focus on *engagement, belonging* and *learning*. We recognise that these three key strategies or prongs have been forged from our overarching philosophies of social justice and flourishing.

Principles for *engaging* students from low socioeconomic and first-in-family backgrounds (a large contingent of the enabling cohort), include a focus on curriculum that is relevant, authentic, accessible, explicit, and that provides clarity around expectations and progress (Devlin, Kift, Nelson, Smith, & McKay, 2012; O'Shea, 2016). According to Tinto (2003), *belonging*, which can be intentionally fostered through learning communities, can increase engagement and enhance the quality of learning. Lastly, timely access to *learning* involves understanding that students construct knowledge within the Zone of Proximal Development (ZPD) (Vygotsky, 1978) and ensuring scaffolding matches their incremental growth. Pedagogy and curriculum that draws from educational psychology too can explicitly address gaps in socio-emotional learning through the development of metacognitive skills (Ee, 2009), emotional intelligence, resilience or 'grit' (Duckworth, Peterson, Matthews, & Kelly, 2007) and a growth mindset (Dweck, 2007, 2012) – growing not just academic skills but academic self-efficacy. This three-pronged pedagogical approach is demonstrated in the Figure 3.1 below:

How we enact the EP strategies in practice has differed depending on the needs of specific student cohorts, the nature of the programs (e.g. online versus face-to-face)

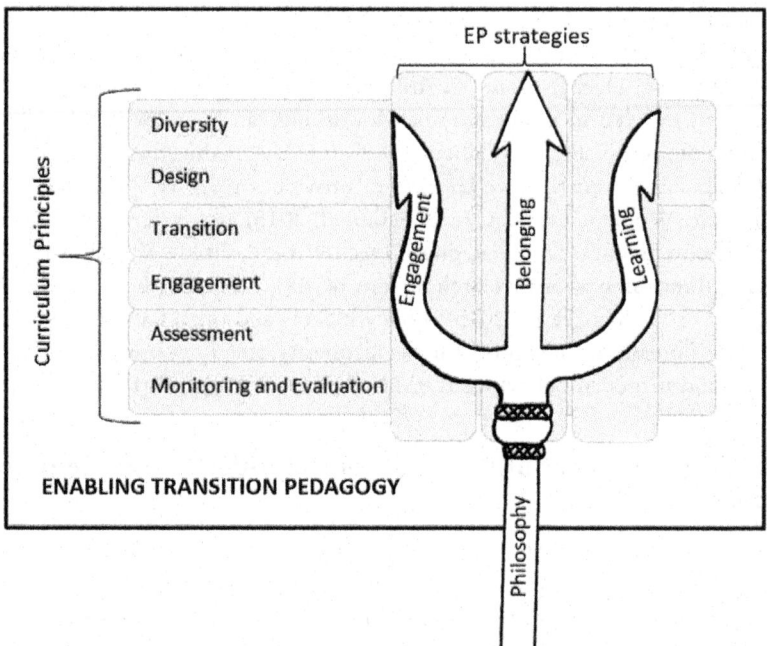

FIGURE 3.1 Enabling transition pedagogy model: The trident[2]

and the resources available. In Greek and Roman mythology, the three-pronged trident is a symbol associated with the power wielded by marine deities like Poseidon or
Neptune (Walters, 2013). In more contemporary depictions, such as the DC Comic
superhero 'Aquaman' and Marvel's 'Odin' (Thor's father), the trident is the symbolic
source of power (Wan, 2018). Within our team we conceptualised the "Engagement
Zone" (EZ) as our pedagogical 'trident'. This zone simultaneously enacts all three
pedagogical prongs of *engagement, belonging* and *learning* and empowers students to
flourish in this transitional educational space, thus aligning curriculum pedagogy with
our ultimate philosophical aims.

The EZ designates a space of shared interest between the educator and their students. It is a place where together we can work towards emancipation and flourishing.
It uses student knowledge and passions to acculturate students into a space of the
unknown and empowers them to become actively involved in their own learning
(Jones et al., 2016). Notably, the examples given in Figure 3.2 below of shared 'passions' falling within the EZ included music, humour and storytelling, but this could
differ depending on the cohort and staff. An understanding of the learner is the first
step to determining which passions and interests fall within the EZ.

The EZ first builds student engagement by meeting the student in a space which is
inclusive, familiar, interesting and relevant to them, and which values and unleashes the
potential in their diverse 'capitals'. Second, because it is a space of shared passions where
students can find commonalities, anxieties can be alleviated through the use of humour,

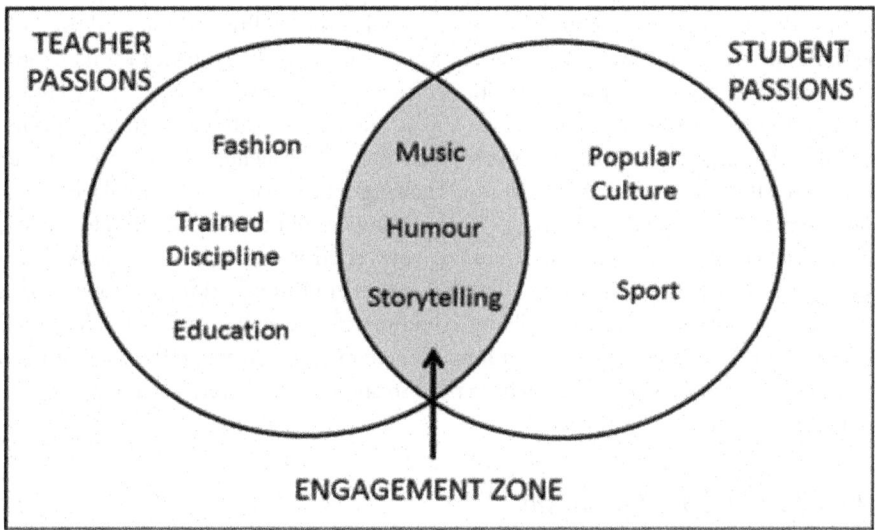

FIGURE 3.2 The Engagement Zone (Jones et al., 2016)

and 'inside' jokes can be created and understood. Essentially, it is a powerful space where connection and belonging can be fostered authentically and naturally, and all the benefits of a learning community can be realised. Lastly, the EZ scaffolds new learning within the ZPD by an active and collaborative process that "create(s) new cognitive pegs for students to hang (their) academic knowledge on" (Jones et al., 2016, p. 27).

The following paragraphs demonstrate our pedagogical trident in action through examples of the EZ at play in two internally delivered enabling programs. Each example reflects our shared philosophies of flourishing and emancipation.

The OnTrack program

The OnTrack program is a single holistic curriculum delivered in full-time, internal mode with students working with a single tutor and group of peers for the entire 14-week course. Although it is resource intensive, it is a program that has delivered consistently high retention and progression rates for thousands of non-traditional, equity and first-in-family students over its lifespan; an effect largely attributed to the way in which it fosters community, learning and engagement (Lisciandro & Gibbs, 2016).

One way in which the EZ is applied in this context is through the sharing of stories to normalise the struggles associated with learning, and reframe previous negative narratives and beliefs around learning, achievement and whether the student belongs at university. For example, in the first week, students attend a lecture titled 'Footprints into Learning' in which educators recount their own learning journey and learning struggles for students. Students are then introduced to evidence from the field of neuroscience that demonstrates how neurons can grow and form new connections when learning (i.e. the premise that intelligence can be developed), as well as theory from educational psychology that cultivating a 'growth' mindset results in behaviours that enhance learning. Students are regularly asked to produce written reflections about their own learning journey, their motivations, goals, and aspirations, and to identify areas for growth and specific strategies that they will employ to attempt to overcome challenges. In this process, students come to understand that struggles and challenges are a shared and normal part of the learning process, as well as develop self-awareness and insight that allows them to reframe their own narrative and feel empowered to have control over their learning which is perhaps contrary to past experience. The EZ enacted in this way through storytelling is successful in engaging learners, building community connection and scaffolding their learning journey. Further, the opportunity for reframing emancipates the student from any self-limiting beliefs, allowing them to flourish and feel empowered as a learner in this transitional learning environment.

The OnTrack Sprint program

OnTrack Sprint is a full time, four-week intensive enabling program offered at the start of the academic year. It aims to upskill near-miss ATAR[3] students for university readiness. For students who pass, it is an opportunity to start university at the beginning of the academic year with their peers. In order to achieve the greater goals of flourishing and emancipation, every minute of Sprint is valued as a teachable moment in a pressured timetable that builds engagement, belonging and scaffolds learning.

Drawing on popular culture in the Sprint space is vital for it ensures a way to connect with the adolescent cohort and attach new knowledge to their already existing cognitive pegs. Popular culture music, sitting squarely in the middle of the EZ central zone, is exploited to scaffold major concepts and foundational skills, engage learners, and build community. In previous iterations of Sprint, theme songs linked to lecture concepts were played before every lecture. For example, in the week 2 lecture, students viewed a satirical rap-battle, the *Hiphopopotamus vs. Rhymenoceros* by Flight of the Conchords. Students were then invited to imagine they were starring on a rap battle TV show. They were asked what steps would need to be taken in order to win. Drawing on their existing knowledge of rap, a picture and awareness of language conventions specific to the genre emerged. Students were then asked to transfer this awareness of language conventions to academic writing and explicit instructions on academic language were given. In later classes, as the skill of academic writing strengthened, references to rap culture continued. Where students missed an opportunity to modify a noun in their writing, we joked, "where's the pimping?" When we started exploring the concept of creating positive social change and the historic figures that fought for justice, Bliss and Eso's *Sea is Rising* was played. Students embraced the popular culture analogies quickly, and often in following weeks as the concept of positive social change deepened, offered protest songs of their own. Creative approaches such as these acknowledge and build on learner capitals, and cultivate shared 'insider' languages for learning communities, but on more macro levels, build relatedness, a virtue of flourishing.

Final thoughts

Why is a shared philosophy between interdisciplinary academics so important? We have found within our own teaching context that coherence in philosophies and pedagogies/practice leads to the best possible outcomes for students including emergence of successful learning communities, and evidence of high student engagement, retention, achievement, growth and transformation (Lisciandro & Gibbs, 2016). These realisations guide staff recruitment to our 'Social Justice League'. Interview questions are designed to locate staff that care deeply about student flourishing and social justice. Our unifying philosophies build camaraderie, culture, and a community attitude that infiltrates the work (Freire, 1973). Ultimately, this enables us to remain inspired and to weather the challenges of the space.

We hope that this chapter has offered readers a way through the mire of complex choices when working in the transitional education space. The Social Justice League is a playful superhero metaphor, but is also grounded in philosophical roots of social justice and flourishing. We believe that the EZ as a pedagogical trident offered us, as educators, a powerful way to connect in a disciplinary, educationally and politically diverse environment. Finding a shared philosophy and a pedagogical trident, not only enabled us to navigate this terrain with humour, and rigour, but provided us with the opportunity to create transformative educational experiences for our students.

Notes

1 An Australian Tertiary Admissions Rank (ATAR) is generated based on performance in final high school exams, and used as a basis for admission to Australian universities. The rank gives an indication of how well the student performed compared to their peers across the country. For example, a rank of 70 means that the student performed better than 70 per cent of their peers.
2 This is with a view that students will receive a first-year transition pedagogy (Nelson et.al., 2014), once they achieve university entrance and commence their undergraduate program.
3 Near-miss ATAR students are those that received an ATAR score within 10 points below the university's minimum entry standard

References

Australian Government (2018). *Higher education statistics*. Retrieved from https://www.educa tion.gov.au/higher-education-statistics.
Bandura, A. (2006). Toward a psychology of human agency. *Perspectives on Psychological Science*, 1(2), 164–180. doi:10.1111/j.1745–6916.2006.00011.x.
Bell, L. A. (2016). Theoretical foundations for social justice education. In M. Adams & L. A. Bell (Eds), *Teaching for diversity and social justice* (pp. 1–22). New York: Routledge.
Bennett, R., Hobson, J., Jones, A., Martin-Lynch, P., Scutt, C., Strehlow, K., & Veitch, S. (2016). Being Chimaera: A monstrous identity for SoTL academics. *Higher Education Research & Development*, 35(2), 217–228. doi:10.1080/07294360.2015.1087473.
Blyth, K. (2014). Selection methods for undergraduate admissions in Australia. Does the Australian predominate entry scheme the Australian Tertiary Admissions Rank (ATAR) have a future? *Journal of Higher Education Policy and Management*, 36(3), 268–278. doi:10.1080/01587919.2014.899049.

Bourdieu, P. (1984). *Distinction: A social critique of the judgment of taste.* Cambridge, MA: Harvard University Press.

Bradley, D., Noonan, P., Nugent, H., & Scales, B. (2008). *Review of higher education in Australia, final report.* Canberra: Australian Government.

Brighouse, H. (2006). *On education: Thinking in action.* New York: Routledge.

Coello, H. M., & Casanas, J. A. (2004). Educational philosophies. *Radiologic Technology, 75*(5), 385–392.

Cohen, D. K. (1988). Teaching practice: Plus ça change. In *Contributing to educational change: Perspectives on research and practice* (pp. 27–84). Berkeley, CA: McCutchan.

Deci, E. L., & Ryan, R. M. (2000). The "what" and "why" of goal pursuits: Human needs and the self-determination of behavior. *Psychological Inquiry, 11*(4), 227–268. doi:10.1207/S15327965PLI1104_01.

DeHaan, C. R., Hirai, T., & Ryan, R. M. (2016). Nussbaum's capabilities and self-determination theory's basic psychological needs: Relating some fundamentals of human wellness. *Journal of Happiness Studies, 17*(5),2037–2049. doi:10.1007/s10902–015–9684-y.

Devlin, M., Kift, S., Nelson, K., Smith, L., & McKay, J. (2012). *Effective teaching and support of students from low socioeconomic status backgrounds: Resources for Australian higher education.* Sydney: Australian Government Office for Teaching and Learning. Retrieved from: http://vuir.vu.edu.au/37543/1/ALTC%20LSES%20Final%20Report%202012.pdf.

Duckworth, A. L., Peterson, C., Matthews, M. D., & Kelly, D. R. (2007). Grit: Perseverance and passion for long-term goals. *Journal of Personality and Social Psychology, 92*(6), 1087. doi:10.1037/0022–3514.92.6.1087.

Dweck, C. S. (2007). Boosting achievement with messages that motivate. *Education Canada, 47*(2), 6–10.

Dweck, C. S. (2012). *Mindset: How you can fulfil your potential.* London: Hachette.

Ee, J. (2009). *Empowering metacognition through social-emotional learning: Lessons for the classroom.* Singapore: Cengage Learning.

Freire, P. (1973). *The pedagogy of the oppressed.* New York: Continuum International Publishing Group.

Hanley, L. (2011). Mashing up the institution: Teacher as bricoleur. *Radical Teacher, 90*(1), 9–14.

Hodges, B., Bedford, T., Hartley, J., Klinger, C., Murray, N., O'Rourke, J., & Schofield, N. (2013). *Enabling retention: Processes and strategies for improving student retention in university-based enabling programs.* Sydney: Australian Government Office for Teaching and Learning. Retrieved from: https://eprints.usq.edu.au/26824/.

Jones, A., Olds, A., & Lisciandro, J. (2016). Understanding the learner: Effective course design in the changing higher education space. *International Studies in Widening Participation, 3*(1), 19–35.

Kristjansson, K. (2016). Flourishing as the aim of education: Towards an extended, 'enchanted' Aristotelian account. *Oxford Review of Education, 42*(6), 707–720. doi:10.1080/03054985.2016.1226791.

Lisciandro, J. G., & Gibbs, G. (2016). OnTrack to university: Understanding mechanisms of student retention in an Australian pre-university enabling program. *Australian Journal of Adult Learning, 56*(2), 198–224.

Naidoo, R., & Jamieson, I. (2005). Empowering participants or corroding learning? Towards a research agenda on the impact of student consumerism in higher education. *Journal of Education Policy, 20*(3), 267–281. doi:10.1080/02680930500108585.

Nelson, K. J., Creagh, T., Kift, S. M., & Clarke, J. A. (2014). Transition pedagogy handbook: A good practice guide for policy and practice in the first year experience at QUT. Retrieved from https://eprints.qut.edu.au/76333/1/Transition_Pedagogy_Handbook_2014.pdf.

Rea, J. (2016). Critiquing neoliberalism in Australian universities. *Australian Universities' Review*, 58(2), 9.

O'Shea, S. (2016). *Overarching principles and strategies for supporting first-in-family students and their families.* Sydney: Australian Government Office for Teaching and Learning. Retrieved from: http://www.firstinfamily.com.au/docs/Final%20-%20Overarching% 20Principles%20and%20Strategies%20for%20Supporting%20First-in-Family%20Students% 20and%20Their%20Families.pdf.

Tinto, V. (2003). Learning better together: The impact of learning communities on student success. *Higher Education Monograph Series*, 1(8). doi:10.12691/education-2-6-13.

Vernon, L., Watson, S. J., Moore, W., & Seddon, S. (2018). University enabling programs while still at school: Supporting the transition of low-SES students from high school to university. *The Australian Educational Researcher*.doi:10.1007/s13384-018-0288-5.

Vygotsky, L. S. (1978). *Mind in society: The development of higher psychological processes.* Cambridge, MA: Harvard University Press.

Walters, H. (2013). Poseidon's trident. *The Journal of Hellenic Studies*, 13, 13–20. doi:10.2307/623886.

Wan, J. (Director). (2018). *Aquaman* [DVD]. USA: Warner Bros Pictures.

Wolbert, L. S., De Ruyter, D. J., & Schinkel, A. (2015). Formal criteria for the concept of human flourishing: The first step in defending flourishing as an ideal aim of education. *Ethics and Education*, 10(1), 118–129. doi:10.1080/17449642.2014.998032.

4

TRANSITIONING TO THEIR FUTURE

Creating an environment of 'possibilities' for enabling students

Dr Julie Willans

Introduction

Students in university-based enabling courses that prepare them for undergraduate studies have the potential to greatly benefit from active engagement in pedagogical practices that generate greater insights into self as learner. This chapter illustrates how a formal learning environment philosophically underpinned by tenets of transformative learning theory, and infused with humanistic and adult learning principles, utilises specific pedagogical practices with adult students to generate greater insights about self as learner. This enables many learners to conceptualise new possibilities for themselves. The discussion in this chapter is based on qualitative research revealing the impact of including pedagogical practices and strategies such as the Myers-Briggs Jung Typology test and Felder-Soloman Index of Learning Styles in *Preparation Skills for University* (PSU), the core unit in the Skills for Tertiary Education Preparatory Studies (STEPS) pre-university enabling course at CQUniversity Australia. Student responses to these approaches, gathered from unit evaluation data, were identified and analysed. Richie and Spencer's (2002) framework model was applied to 'sort and sift' the data and distil salient themes. Results suggest that students placed an exceptionally high value on the use of online tools including the Typology Test, Index of Learning Styles Questionnaire and specific career websites. With the overarching goal of enhanced self-awareness, these tools purposively guided students in exploring their personal learning style preferences, personality traits, and career and future objectives. The following sections provide a context, a description of philosophies and principles underpinning STEPS, the methodological approach that enabled the use of the student voice as data, and the salient research findings.

Contextualisation

As a consequence of more equitable access to higher education, growing numbers of non-traditional students are enrolling in university study. Many of these 'first in family' to study at university are from a low socioeconomic status background (LSES) and are not recent school learners. Most have broad prior life and work experiences but are underprepared for the expectations of university study, necessitating extra technical and personal support. This prompts some to access enabling courses to increase their knowledge, skills and confidence as preparation for undergraduate study. According to Universities Australia (2018), in 2016 almost 28,500 Australian students participated in enabling courses, representing approximately 2.7 per cent of all students in Australian universities for that year (excluding post-graduate students). Pre-university pre-paratory/bridging/access courses are offered by the majority of Australian universities, providing an authentic experience of what study at university is likely to entail. STEPS at CQUniversity is one such course, with the aim of preparing adult learners with the skills, knowledge, and confidence to gain entry to, and competently participate in university studies. This fee-free, online or on-campus, full- or part-time course also promotes the student's social, cultural and physical wellbeing.

For many STEPS students, returning to a formal learning environment can be very intimidating and disorienting. While low socio-economic status does not necessarily equate to low achieving, a commonality for many students from such backgrounds is a feeling of anxiety about returning to formal study. Despite their broad diversity of knowledge and life experiences, many underestimate their abilities as 'student' (Burke, 2015; Burke, Bennett, Burgess, Gray & Southgate, 2016; Merrill, 2004; Read, Archer & Leathwood, 2003; Scanlon, 2008; Tett, 2000). As Blair, Cline and Wallis (2010) note, embodiment of a student identity is significantly affected by past and present life outside university, and although typically bringing much experiential capital (O'Shea, 2016) to the learning environment, many STEPS students are unfamiliar with institutional protocols and practices. This lack can be further exacerbated by issues associated with past school experiences, and an absence of family support and perception of what higher education study entails. In combination, these factors can negatively impact a student's motivation and encouragement in the consideration of higher education studies (Bennett, Motta, Hamilton, Relf, Gray, Leroy-Dyer & Albright, 2017; Burke et al., 2016; Merrill, 2004; Motta & Bennett, 2018; Willans & Seary, 2007, 2011).

In STEPS, student anxiety and ill-preparedness are taken into consideration in inclusive learning environments that focus on preparing the 'whole' student. Informing the pedagogical practices that aim to empower students to contemplate new possibilities of self as learner is a synthesis of humanism (Gage & Berliner, 1991), transformative learning theory (Cranton, 2016; Dirkx, 2008; Willans, 2010) and adult learning principles (Cranton, 2016; Knowles, 1980). Humanism purports that individuals possess within them all that is necessary to grow and develop their unique capabilities (Huitt, 2009). It holds that students learn best in a learning environment that is physically, psychologically and emotionally non-threatening

(Gage & Berliner, 1991, cited in Huitt, 2009). Humanistic principles are embodied in STEPS learning environments through pedagogical practices that encourage students to reflect on how some of their personal worldviews, perspectives and beliefs may have been limited by life circumstances, upbringing, schooling, work, and many other lived experiences. This is the genesis of transformative learning, theorised as the cognitive, developmental, constructivist, extrarational, emotional, and spiritual process that ensues when disruption or challenge to a long held personal assumption or perspective occurs. An indeterminate period of disorientation can afford opportunities for critical self-reflection. Acting upon a revised or new perspective signifies a personal transformation (Cranton, 2016; Dirkx, 2008).

Underpinning STEPS is an 'inclusive' conception of transformative learning theory (Cranton, 2016; Willans, 2010) that encompasses the cognitive, developmental and extrarational dimensions of learning. When their unexamined personal perspectives and long held worldviews become challenged or unsettled, students are encouraged to critically reflect on themselves, others and the world around them. Cranton (2016) suggests that any strategies that provide opportunities to open up new perspectives and challenge existing assumptions have the potential to encourage reflection and personal transformation. This can be extremely liberating for adult learners returning to study, releasing them from previous perspectives that have possibly limited their potential. Such agency exposes new possibilities and opportunities that can empower them with ways to see and act within a more open world (Cranton, 2016).

Premised on the principles of adult learning, STEPS adopts a philosophical approach akin to other 'enabling' educators (Bennett et al., 2017; Lane & Sharp 2014; Lisciandro & Gibbs, 2016; O'Shea, 2016), wherein existing knowledges and experiences of students are welcomed, valued and built upon. Grounded in the notion that adult learners need justification for learning something before committing to learn it (Cranton, 2016; Knowles, 1980), the view is taken in STEPS that despite non-success in previous academic studies, a student's life experiences actively contribute to their future successes. Thus, experiential knowledge is valued, and in recognition that adult learners respond best to learning that makes sense of new knowledge in the context of their own lives (Cranton, 2016; Knowles 1980), pedagogical practices in STEPS focus on helping students draw from their wealth of prior knowledge and life experiences to critically reflect upon themselves as learners, and why they think, believe and act as they do.

Preparation Skills for University (PSU) is the only compulsory unit for all STEPS students, the rationale being that the skills, concepts and knowledge that these adult learners stand to gain from this unit are deemed fundamental in optimising their future success as a university student. In promoting strategies that reveal greater insight into one's personal learning potential, and addressing personal and other life challenges, PSU actively challenges its adult learners to reflect on past, present and future, and envision their possible future selves (Millman & McNamara, 2018). Consequently, many pedagogical practices in PSU focus exclusively on the student, their unique learning needs, abilities, and prior experiences providing springboards for their learning. Not only are opportunities provided in PSU for the development of relevant technical and academic skills and knowledge, and the application of information literacy skills, but pragmatic skills also, such as effective communication and self-management skills. However, the focus of this chapter is on pedagogical practices in the form of online tools that assist students in discovering more about their unique learning style preferences and personality types, and future study options and possible career paths. The intention of incorporating these pedagogical practices into the curriculum is to critically evaluate and envisage future possibilities in light of new knowledge of self as learner.

In PSU, the view is taken that self-awareness is fundamental to being an effective student. To elicit a greater level of consciousness, specific online pedagogical tools are utilised by students as a catalyst for critical reflection about self as learner. These tools include the Felder-Soloman Learning Styles Inventory (Felder & Soloman, n.d.) and the Jung Typology Test (Myers & Briggs Foundation, n.d.), chosen as appropriate tools because they assist students in understanding how they learn best and experience their world. When in receipt of new insights about themselves as learners, critical reflection can help students deconstruct past learning experiences, both positive and negative, and project ways in which their future learning potential could be enhanced. Greater knowledge of self as learner and contemplation of potential can allow students to see themselves from a different point of view, leading to consciousness-raising (Cranton, 2016).

In terms of guiding students in clarifying their future career prospects, key career websites featuring information regarding possible job opportunities (see, for example, Career Voyage Tool; The Job Outlook; Graduate Careers Australia; My Health Career; Graduate Opportunities) are used. These online tools can encourage students to challenge habitual expectations about careers they have previously felt restricted to and explore alternative possibilities that might enhance their potential. The importance of appropriate, relevant guidance for adult learners in higher education cannot be underestimated. As Cherastidtham and Norton (2018) caution, given the general tendencies of many adults to transition in and out of work and education, lack of suitable career advice contributes to student disengagement and attrition at university.

Methodology

Research informing this chapter was conducted within a qualitative research paradigm, underpinned by a constructivist framework. Transformative learning theory is premised on constructivist assumptions, for as Cranton (2006, p. 23) explains, "meaning is seen to exist within ourselves, not in external forms" and making sense of our world occurs through our "perceptions of our experiences". As such, a qualitative research paradigm allowed for the generation of a corpus of data that embodied the student voice in terms of their perceptions of the impact of certain pedagogical practices utilised in PSU. The data on which findings in this chapter are based were drawn from anonymous, voluntary responses obtained from approximately 562 end of unit (subject) evaluations completed by students enrolled in the core STEPS unit, Preparatory Skills for University over the period Term 1 2016–Term 1 2017.

To protect the privacy of those completing the evaluations, no specific demographic data was collected about age, gender, or study mode status of those responding. However, the age range in STEPS typically spans 17–69 years of age, so responses are likely representative of a very broad age range. The evaluation survey asked students for free text responses about what they considered to be the "Best Aspects of PSU", and "Suggestions for Improvement". Fifty per cent of all enrolled students completed the PSU unit evaluation, and their comments on what they considered to be the "Best aspects of PSU" were retrieved from the evaluation data for use in this chapter. This occurred once ethical clearance was formally granted by the university, and approval from the Head of STEPS was provided.

Organisation and analysis of data

The 'framework model' espoused by Richie and Spencer (2002) was used to categorise and scrutinise data, allowing for the determination of "meaning, salience and connections" (p. 307) relating to the personal impacts of certain pedagogical practices students engaged in while in PSU. Analysis entailed data familiarisation; generation of initial codes; the search for recurring themes; revision of those themes; theme definition and naming; and, production of the final account. Data familiarisation was conducted by iterative readings of student comments, culminating in the establishment of data categorisation and coding. Categorisations were then tallied to consolidate pedagogical practices in PSU most commonly valued by students, then combined and revised to distil salient themes. In relation to pedagogical practices focused on new knowledge of self as learner, data findings revealed that 'empowerment' was a dominant theme, student responses suggesting that enhanced self-knowledge gained through the use of these practices empowered them as students and as people. The following section provides a discussion of this theme, namely *Empowerment through enhanced self-knowledge*. Excerpts from the data representing student viewpoints are interspersed throughout (denoted by quoted text).

Empowerment through enhanced self-knowledge

One reoccurring finding was the students' appreciation for pedagogical practices that enabled them to use online tools to purposefully explore their personal learning style preferences, personality traits and future career options. Multiple students applauded the inclusion of these tools, describing the acquisition of new knowledge about themselves as "insightful; invaluable and had a positive effect on my everyday life"; enabled the ability to "make the most of them [learning styles] as an individual; continuously taught me something new about myself"; "greatly helped my learning and to improve myself"; and in "learning more about myself, achieving more than I thought I was capable of". Embodying the emancipatory goal of transformative learning (Mezirow, 2000), some students indicated that greater self-knowledge led to personal empowerment and motivation, and the consideration of new perspectives. As one wrote: "after completing the Learning and Personality testing, I felt I understood more about myself and it made me want to learn more". In reflecting the importance of embedding adult learning principles in enabling pedagogy, another student shared that the "information was relevant and reflected so much of life, either in one's personal life or the world around us and I found that this is what made learning easy". This was similarly expressed by another who appreciated new self-knowledge and its applicability to contexts beyond STEPS, reflecting that "it is not only valuable for student life but I believe it provides wonderful skills for life in general". This insight was iterated by another, who disclosed that "I learnt a lot about myself as a person and my learning styles which I believe will help me immensely during an undergraduate degree". Indicative of self-reflection evoked in the process of transformative learning, for some students, introspection helped them "to look deeper into myself"; "to understand different ways in which I learn"; or, for another, "to think deeper into myself".

The focus on "self" through relevant meaningful pedagogical practices aimed at self-development and self-awareness was found to be highly valued by many students. In espousing humanistic principles, Gage and Berliner (1991) remind us that knowing how to learn is more important than acquiring a lot of knowledge. This was reflected by student comments such as: "I like that you spend a lot of time learning about yourself to be able to develop the skills you don't necessarily naturally have" and, "I really enjoyed learning about personality types and learning styles. I feel it greatly helped my learning and to improve myself". However, for others, compassion was awakened, and the examination and questioning of long held perspectives, so integral to transformative learning, led to more profound understanding of self. One student confided that they became "very encouraging and accepting of each other's weaknesses", while another felt it was "enlightening to see who shared the same learning styles". As evidence of a revised perspective that encompassed greater inclusivity and compassion, one shared that "discovering how I learn best and applying that to my study has really helped me understand others". This is indicative of a change in the student's understanding of themselves and their world, "seeing familiar things from a different perspective, thereby increasing one's self-awareness" (Cranton, 2016, p. 111).

Armed with greater understanding and knowledge of self and potential, adult learners can come to deconstruct previous perspectives of school, work or life that may have acted as barriers to personal growth. Dirkx (2008), whose work focuses on the meaning and role of emotions in adult learning, cautions that previous humiliation in school classrooms can cause great angst for some students. This appeared so for some students in this research, yet as Millman and McNamara (2018, p. 45), explain, in purposively reflecting on self as learner, "new ways of imagining the self and reimagining the future self can occur". At its core, transformative learning is concerned with meaning making from experience and the questioning of assumptions based on prior experience (Cranton, 2016). This was evidenced by one student, who in reflecting on past experiences, described themselves as "terrible at school", yet upon critical reflection, shared that "this is probably the reason why I've put-off wanting to better myself". Testimony to the influence of pedagogical practices encouraging students to critically reflect on past, present and future selves, was another student's revelation that "STEPS has made an incredible impact in my life ... learning more about myself and also achieving more than I thought I was capable of". The value of using pedagogical practices to elicit more insight about self as learner, and the emancipatory effect such practices can have, was validated by one student who shared that these "made me reflect about myself, that I would not have ever thought of doing before and given me confidence to fore-fill [sic] my dream to complete an undergraduate degree". The suggestion that empowerment can be instigated when long held personal perspectives of self are challenged, examined, and transformed, was similarly expressed by another student who reflected that "I have learned so much about myself and can feel the positive changes already ... I have learned to change my negative thoughts into positive ones".

It was found that many students not only highly valued pedagogical practices that generated new knowledge about themselves as learners, but also highly valued targeted information about their future possible careers. Such practices purposefully cater to the specific needs of the adult learner, and the value of using online tools to explore career options was evident. Students commented about the clarity and decisiveness they gained regarding their future career's intentions. They revealed that *they* [online tools] "were able to help me finally decide what I wish to do for my undergrad"; "helped me to gain a greater understanding of where I want to head career wise and how to achieve these things"; "will hopefully help me to continue as I seek to pursue nursing as a career" and, "gave me a clearer picture of what I need to do and what some job specifics are". For others, it appeared that unexamined perspectives of self as learner were challenged, then revised to encompass a more focused personal projection. As one student articulated: "career profiling has changed my world for the better [as] I now have a clear path towards my future in Business". Transformed perspectives of self as learner and consequent empowerment to envision new future selves were also manifested in student comments: "I can now start dreaming about my career"; "I feel really inspired"; "now I have my goal"; and, "I have gained the confidence to further achieve my dream job". Revised perspectives of self as learner seemingly opened the door of possibilities for some students.

Conclusion

Enabling students are a unique cohort of learners with specific needs, and in their quest to re-engage with formal education, could be said to be ripe for transformation. Findings in this chapter have revealed that greater knowledge of learning style preferences and personality types, alongside greater clarity regarding future career goals and options can be very liberating for adult learners. Providing opportunities to engage in pedagogical practices infused with adult learning, transformative learning and humanistic philosophies can provide valuable opportunities for adult learners to identify and deconstruct unexamined assumptions about themselves as learners. In turn, critical self-reflection on how such perspectives have possibly limited their potential can be more fully explored, and such learners can come to embrace and act upon new or revised perspectives about themselves. This transformative learning process fosters personal growth and the capacity to empower adults learners to more confidently visualise and enact their possible futures.

References

Bennett, A., Motta, S., Hamilton, E., Burgess, C., Relf, B., Gray, K., Leroy-Dyer, S., & Albright, J. (2017). *Enabling pedagogies: A participatory conceptual mapping of practices at the University of Newcastle, Australia.* University of Newcastle, Australia. Retrieved from https://nova.newca stle.edu.au/vital/access/manager/Repository/uon:32947.

Burke, P. (2015). Re/imagining higher education pedagogies: Gender, emotion and difference. *Teaching in Higher Education,* 20(4), 388–401, doi:10.1080/13562517.2015.1020782.

Burke, P., Bennett, A., Burgess, C., Gray, K., & Southgate, E. (2016). *Capability, belonging and equity in higher education: Developing inclusive approaches.* Centre for Excellence for Equity in Higher Education. Australia: The University of Newcastle.

Blair, E., Cline, T., & Wallis, J. (2010) When do adults entering higher education begin to identify themselves as students? The threshold-of-induction model. *Studies in Continuing Education,* 32(2), 133–146, doi:10.1080/0158037X.2010.488355.

Cherastidtham, I., & Norton, A. (2018). *University attrition: What helps and what hinders university completion?*Grattan Institute. Retrieved from https://grattan.edu.au/wp-content/up loads/2018/04/University-attrition-background.pdf.

Cranton, P. (2006). *Understanding and promoting transformative learning* (2nd ed.). San Francisco, CA: Jossey-Bass.

Cranton, P. (2016). *Understanding and promoting transformative learning* (3rd ed.). Virginia: Stylus Publishing.

Dirkx, J. (2008). The meaning and role of emotions in adult learning. *New Directions for Adult and Continuing Education,* 120, Winter, 7–18.

Felder, R., & Soloman, B. (n.d.). *Index of Learning Styles Questionnaire.* North Carolina State University. Retrieved from https://www.webtools.ncsu.edu/learningstyles/.

Gage, N., & Berliner, D. (1991). *Educational psychology* (5th ed.). Boston: Houghton, Mifflin.

Huitt, W. (2009). *Humanism and open education.* Educational Psychology Interactive. Valdosta, GA: Valdosta State University. Retrieved from http://www.edpsycinteractive.org/topics/affect/humed.html.

Knowles, M. (1980). *The modern practice of adult education: From pedagogy to andragogy* (2nd ed.). New York: Cambridge Books.

Lane, J., & Sharp, S. (2014). Pathways to success: Evaluating the use of 'enabling pedagogies' in a university transition course. *GSTF Journal on Education,* 2(1), 66–73.

Lisciandro, J., & Gibbs, G. (2016). 'OnTrack' to university: Understanding mechanisms of student retention in an Australian pre-university enabling program. *Australian Journal of Adult Learning,* 56(2), 198–224.

Merrill, B. (2004). Biographies, class and learning: The experiences of adult learners. *Pedagogy, Culture and Society,* 12(1),73–94.

Mezirow, J. (2000). Learning to think like an adult – core concepts of transformation theory. In J. Mezirow and Associates (Eds) *Learning as transformation: Critical perspectives on a theory in progress* (pp. 3–31). San Francisco, CA: Jossey-Bass.

Millman, T., & McNamara, J. (2018). The long and winding road: Experiences of students entering university through transition programs. *Student Success,* 9(3), 37–49, doi:10.5204/ssj. v9i3.465.

Motta, S., & Bennett, A. (2018). Pedagogies of care, care-full epistemological practice and "other" caring subjectivities in enabling education. *Teaching in Higher Education,* 23(5), 631–664.

Myers & Briggs Foundation (n.d.). *Jung typology test.* Retrieved from http://www.humanm etrics.com/cgi-win/jtypes2.asp.

O'Shea, S. (2016). Navigating the knowledge sets of older learners: Exploring the capitals of first-in-family mature age students. *Widening Participation and Lifelong Learning*, 18(3), 34–54, doi:10.5456/WPLL.18.3.34.

Read, B., Archer, L., & Leathwood, C. (2003). Challenging cultures? Student conceptions of "belonging" and "isolation" at a post-1992 university. *Studies in Higher Education*, 28(3), 261–277, doi:10.1080/03075070309290.

Richie, J., & Spencer, L. (2002). Qualitative data analysis for applied policy research. In A. Huberman & M. Miles (Eds), *The qualitative researcher's companion* (pp. 305–329), doi:10.4135/9781412986274.

Scanlon, L. (2008). Adults' motives for returning to study: The role of self-authoring. *Studies in Continuing Education*, 30(1), 17–32.

Tett, L. (2000). "I'm working class and proud of it". Gendered experiences of non-traditional participants in higher education. *Gender and Education*, 12(2), 183–194.

Universities Australia. (2018). *Data snapshot 2018: Australia has one of the best higher education systems in the world*. Retrieved from https://www.universitiesaustralia.edu.au/australias-universities/key-facts-and-data#.XD6UDsRS-Uk.

Willans, J. (2010). *Navigating personal change: Transforming perceptions of self as learner*, (Doctoral dissertation), CQUniversity Australia.

Willans, J., & Seary, K. (2007). I'm not stupid after all – changing perceptions of self as a tool for transformation. *Australian Journal of Adult Learning*, 47(3),433–452.

Willans, J., & Seary, K. (2011). I feel like I'm being hit from all directions: Enduring the bombardment as mature-age learner returning to formal learning. *Australian Journal of Adult Learning*, 51(1), 119–142.

5

LIBERATION AND CONNECTION

Fostering critical students as active agents of their own learning

Dr Sarah Hattam and Jennifer Stokes

> The learning process should be one that enables students to contend with their actual conditions, in order to move toward greater critical consciousness and a critical literacy that prepares them to engage effectively with more complex forms of knowledge and to enact practices in their lives in sync with a more just world.
>
> *(Darder, Mayo, & Paraskeva, 2016, p. 3)*

Introduction

Many enabling programs adopt fundamental principles from pedagogies of social justice and other empowering philosophies. As educators, we have drawn upon critical pedagogy to inform the design and development of key courses that serve to embed criticality in our enabling teaching and support the transition of students into Higher Education (HE). While our university delivered a preparatory program for many years prior to the establishment of our school in 2011, we realised early into our own teaching in enabling education that we had been given a rare and special opportunity. Enabling education is characterised by its separation from mainstream HE as well as freedom from constraints of a standardised, government-regulated year 12 curriculum. As an alternative pathway into university, we realised we had the potential to engage and capture an audience with teaching approaches and curriculum that could be labelled 'radical' within higher education (Shor, 2007, 2013). We are not alone in this quest, as there are other 'radical' teachers in HE that also advocate for and adopt critical pedagogical approaches (Brookfield, 2004; Mayo, 1999; Finger & Asun 2001; Hattam, Shacklock & Smyth, 1997; Degener, 2001). Traditional educational pedagogy relies on the 'banking method' (Freire, 1974) and prior to widening participation initiatives, the 'traditional' Australian university student was more likely to be of Anglo-Saxon origin, middle-class and able to compete in a masculine, competitive culture (Bennett et al., 2016; Burke, Bennett, Burgess, Gray & Southgate, 2016). Widening participation warrants a redesign of educational pedagogy to better support and value students from diverse backgrounds and extend the knowledges valued within the university in line with socially inclusive approaches. This chapter shows how our linking of philosophy, pedagogy, and practice radically shifts away from established pedagogy as we unsettle the notion of the 'traditional' university student subject. This chapter considers the role of strong educational philosophy in pedagogy and practice, which provides spaces for students to explore relevant issues, develop class consciousness and critique systems, so that they may engage with societal change.

We have applied these pedagogical and philosophical approaches in the design and delivery of critical, digital, and information literacy courses. We provide examples from practice in the courses *Digital Literacy: Screen, Web and New Media, Future Ideas: Information and the Internet* and *Critical Thinking: Media and Academia*. Constructing meaningful experiences through exploring contemporary texts and interpreting these in an academic context assists the students to "read the word through a reading of the world" (Freire, 2004, p. 29). Supporting the development of respectful dialogue in enabling classrooms assists in the development of learning communities wherein each learner is valued and feels safe to develop their critical understanding of the world. Through carefully designed curricula that respond to students' needs and develops awareness, this approach encourages passionate engagement leading to deep learning experiences (Ramsden, 2003). This chapter will explore the role of educators as change-makers, the students' adoption of critical approaches, and the potential this presents for the development of active learning communities.

The need for critical pedagogy

In adapting critical pedagogy for the present, we reflect upon how Freire's philosophy was born in revolutionary 1960s South America. Additionally, Shor speaks of his earlier experimentation with critical pedagogy in the 1970s in a time of counter culture in American colleges. As sociologists, we identify the need for resistance, activism, and a questioning of the status quo in our contemporary global economic and political times. We are in an era of 'Fake News', the rise of social media, Brexit, growing nationalist rhetoric across Europe, and changes to media ownership laws limiting the diversity of voices presented to the Australian public (Evershed, 2018). Alongside similar Western nations, politics of division, fear, and the culture wars (Johnson, 2007) dominate Australian political discussion. This is a time to question dominant messages and ask why we are being distracted from critical global issues, such as climate change, and the widening gap between rich and poor in many wealthy nations. These are times to encourage our students to seriously question the world around them and to imagine a more equal and caring society. It is through education that we can co-create dialogue, extend opportunity, and support our students to make a difference in their own lives and the lives of others, in the hope of building a better world together.

Our teaching approaches and course design are underpinned by the philosophical work of Ira Shor and Paulo Freire (1987a) who believe in the liberating and transformational role that education can play. This educational philosophy inspires us to employ critical approaches which lead to transformative experiences wherein students can critique power structures and gain agency:

> as conscious human beings, we can discover *how* we are conditioned by the dominant ideology. We can gain distance on our moment of existence … we can struggle to become free precisely because we can know we are not free! That is why we can think of transformation.
>
> *(Shor & Freire, 1987a, p. 13)*

This chapter will explore the liberatory potential of informed course design, which can support student transformation into critical and active agents of their own learning.

Drawing on Freire and Shor's teachings of critical pedagogy provides opportunities for radical teaching, as their approaches are underutilised in mainstream HE or secondary schooling pedagogy. Arguably, by their nature enabling programs are a radical space, designed to widen participation and challenge the status quo of who 'belongs' at university. Through practice and research, we learnt our students often had negative experiences at high school (Smyth & Hattam, 2004), which led them to question their capability and intelligence and whether they belonged at university (Burke et al., 2016). We could see that often the 'problem' of our students' prior lack of educational attainment was framed in deficit terms (Bacchi, 1999; 2009); that students from low socio-economic backgrounds could be perceived as lacking the cultural capital to succeed at university (Bourdieu, 1977). Yet, we could also see opportunities to value the diverse capitals students bring through a 'funds of knowledge' approach (Moll, Amanti, Neff & Gonazales, 1992), which would assist them to connect with university. We realised that we needed to implement an alternative method to connect with our students who had previously disengaged or encountered barriers in their education. Challenging traditional methods has its own issues, as Shor and Freire observe:

> there is a lot of pressure to teach the traditional way, first because it is familiar and already 'worked out', even if it doesn't 'work' in class. Second by deviating from the standard syllabus you can get known as a 'rebel' or 'radical'.
>
> *(1987a, p. 7)*

While we work to empower students through an understanding of the political nature of education and social systems, we share Long's understanding that we must

> be careful not to distort the spirit of Freire's radical pedagogical agenda by taking for granted that empowerment and liberation are synonymous with autonomous actors engaging in militant, counterhegemonic activity … the call of the radical teacher is therefore to challenge and enable students to take

responsibility for their own education so that students become both willing and able to make difficult, perhaps even life-changing decisions.

(Long, 1998, p. 114)

In this way, we can work toward greater social justice; as Shor (2007, p. 39) argues "questioning the status quo is the central goal" of radical teaching.

Freire and Shor's empowering education

Freire has inspired critical educators and those working toward greater social inclusion through a commitment to utopian ideals wherein we actively "imagine a world not as it is now but as it should and can be" (Mayo, 2012, p. 9). In Freire's work, societal change is progressed through critical pedagogy, which understands education as a political system that privileges some and disempowers others. Through respectful praxis and critical consciousness raising, educators can work with the oppressed to transform the world (Freire, 2004). Freire's critical pedagogy was developed through teaching experiences with oppressed peoples in 1960s South America (Mayo, 2012), and his approach conveys the radical ideals of the time. His hopeful approach has been adapted and implemented around the world, while maintaining its commitment to societal betterment: "critical pedagogy is fundamentally concerned with the relationship between education and power in society and, thus, uncompromisingly committed to the amelioration of inequalities and social exclusions in the classroom and society at large" (Darder et al., 2016, p. 1).

Rejecting a 'banking' approach to education, Freire (2004) focuses on the importance of respectful dialogue to better understand students' subjective position, progress understanding, and support active critique of systems. Working with students to develop tools to analyse and overcome the structural limitations of existing systems, critical educators encourage agency and facilitate societal transformation (Darder et al., 2016, p.3). In this way, educators continue to develop understanding and critique to better support marginalised students: "through dialogue, problem posing and reflection (a form of praxis), students can come to a deeper understanding of the factors that contribute to their marginalisation and the steps they might take to eliminate them" (Degener, 2001, p. 13). In implementing critical pedagogy for teaching in the developed world, educators have maintained the revolutionary spirit and commitment to hope and societal change embodied in Freire's work.

Like Freire, Shor's critical teaching framework strongly emphasises the 'empowering' role that education can play. The history of Freire and Shor's intellectual relationship is revealed in their co-authored book *A pedagogy for liberation* (Shor & Freire, 1987a), a transcript and record of their conversations about their shared dream of liberating education. The book provides an insight to both Freire and Shor's classroom experiences, as they experimented with liberatory pedagogies. Shor followed this up with a practical 'guide' (Shor, 1992) of how to apply critical pedagogy to teaching, which was valuable in the development of our own praxis.

In *Empowering education: Critical teaching for social change* (1992), Shor offers explicit methods for how to implement key aspects of Freire's philosophy.

In this chapter we demonstrate how we implement four of these elements: participatory, problem-posing, dialogic, and change-agency. The following sections demonstrate how we have adopted Shor's model to produce positive outcomes for our students, to inspire a sense of liberation and to re-assess their own place in the world.

Liberation through critical literacy

Critical Thinking: Media and Academia is a critical literacy course which focuses on the media for the first seven weeks, followed with six weeks of analysis of the academic genre. The course aims to develop the criticality of the students across the genres so they learn that some are more credible sources of information than others. From a social justice perspective, teaching critical literacy in a university widening participation program, targeted at people who were historically marginalised, is fundamentally important. The diversity of our student cohorts is substantial with approximately over 50 per cent from low socio-economic backgrounds, 40 per cent from culturally and linguistically diverse (CALD) backgrounds, 10 per cent on humanitarian visas and 5 per cent Aboriginal.

This course highlights who benefits from the status quo "by disrupting commonplace notions of socially constructed concepts such as race, class, gender and sexuality" (Wallowitz, 2008, p. 1). The tools developed in the course assists the recognition of how "language use is one social force constructing us" (Shor, 1999, p. 2) and critical literacy can "teach oppositional discourses so as to remake ourselves and our culture" (Shor, 1999, p. 2). This element of critical literacy is liberatory as students engage in dialogue regarding the social constructions of race, gender, sexuality, social class, age, and religion in the texts around them and question the 'truth' claims that are being told in these narratives that may be contributing to their own marginalisation in Australian society.

In the development of the curriculum of *Critical Thinking*, where it is possible, the students are encouraged to select their own topic for assessment to enhance the participatory element in the course. The 'participatory' element highlights the political importance of 'talking' that occurs in the teaching space, as "the rules for talking are a key mechanism for empowering or disempowering students" (Shor, 1992, p. 21). If participating in a group text analysis, we select a topic that connects with their life-worlds. This demonstrates Shor's connection also between generative issues, topical themes and academic themes. When taught in isolation from the other two themes, the academic theme can be abstract and 'alien' (Krause, 2006) to students new to university.

A topical theme we explore to highlight how the media utilises language techniques (or discourses) that produces harmful consequences for groups of people is the link between young people and 'hoon drivers' (a term commonly employed to describe people who drive above the speed-limit and break road-safety laws). We problem-pose collectively what is the 'truth' about young people in contemporary times? We show clips from mainstream current affair shows that regularly repeat the same stories about young people (specifically working-class young men) engaging in dangerous practices on the roads. The students observe that the repetitive representation of young people as 'hoons' by the media is damaging with the increased cost of insurance for all male drivers under the age of 25 as well as 'hoon' driver laws that mean all drivers under 25 cannot drive with other young people after 9 pm at night.

We connect the discussion with an 'academic theme' by introducing Cohen's (2002) theory of moral panics to show how politics and the media historically construct 'folk devils'. Cohen's theory outlines the steps involved in constructing 'folk devils' with the media shaping the opinion of particular groups of people, creating a panic amongst the viewers (and voters) who then lobby the government for change of laws and policies. This often produces an 'a-hah' moment for the students. They see how the media works along a continuum of condemnation and commendation and people and issues are presented to us in simple binary terms, as we are encouraged to 'choose a side'. They see how particular groups are continually positioned in particular ways (refugees, Aboriginal Australians, women, young people), and the audience is only presented with narrow perspectives on issues (marriage equality, abortion, politicians, welfare support).

Students often reflect on completion of the course of how they have come to identify the media as a key proponent of racism, sexism, Islamophobia and homophobia. Giving the students opportunities to analyse and critique the power structures (media, government, education, church) that they interact with on a daily basis empowers them as they realise they can resist and challenge the dominant messages communicated within and by these structures. Choosing themes that connect strongly with their lifeworlds means the students see that learning about political ideologies is important to them. This inspires students to challenge what is being presented as the 'truth' in the media across a whole range of issues. In Freire's terms, through the course students can become 'masters of their own thinking' (1974, p. 124), as their consciousness has been raised and they are empowered to create their own 'truth' claims, or narrative, about the world and their place in the world.

Building agency through digital and information literacies

In developing content for enabling programs, dialogic processes are employed to build trust and rapport with students, embed elements of learner choice, and work with students to co-create content, which builds learner agency. Students develop digital literacies and production practices through *Digital Literacy: Screen, Web and New Media*, while *Future Ideas: Information and the Internet* focuses on innovation through information literacy and university research practices.

To support participation, it is important to establish trust early on, particularly for students with negative past educational experiences. The first two weeks of teaching are critical for retention of students transitioning to university through enabling pathways (Hodges et al., 2013, p. 53), so it is important to rapidly establish a welcoming environment wherein diverse voices are valued. Embedding inclusive strategies better supports all learners (Hockings, 2010), and techniques can be employed from the first interaction. As Freire states:

> at the moment you say *Hello! How are you?* to the students you necessarily start an aesthetic relationship. This is so because you are an educator who has a strategic and directive role to play in liberating pedagogy. Then, education is simultaneously a certain theory of knowledge going into practice, a political and aesthetic act.
>
> *(Freire in Shor & Freire, 1987b, p. 31)*

Learning names, goals and motivations for study helps educators tailor learning toward student interests. As an introduction to our inclusive learning environment, university codes of conduct are unpacked and connected to classroom practice. From the first tutorial, academic culture is introduced, such as the '50-minute-university-hour' and use of first names, and linked to a supportive learning environment. While especially relevant for first-in-family students, this explication acts to reassure all students that individuality is respected. Establishing an inclusive learning environment opens space for dialogue wherein students actively contribute, and their knowledges are valued.

With trust established, we move to problem exploration of complex and emerging digital and information issues, assisting students to build academic literacies, knowledge and argumentation. For example, in a 2018 *Digital Literacy* lecture we explored the 'moral panic' and reportage on video game *Fortnite* on current affairs television and by YouTube vloggers. Students drew upon gaming experience and familial relationships to bring valued perspectives to the discussion. Ultimately, we reached a consensus that the issue was around parental supervision, lax enforcement of game ratings, and misunderstanding of game content. Here, the dialogic classroom provided learning outcomes for both students and academics, working together to determine the best way forward from a combination of lived experience and theory.

Course assessments provide opportunities for students to generate concepts and address student-identified problems. In *Future Ideas*, learning analytics is used to capture responses to questions posed in the lecture and online, and students form teams based on topic interest, using research to better understand and address these 'wicked problems'. Students are encouraged to use design thinking and diverse perspectives to approach their research question, which underpins their engagement with academic sources. In *Digital Literacy* students develop an individual pitch for a digital project, which supports personal or professional interests, including advocacy for disempowered groups. Recent examples include infographics to further understanding of diverse sexual orientation, anti-bullying, or breaking the cycle of drug dependency, websites for environmental action or mental health, and virtual reality excursions for bedridden patients. The students welcome elements of choice and this underpins heightened commitment to producing high quality assignments, which support student agency and facilitates deep learning outcomes (Ramsden, 2003). Through connecting with student lifeworlds and a commitment to change through informed action, the tutorial room becomes a space for innovation and new understandings are built through respectful co-construction of knowledge.

Conclusion

We look with hope to the diverse knowledges and perspectives these new students bring through successful transition to and connection with university. Engaging with students' lived experience supports transformation of self and society through education: "the students' lives and language were social texts ... the liberatory process could be a window and a road to the students, to see their own conditions and to envision a different destiny" (Shor, 1992, p. 24). As students from marginalised backgrounds enter the academy through enabling education, they also make a valued and unique contribution through connecting their existing knowledges with those of the university, and the liberatory potential of widening university participation is evident. As Shor and Freire (1987b) argue, "the critical development of these students is absolutely fundamental for the radical transformation of society" (p. 23). At a time when trust in significant institutions has fallen, there is growing evidence of activism for societal betterment around the world. From #MeToo to #NeverAgain, young people are mobilising through technology and developing agency. As educators, we can play a significant role through philosophically informed pedagogy and practice that supports students to develop critical consciousness, and informed action to create change for a better future. Let's begin!

References

Bacchi, C. (1999). *Women, policy and politics: The construction of policy problems.* London: Sage.

Bacchi, C. (2009). *Analysing policy: What's the problem represented to be?* NSW: Pearson.

Bennett, A., Motta, S. C., Hamilton, E., Burgess, C., Relf, B., Gray, K., Leroy-Dyer, S., & Albright, J. (2016). *Enabling pedagogies: A participatory conceptual mapping of practices at the University of Newcastle.* Australia: University of Newcastle.

Bourdieu, P. (1977). *Outline of a theory of practice.* Cambridge: Cambridge University Press.

Brookfield, S. D. (2004). *The power of critical theory: Liberating adult learning and teaching.* Indianapolis: An Imprint of Wiley.

Burke, P., Bennett, A., Burgess, C., Gray, K., & Southgate, E. (2016). *Capability, belonging and equity in higher education: Developing inclusive approaches.* Australia: University of Newcastle.

Cohen, S. (2002). *Folk devils and moral panics: The creation of mods and rockers* (3rd ed). Canada: Routledge.

Darder, A., Mayo, P. & Paraskeva, J. (2016). *International critical pedagogy reader.* New York: Routledge.

Degener, S. (2001). Making sense of critical pedagogy in adult literacy education. In J. E. Comings, B. E. Garner, & C. E. Smith (Eds), *Annual review of adult learning and literacy.* Volume 2. The Jossey-Bass Higher and Adult Education Series (pp. 26–62). San Francisco: Jossey-Bass Publishers.

Evershed, N. (2018, 3 August). How the Fairfax takeover will further concentrate Australia's media. *The Guardian.* Retrieved from https://www.theguardian.com/news/datablog/2018/aug/03/the-fairfax-takeover-and-how-it-will-worsen-australias-media-industry-squeeze.

Finger, M. & Asun, J. M. (2001). *Adult education at the crossroads: Teaching our way out.* New York: Palgrave.

Freire, P. (1974). *Education for critical consciousness.* New York: The Crossroads Publishing Company.

Freire, P. (2004). *Pedagogy of hope: Reliving pedagogy of the oppressed.* Trans. R. B. Barr, London: Continuum.

Hattam, R., Shacklock, G., & Smyth, J. (1997). Towards a practice of critical teaching about teachers' work. *Teaching in Higher Education*, 2(3), 225–241.

Hodges, B., Bedford, T., Hartley, J., Klinger, C., Murray, N., O'Rourke, J., & Schofield, N. (2013). *Enabling retention: Processes and strategies for improving student retention in university-based enabling programs.* Canberra: Office for Learning and Teaching, Commonwealth of Australia.

Hockings, C. (2010). *Inclusive learning and teaching: Research synthesis.* York: Higher Education Academy.

Johnson, C. (2007). *Governing change: From Keating to Howard.* Perth: Network.

Krause, K. (2006). *Transition to and through the first year: Strategies to enhance the student experience*, Keynote Paper Inaugural Vice-Chancellor's Learning and Teaching Colloquium 2006. Queensland, Australia: University of the Sunshine Coast.

Long, D. (1998). A radical teacher's dilemma. Response to "Practicing radical pedagogy: Balancing ideals with institutional constraints". *Teaching Sociology*, 26(2), 112–115.

Mayo, P. (1999). *Gramsci, Freire and adult education: Possibilities for transformative action.* London: Zed Books.

Mayo, P. (2012). *Echoes from Freire for a critically engaged pedagogy.* London, Bloomsbury Publishing.

Moll, L., Amanti, C., Neff, D., & Gonazales, N. (1992). Funds of knowledge for teaching: Using a qualitative approach to connect homes and classrooms. *Theory into Practice*, 3(2), 132–141.

Ramsden, P. (2003). *Learning to teach in higher education* (2nd ed). London: Routledge Falmer.

Shor, I. (1992). *Empowering education: Critical teaching for social change.* Chicago: University of Chicago Press.

Shor, I. (1999). What is critical literacy. *Journal of Pedagogy, Pluralism, and Practice*, 1(4), 2–32.

Shor, I. (2007). Can critical teaching foster activism in this time of repression. *Radical Teacher: A Socialist, Feminist, and Anti-racist Journal on the Theory and Practice of Teaching*, 79(Fall), 39.

Shor, I. (2013). Occupy in one classroom. *Radical Teacher: A Socialist, Feminist, and Anti-racist Journal on the Theory and Practice of Teaching*, 96(Spring), 54–58.

Shor, I. & Freire, P. (1987a). *A pedagogy for liberation: Dialogues on transforming education.* Westport, Connecticut: Bergin Garvey.

Shor, I. & Freire, P. (1987b). What is the 'dialogical method' of teaching? *The Journal of Education*, 169(3), 11–31.

Smyth, J. & Hattam, R. (2004). *Dropping out, drifting off, being excluded: Becoming something without school.* New York: Peter Lang.

Wallowitz, L. (2008). *Critical literacy as resistance.* New York: Peter Lang.

THE EDUCATORS' TIPS FOR FLOURISHING STUDENTS (PART I)

...learning communities, when properly implemented, offer the promise of significant improvement in both the quantity and quality of student learning.

(Tinto)

Be unified in a belief about the role of enabling education to uncover students' potential and unlock their agency.

(Olds, Jones, & Lisciandro)

When recruiting new staff to work in the space of transition, the most important thing that you need to know is what their values and beliefs about education are. Ask questions that drill down into their philosophy. Ask questions about how they go about their practice. Is there clear alignment and do they care about students and their outcomes? Do they embody a growth mindset and a commitment to social justice and flourishing of their students?

(Olds, Jones, & Lisciandro)

Build student engagement by meeting students in a space which is inclusive, familiar, interesting and relevant to them. Make a space of shared passions where students can find commonalities, where anxieties can dissipate through the use of humour. Ensure this space values and unleashes the potential in their diverse 'capitals'.

(Olds, Jones, & Lisciandro)

At all times, enabling educators should know and respect their students and the knowledge, experiences and possible anxieties they bring to the learning environment.

(Willans)

Dialogue is key to understanding student perspectives and subjective experience. There is a wealth of knowledge in your classroom. Creating a welcoming and respectful learning environment through clear expectations will encourage students to feel safe to share their experiences.

(Hattam & Stokes)

Find out what is important to students in your course and build your curriculum around their concerns that can then be connected to academic themes.

(Hattam & Stokes)

PART II
Engaging diverse cohorts

INTRODUCTION

Dr Angela Jones

When delivering a professional development session to a team of online tutors, I asked the question: "What does engagement in the online space look like to you?" A room of blank faces blinked back at me as if I was speaking a foreign language. One gingerly replied: "An active forum?" To which I asked: "Is that only place where we can see engagement? Can engagement be seen anywhere else?"

If we, as educators, do not know what engagement looks like in the context of our teaching, how can we effectively engage students? There is no one-size approach for transition in/to higher education or the world of enabling located within this paradigm. *What* engagement looks like in different contexts, *how* we effectively engage diverse cohorts and *what* impacts engagement can often feel like constantly changing elements. Diverse cohorts need diverse approaches and this is the focus of this section. Within these pages we weave pedagogical approaches that are uniquely framed around the philosophical, cultural and political context in which these cohorts and educators are located. Deeply rooted in ideas of student-centred learning, these chapters rigorously theorise why different philosophical stand points – beyond that of the educator – are necessary to create authentic and engaging programs that value and celebrate diverse ways of thinking and knowing, while building new knowledge and transitioning students to the university environment.

This section begins with Forrest and Hogue's chapter "Bridging Cultures Over-Under", which provides a context for Indigenous enabling programs in Australia and Canada, and shares the authors' philosophically driven two-eyed ways of seeing pedagogy. They look at the value of diverse cultural capitals and the need for engaging both Indigenous and Western knowledge systems when curating the transitional experience. These authors share their experience in bridging cultural worlds, and developing shared spaces of knowledge in their collaboration between Canadian and Australian enabling programs. Bennett and Bennett's chapter extends the discussion on engaging Indigenous cohorts. Through their philosophical rationale for 'Big Ideas' (a subject in K-Track, an Indigenous enabling program in Western Australia) they offer the reader an alternative framework for engaging learners. Their discussion on intersectionality demonstrates how curriculum that situates Aboriginal and Torres Strait Islander (ATSI) experience within discussions of socio-political and cultural 'big ideas', can challenge stereotypes that can impact Aboriginal university students' capacity for success. Beals and Perrot, through their conversational vignettes, write through the experience of drawing on the Pasifika philosophies of Va and Talanoa to engage students in paradigms that 'make sense' to the student and support the transition to tertiary education within a New Zealand context.

Monteith and Geerlings' journey us to the world of high school enabling students. Their *newness* to the space and socio-cultural location on the edge of Perth, Western Australia, place them physically and metaphorically on the fringe of transitional education. This chapter concretises the role of enabling educator as both facilitator and mentor, demonstrating the importance of the practitioners' philosophical and pedagogical position when engaging students in an enabling program. Irwin and Hamilton's chapter shifts gear and ponders the impacts of neoliberalism in the uncomfortable pedagogical space of online enabling education. Jones and Olds continue this conversation in the final chapter of the section. They offer the philosophical response of EduPunk as a way for curriculum designers and educators to culture jam the neoliberalist agenda and (re)engage enabling learners in the oft flat space of online learning.

These chapters offer nuanced conceptualisations and applications of philosophy to pedagogy, and provide snapshots of what diversity looks like within the space of transitional education: culturally, politically, digitally and theoretically. At the conclusion of this section you will find some pithy tips for engaging diverse cohorts in transitional tertiary spaces. So, we invite you dear reader "to come with us on a journey through time and space" (Barratt, 2004), and peak through diverse lenses into the engaging and dynamic world of enabling education across Australia, New Zealand, and Canada.

Reference

Barratt, J. (2004). *Mighty Boosh theme*. United Kingdom: BBC Three.

6

BRIDGING CULTURES OVER-UNDER

A unique collaboration between two Indigenous academic enabling programs in Canada and Australia

Dr Michelle M. Hogue and Joanne Forrest

Disrupting the glass ceiling imposed by traditional Eurocentric-based Western education for Indigenous students requires a different approach to teaching and learning; one that is culturally relevant and that attends to Indigenous Ways of Knowing and Learning (IWKL). Such work is not for the faint of heart as it requires stepping back and critiquing historically embedded philosophy, pedagogy and practice and reframing it in an ethical and equitable way that bridges cultures and connects the learner with both knowledge systems in ways that are transformative and enable success.

Introduction

In Canada and Australia, as well as globally, there is an increasing demographic of Indigenous students preparing for university through enabling courses or programs as an entry point. The greatest success is seen when such programs create bridges between Indigenous knowledge systems and Western education that are inclusive of IWKL (Aikenhead, 2001; Bartlett & Marshall, 2009; Bartlett, Marshall & Marshall, 2012; Hogue, 2018; Ober & Bat, 2007) rather than expecting Indigenous students to assimilate into the Western system. The Preparation for Tertiary Success (PTS) program is designed and delivered by Batchelor Institute for Indigenous Tertiary Education (BIITE), located at Charles Darwin University in Darwin, Northern Territory, Australia. This program has the underpinning philosophy of *Both Ways* (Ober & Bat, 2007; Ober, 2009), which resonates with the *Two-Eyed Seeing* philosophy (Bartlett & Marshall, 2009; Bartlett, Marshall & Marshall, 2012) incorporated into the First Nations Transition Program (FNTP) at the University of Lethbridge, in Lethbridge, Alberta, Canada. Both programs are dedicated Indigenous cohort programs comprised exclusively of, in Canada, First Nations, Métis and Inuit (FNMI) and, in Australia, Australian Aboriginal and Torres Strait Islander (AATSI), students. Our collaboration began when Michelle was on an international scoping research trip in 2016 to explore models of Indigenous academic success; research that led her to Darwin. Although located on polar opposite sides of the world, we had no idea that the Indigenous story (socioeconomic and educational status) interestingly, although sadly, mirrored each other. Fascinated by our extra-ordinarily similar and parallel teaching experiences, we recognised that we, as educators, and our students, could learn much from each other. This vision initiated the building of relationships and sharing between the two programs through curriculum development, instructor exchanges, and student connections via classroom Skype sessions and a closed Facebook website. In addition to sharing our own philosophy as well as our pedagogy and practice, we wanted our students, in connecting with each other, to develop relationships so that they might share their own experiences, learn from each other, and support and encourage each other to achieve their goals. In this chapter we share our integrated philosophy of Two-Eyed Seeing (TES) *for* Both Ways Knowing (BWK) through the pedagogy and practice of our collaborative, co-learning, three-year project entitled *Bridging Cultures Over-Under*. This chapter reveals a unique story of friendship, knowledge sharing, and co-learning that validates IWKL.

Background

In both Canada and Australia, Indigenous peoples have historically been seen to be lesser on all levels, and their way of learning, life and living not equitable to that of the dominant coloniser population. This philosophy of superiority, coupled with the expressed intention to take the land and resources rightfully belonging to the Original Peoples, became the root of assimilationist policies and erasure of Indigenous identity. In Canada this happened through residential schools (Truth and Reconciliation Commission (TRC), 2015) and in Australia through mission schools (Cassidy, 2006). Intergenerational impacts of residential and mission schools have resulted in educational and socioeconomic inequities for Indigenous peoples at all levels. In Australia, of the Indigenous students who have successfully navigated a predominantly Western education system, it is reported that while enrolment is up by 1.2 per cent from a decade ago, Aboriginal people still only make up 1.6 per cent of university student enrolments (Universities Australia, 2017). This low figure is correlated to the low year twelve Indigenous student completion rates (Helme & Lamb, 2011) which directly impact their preparation for, and access to, higher education. In Canada, Indigenous students are seemingly doing better with respect to entrance, retention, and completion at the post-secondary level. Between the 2006 and 2016 Canadian census, FNMI people aged 25 to 64 made gains at all levels of education. Of significant importance for this demographic was the increase in the completion of at least an undergraduate bachelor's degree, up from 7.7 per cent in 2006 to 10.9 per cent in 2016. A similar increase for this demographic was seen in those obtaining a college diploma with an increase to 23.0 per cent in 2016 from 18.9 per cent in 2006 (Statistics Canada, 2016). As in Australia, there is a high attrition rate at the secondary level relative to the non-Indigenous mainstream population, with those living in community being at a greater risk for dropping out (Statistics Canada, 2016). For many socioeconomic reasons, those who do complete high school often do not pursue post-secondary education until much later, and those who do enter directly from high school are often less successful. In both countries, it still remains that Indigenous learners entering into tertiary education, even with a high school diploma, struggle greatly in creating bridges between IWKL and Western expectations. This is due in part to the context of entrenched Euro-Western ways of teaching and learning expectations, as well as the culturally irrelevant curriculum (Aikenhead, 2001; Aikenhead & Michell, 2011; Bartlett & Marshall, 2009; Guenther, 2013; Hogue, 2018; Statistics Canada, 2016). Programs such as the FNTP and PTS, that create bridges between IWKL and Western expectations through intentional design and delivery in a culturally relevant and respectful environment, are critical pathways to university for Indigenous learners (Hogue, Calver, Gomez-Riviere, Lamb & Mellow, 2014; Ober & Bat, 2007; Ober, 2009). While successful, these programs are still few in number and are often viewed through a deficit lens as remedial. This can be a challenge for educators in such programs as there is little opportunity for collaboration and sharing. Our fortuitous meeting in 2016 was important as it opened a door to a unique collaboration between ourselves and the students in our programs. It created a space for us to learn from each other in ways that have greatly enhanced our Scholarship of Teaching and Learning particularly in terms of our philosophy, pedagogy and practice.

Philosophy

Two-Eyed Seeing (TES) is a philosophy established by elders Albert and the late Murdena Marshall, and Dr Cheryl Bartlett at Cape Breton University in Canada nearly three decades ago – a philosophy that since the 2015 Truth and Reconciliation Report and the 94 Calls to Action is finally gaining national momentum. TES refers to seeing with one eye through an Indigenous lens, and the other through a Western lens, using both eyes together for a respectful, equal, shared, and deep vision. It moves beyond perception and perspective to a truly informed, holistic, and binocular vision (see Figure 6.1).

Similarly, Both Ways (BW) was established in the Yirrkala community by the Yolngu people working with the *balanda* (non-Yolngu) people in Northeast Arnhem Land, in the Northern Territory, as a way of working with others (see Figure 6.2). It was further developed by Ober and Bat (2007) and is the underpinning philosophy of BIITE, not only for teaching, but in everything they do. As a teaching and learning practice, BW is an equitable and constantly shifting collaboration with intersections of learning between Indigenous and Western knowledge systems. Students leave BIITE having experience with both knowledge systems upon return to their community. It is a philosophy and practice underpinned by relationships built on understanding, commonality, and respect.

TES (Figure 6.1) (Bartlett & Marshall, 2009; Bartlett, Marshall & Marshall, 2012; Knapp, 2013) and BW (Figure 6.2) (Ober, 2009; Ober & Bat, 2007) as parallel philosophical frameworks, shape the teaching and learning spaces for respectful and rigorous engagement of both Indigenous and Western ways of knowing (world-

FIGURE 6.1 TES philosophical framework (Bartlett & Marshall, 2009; Bartlett, Marshall & Marshall, 2012).

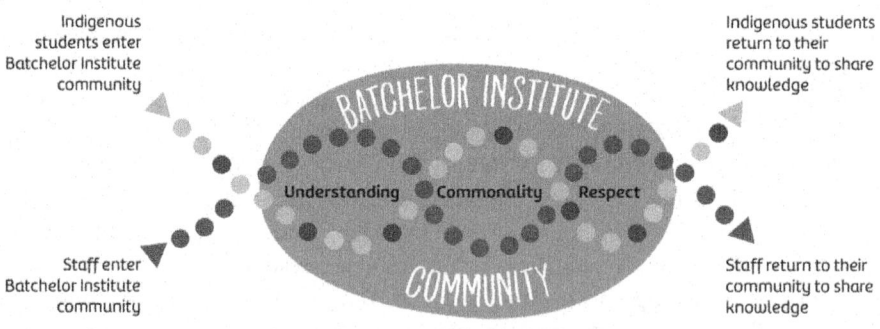

FIGURE 6.2 BW as a philosophical framework (Batchelor Institute, 2019).

views and personal lenses). Elder Albert Marshall best articulates such a collaborative philosophy when he describes co-learning as nurturing collective, relational capacities to understand and to collaborate. "It's about … learning together … with and from each other …" (Bartlett, 2017 as cited in Hogue & Forrest, 2018). The combined philosophies of TES *for* BWK are foundational to our collaboration that informs our pedagogy and shapes our practice.

Pedagogy

Educational pedagogy, is traditionally rooted in the Euro-Western approach – that of theory before practice. Such a pedagogical approach is counterintuitive to the oral, hands-on, practical learning style of Indigenous cultures (Aikenhead, 2001; Aikenhead & Michell, 2011; Bartlett & Marshall, 2009; Beckwith, Halber, & Turner, 2017; Cajete, 1994; Hogue, 2018) resulting in a paradigm clash. This paradigm clash is a critical reason for a multitude of the challenges Indigenous learners experience in the Western education system, particularly in the science, technology, engineering and mathematics (STEM) disciplines where Indigenous peoples are grossly under-represented (Aikenhead, 2001; Bartlett & Marshall, 2009; Hogue, 2018). Freire (2000), suggested that traditional Euro-Western education oppresses the learner by treating them as an *empty vessel* that needs to be filled rather than acknowledging the strengths and knowledge each brings to the table. Freire also advocated for a more world-mediated, co-creation of knowledge whereby the educator is aware of, and acknowledges, their incompleteness of knowledge thus opening a space to learn together. Cooperation, unity, organisation and cultural synthesis, he suggests, lead to decolonisation of the oppressor (Freire, 2000). If we are to enable the success of Indigenous learners in the Western system, then it is critical that our pedagogical approach to teaching, as Freire suggests, be decolonised. For many educators, particularly those of non-Indigenous heritage working in the bridging space, this can be a challenge. To address the historical and current inequities and ensure equitable futures calls one to explore methodological approaches to teaching that often require one to step out of the comfort zone of their traditional pedagogical teaching practice. It challenges one to be open to different ways of seeing and be creative, purposeful, and knowledgeable in that endeavour. In creating bridges within the dominant education system, Nakata (2004) suggests that,

> To defend Indigenous peoples, Indigenous students require understanding of the concepts and methodologies of both systems of knowledge. That is, one can't do battle with Western systems of thought without understanding it, likewise, its inconsistencies cannot be turned around and an Indigenous perspective substituted without rigorous understanding of Indigenous concepts.
>
> *(p. 9)*

Biermann and Townsend-Cross (2008) advocate that Nakata's statement is true also for non-Indigenous educators and students; that in working collaboratively they can create a transformative critical thinking shift, which could be to the benefit of all. Nakata (2007) suggests that the *irreconcilable* nature of the two knowledge systems occurs through misunderstandings when one looks only at the surface level of Indigenous Knowledges. TES for BWK requires that educators deeply explore inclusive and equitable ways of practice.

The recognition, apologies, and acknowledgement of the wrong-doings done to Indigenous people through the enforced assimilative educational practices in both countries has resulted in non-Indigenous people slowly becoming more cognisant of the many socioeconomic, cultural and political reasons, both historically and currently, that have resulted in the discrepancy in educational achievement between Indigenous and non-Indigenous peoples. Senator Murray Sinclair, former Chair of the Truth and Reconciliation Commission of Canada (2015), advocates that it is education that got us into this and education that will get us out. The question then becomes: *Who should be doing this?* Senator Sinclair says that we are all Treaty people and so it is everyone's responsibility; it is not just Indigenous peoples' issue. This calls everyone to action to co-learn, collaborate, and work together. In Australia, it is a call to Treaty through reconciliation and resistance to make education key to moving forward (Worby, Rigney & Tur, 2010). It means decolonising traditional Eurocentric practice in favour of practice that attends to IWKL in a culturally relevant context. Actualising philosophy and pedagogy into ethical and equitable practice can be a challenge for non-Indigenous educators and allies who struggle with how to do this; how to move away from historically embedded practice. The story woven from the statistics of Indigenous success, or lack of, on both sides of the equator, is always through a negative lens of comparison; how they [Indigenous students] don't measure up; how they fall short; what they CAN'T do; always in comparison to the dominant non-Indigenous population. We need to 'Drop the "T" from CAN'T' (Hogue, 2018) and reframe teaching and learning in a different, collaborative, co-learning way; what CAN (and does) work? As educators, one of Indigenous heritage, the other an ally, working in this liminal space of possibility (Hogue, 2018), we share our practice of TES for BWK.

Practice

Both programs as described above, are unique in that they embed the philosophy and pedagogy of TES and BW using the practice of practical, experiential, and applied learning. Our programs are unique in that they are cohort programs which gives us the rare opportunity to explore "what works" with a group of Indigenous learners and adjust our teaching practice to meet the needs and diversity of the cohort. We have entitled our collaboration, as well as the linking of our students in Canada and Australia, as *Over-Under* to represent the polar opposite location of our Indigenous cohorts, yet acknowledge the commonality of their historical and educational experience. Both the FNTP and PTS have been revised continually, survived and grown for a significant length of time (two decades for the PTS and over a decade for the FNTP) to become the successful models of practice they are today.

Creating an over-under learning space

Through technology, we connected our students using Skype sessions and a closed Facebook group. While fraught with challenges such as opposing time zones, opposing academic calendars and thus a limited window of opportunity to connect, as well as extreme weather conditions (i.e. cyclones versus blizzards), and technological issues that impeded connections, we have been able to co-create an amazing learning environment. Students in Darwin are just entering class (the "next" day) when students in Lethbridge are finishing theirs (yesterday). Michelle provides her students with dinner and Joanne provides her students with breakfast for each Skype session. We begin the Skype sessions with introductions made by us as the facilitators and then hand it over to the students. Initially, shyness is an issue but once hesitation dissolves, intrigue and curiosity take over on both sides and the students start talking and asking questions. Students visit with each other *in the real*, see each other's learning spaces, have non-edited conversations, and share their work and projects both visually in real time through Skype as well as on-line in the closed Facebook space. This co-learning has been further augmented through our own exchanges and in-person participation alongside the students in the classroom. Michelle has been able to travel to Darwin and participate extensively in the PTS program four times during the collaborative teaching and learning cycles, and Joanne participated in Michelle's program in Lethbridge for the first time in January and February of 2019. Having a visiting fellow from the other side of the globe that the students have engaged with through Skype sessions and online connections is powerful for the students. This process strengthens relationships through familiarity and context. Importantly, it provides opportunities to ask more in-depth questions. Michelle has more flexibility with the FNTP in terms of design and assessment than Joanne does in the PTS. As such, participation of the FNTP students and presentations to the PTS students in real time, are part of their assessment. In Joanne's PTS there is no assessment associated with the project. Interestingly, regardless of whether there is linked assessment or not, students participate out of interest in co-learning and sharing their culture, stories, projects and assignments. In developing a global connection with other Indigenous students, the project has strengthened their learning identity. A 2018 PTS student reflected,

> … I was intrigued with their future goals … I hope they achieve them. I was fascinated with some of the students' last names especially the names, Eagle Bear and Shot Both Sides. Interesting questions arose from Canada about a treaty and if we are still run by the government. It's funny because we do not know anything about their history and the same applies to them.

One of the most striking, perhaps disconcerting, revelations for the students on both sides is the similarity of their history and current situation. For some, it was a point of anger. *"How can that even be possible?"* is a question asked often by the students in both programs when they hear the history and current realities. For them, it is unbelievable that the same atrocities have happened and still exist. The students recognise that they are not alone, which is a disconcerting point of connection; they have parallel histories and current socioeconomic realities. They gain strength through each other's stories, their histories, learning of their families and importantly their academic aspirations. As one FNTP student in the 2018 session said,

> ... Even though there are big differences in comparison to environment, culture, language and traditions, there are similarities in terms of collectiveness, cultural integrity, and community-based structures ... They were so interested in our culture. It's different because most times we feel our culture isn't part of education, so we don't talk about it. I hope we can continue this.

The Indigenous worldview for the students becomes articulated through the sharing of stories of the past, present and future aspirations.

> I thought it was amazing they [the PTS students] had the same dreams. I always wanted a university degree to make a change for my community, my people, but now I want an education to make a change for all Indigenous people around the world who have been or are being treated like us. That is how they feel too.
>
> *(FNTP student, 2018)*

A 2019 FNTP student said,

> Learning that we aren't the only country with its own Indigenous people who have suffered from colonialism is the thing I really enjoyed. Not that that should be something to be happy about, but it feels like we aren't alone, that we have other as brothers and sisters. Having Joanne in our class was a gift ... we learned of the parallel story, which is important in understanding the resilience of Indigenous people.

Another 2019 FNTP student said,

> The most amazing part of the course was getting to Skype with our Indigenous Australian friends! ... I feel it is important to build relationships not only nationally, but also internationally. I believe that is what makes Indigenous people stronger (our connection with one another).

The depth of student reflections demonstrates engagement in a higher order critical dimension far beyond what might be expected in an enabling program. Both the FNTP and PTS continually attend to *practice*; what works for IWKL. Such a practice has had a positive impact on both retention and success.

Challenging the glass ceiling

Much of the current academic conversation is around Indigenisation (TRC, 2015). What does that really mean and who should be doing it? To truly "Indigenise" requires the knowledge and input of the Indigenous peoples, and importantly, it has to be place and context-based. This requires a critical mass of educated Indigenous people to participate at all levels if we are to truly remove the imposed and existing glass ceiling. While we are slowly moving in that direction, we are not there yet. However, it is possible as educators to change our teaching practice such that it engages Indigenous learners in culturally and contextually relevant ways that attend to IWKL. This means thinking creatively and moving away from traditional teaching practice. For many educators this can be an uncomfortable space that requires a different kind of engagement, one of relationship-building which makes us vulnerable. Some are resistant, as such change is seen as a shift in power dynamics, a loss of control rather than a vision of co-learning and growth. For those in areas that are considered "neutral", devoid of the personal, of culture, such as the sciences and mathematics, it is difficult to see how such a shift in philosophy, pedagogy, and particularly practice can work within their traditional, very structured, framework. Resistance, coupled with fear, produces near insurmountable roadblocks, which can perpetuate the status quo. TES for BWK allows for the messiness of learning, of making mistakes, learning from them and moving forward in a better, more informed way. Summatively, the students in our 2016–2019 Over-Under project reflected,

> Two-Eyed Seeing has helped me translate and incorporate traditional knowledge into my work here at the university … Our ways of knowing and learning were not designed to fit into the institution, but I believe whole-heartedly that one day our ways will be fully embraced and flourish … What I learned in this class is that bridging cultures is more than just filling a hole, it is about building resilience and learning to stand strong … it is really important to understand Two-Eyed Seeing and Both Ways as it is a gateway that can be very beneficial to people; both native and non-native people … this class taught me our ways do fit into education … they count.

Conclusion

Relationships in both enabling programs are established and enriched through developing and sustaining a community of learners. Tinto, Goodsell, and Russo (1994) reflect that having a community of learners is a crucial element for the academic success of students; they need to feel a sense of belonging to something greater or larger than themselves. This has been echoed many times by our students who often say, *"I feel like I have a community"* here. Throughout our work, student discussions continually highlighted the TES for BWK teaching and learning approach. This provided space for continuous questioning (Ober, 2009) that prompted, prodded, provoked, and made us all (students and educators) think outside ourselves through intersectionality and border crossing (Aikenhead, 2001; Aikenhead & Michell, 2011) thus enabling the re-imagining of alternative truths.

Through our Bridging Cultures Over-Under project, our students have strengthened their identity as Indigenous learners. Philosophically, it flips the paradigm and discourse of traditional Eurocentric-based education to one of inclusivity and validity where Indigenous disadvantage is not the dominant and suppressing discourse. Pedagogically, it has opened a space to work with students in critically creative and negotiated ways to build academic literacies through a TES for BWK framework. In practice, it has created a platform for both the students and for us as educators; a digital ethical space to collaborate, co-learn, co-create and co-develop our scholarship of teaching and learning together. Linking intrinsically to our philosophy, it is embedded in our pedagogy, visible and reinforced through our practice.

References

Aikenhead, G. S. (2001). Students' ease in crossing cultural borders into school science. *Science Education*, 85, 180–188.

Aikenhead, G., & Michell, H. (2011). *Bridging cultures: Indigenous and scientific ways of knowing nature*. Toronto, ON: Pearson Canada.

Bartlett, C. & Marshall, A. (2009). Integrative science and Two-Eyed Seeing. Life long learning – from youth to elder; conference on Aboriginal education, organized by the Atlantic Aboriginal Economic Development Integrated Research Program (AAEDIRP) of the Atlantic Policy Congress of First Nation Chiefs Secretariat. Fredericton, NB, 23–25, March 2009.

Bartlett, C., Marshall, M., & Marshall, A. (2012). Two-eyed seeing and other lessons learned within a co-learning journey of bringing together Indigenous and mainstream knowledges and ways of knowing. *Journal of Environmental Studies and Sciences*, 2(4), 331–340.

Batchelor Institute. (2019). Both-ways learning. https://www.batchelor.edu.au/about/both-ways-learning/.

Beckwith, B. R., Halber, T., & Turner, N. J. (2017). Creating agency for environmental sustainability through experiential education, transformative learning, and kincentricity. In H. Kopnina & E. Shoreman-Ouimet (Ed.), *Routledge Handbook of Environmental Anthropology* (1st ed., pp. 412–427). New York and London: Routledge, Taylor & Francis Group.

Biermann, S., & Townsend-Cross, M. (2008). Indigenous pedagogy as a force for change. *The Australian Journal of Indigenous Education*, 37(S1), 146–154.

Cajete, G. (1994). *Look to the mountain: An ecology of indigenous education*. Durango, CO: Kivaki Press.

Cassidy, J. (2006). The stolen generations Canada and Australia: The legacy of assimilation. *Deakin Law Review*, 11(1), 131–178.

Freire, P. (2000). *Pedagogy of the oppressed* (30th anniversary ed.). New York: Continuum.

Guenther, J. (2013). Are we making education count in remote Australian communities or just counting education? *The Australian Journal of Indigenous Education*, 42(2),157–170.

Helme, S., & Lamb, S. (2011). *Closing the school completion gap for Indigenous students*. Canberra, Australian Capital Territory: Closing the Gap Clearinghouse.

Hogue, M. (2018). *Dropping the "T" from CAN'T: Enabling Aboriginal success in post-secondary science and mathematics*. Vernon, British Columbia: JCharlton Press.

Hogue, M., Calver, C., Gomez-Riviere, E., Lamb, M., & Mellow, M. (2014). *Academic Quality Assurance Review (AQAR): First Nations' transition program self study*. Lethbridge, AB: University of Lethbridge.

Hogue, M., & Forrest, J. (2018). Bridging Cultures Over-Under: Digital navigation to create liminal spaces of possibility. *Canadian Journal of Family and Youth/Le Journal Canadien de Famille et de la Jeunesse*, 10(2), 67–84.

Knapp, C. E. (2013). Two-eyed seeing as a way of knowing. *Green Teacher*, (99), 31.

Nakata, M. (2004). Indigenous Australian studies and higher education. *The Wentworth Lectures*, 1–20.

Nakata, M. (2007). The cultural interface. *(Re)Contesting Indigenous Knowledges & Indigenous Studies*, 36(1), 7–14.

Ober, R. (2009). Both-ways: Learning from yesterday, celebrating today, strengthening tomorrow. *The Australian Journal of Indigenous Education*, 38(S1),34–39.

Ober, R., & Bat, M. (2007). Paper 1: Both-ways: The philosophy. *Ngoonjook*, 31, 64.

Statistics Canada. (2016). *2016 Census of population: Aboriginal people*. Retrieved from: https://www12.statcan.gc.ca/census-recensement/2016/ref/98-501/98-501-x2016009-eng.cfm.

Tinto, V., Goodsell, A., & Russo, P. (1994). *Building learning communities for new college students: A summary of research findings of the collaborative learning project*. Syracuse University: National Center on Postsecondary Teaching, Learning and Assessment.

Truth and Reconciliation Commission of Canada. (2015). *Canada's residential schools: The final report of the Truth and Reconciliation Commission of Canada* (Vol. 1). McGill-Queen's Press-MQUP.

Universities Australia. (2017). *Universities unveil Indigenous participation targets*. Retrieved from:https://www.universitiesaustralia.edu.au/Media-and-Events/media-releases/Universities-unveil-indigenous-participation-targets#.XHMEl-gzbIV.

Worby, G., Rigney, L. I., & Tur, S. U. (2010). Where salt and fresh waters meet: reconciliation and change in education. *Australian Cultural History*, 28(2–3), 201–224.

7

BIG IDEAS

Conquering stereotype threat in an Indigenous enabling course

Sian Bennett and Dr Rebecca Bennett

Introduction

There is a significant difference in university success rates between Indigenous[1] and non-Indigenous Australians (Commonwealth of Australia, 2018; Wilks & Wilson, 2015). This fact, commonly described as a gap, is unsurprising given the nation's history of colonisation, marked by systematic discrimination toward Aboriginal and Torres Strait Islander people, together with ongoing marginalisation of Aboriginal culture in popular and political discourses. As part of the national higher education agenda to address this gap, some Australian universities have implemented enabling programs (Wilks & Wilson, 2014; Hodges et al., 2013) to specifically facilitate Aboriginal and Torres Strait Islander student transition into university. These programs are tasked with negotiating a complex set of challenges in addition to increasing participation and retention; they must consider the culture and expectations of both host institution and Indigenous community, as well as the driving pedagogy of the educators who write and teach the curriculum. Additionally, Indigenous students report a range of obstacles to pursuing university study, including financial hardship, stress, study/life balance, family responsibilities, a perceived lack of cultural safety and insufficient health and support services (Wilks & Wilson, 2014; Day, Nakata, Nakata & Martin, 2015). Nonetheless, these programs are a crucial step in bolstering Aboriginal participation at university and closing the educational gap between Indigenous and non-Indigenous Australians (Behrendt, Larkin, Griew & Kelly, 2012).

Although Aboriginal enabling programs share a common goal of improving Aboriginal tertiary participation (Behrendt et al., 2012), they are not nationally regulated, meaning that each university's offering is distinct. Thus, there are significant variations in load, structure, curriculum and content. Data from 2015 indicates that 27 of Australia's 38 public universities offered enabling courses, and 14 of these catered to Indigenous-only cohorts (Pitman et. al., 2017). The length of these vary from ten days to a full year; some combine skills-based and undergraduate units, others offer distinct disciplinary streams, while others direct Indigenous students into mainstream enabling pathways, with supplemental support from the university's Indigenous centre.

This chapter articulates the pedagogical rationale for a humanities subject in a semester-long Indigenous-only enabling program at a medium-sized university in Western Australia. The program comprises four distinct units: *Big Ideas* (Humanities); *Writing Toolkit* (Academic Writing Skills); *Understanding Your World* (Physical and Biological Sciences); and *iHealth* (Health Science). Focusing on *Big Ideas*, as authors who teach into the enabling program (one, Aboriginal; the other, Caucasian), we offer a rationale for the adoption of an intersectional pedagogy for our students, most of whom reside in urban and suburban areas and many of whom have limited or interrupted experience with traditional cultural practices. The aim of our pedagogy is to develop academic self-efficacy, build high expectations of academic success and foster a strong sense of belonging – as Aboriginal students – at university.

To explain our philosophical rationale, we first address the pedagogical challenge of stereotype threat, a psychological construct that can negatively impact educational outcomes for non-traditional students. We then explore intersectionality as a strategy with which to combat negative stereotypes about Aboriginality that may contribute to stereotype threat amongst our student cohort. Finally, we offer three curriculum exemplars to explain how the pedagogy translates into practice. Each exemplar is analysed in light of teaching experience and data collected from 30 student journals, including weekly reflections and feedback submissions over seven semesters. As the data-pool is relatively small, the student reflections are illustrative only. However, they suggest that our intersectional pedagogy increases students' sense that they – as Aboriginal people – belong at university. Through judiciously chosen curriculum topics, activities and assessments, students explore a common misconception that many of the obstacles they face are linked solely to their Aboriginality. This creates a space for Aboriginal students to inhabit where deficit stereotypes about Aboriginality and education are nullified and replaced by contextual alliances with other students. We call this strategy a strengths-based approach, in that it challenges the assumption that being Aboriginal is intrinsically pejorative to academic achievement.

A clear aim of the *Big Ideas* pedagogy is to replace deficit narratives about Indigenous Australians with stories of success, including persistence in spite of obstacles and empowerment through knowledge. To achieve this aim, it is important to acknowledge the impact that deficit stereotypes regarding Aboriginal and Torres Strait Islanders might have on our students' capacity for success. This understanding was developed through the conceptual framework of stereotype threat.

Stereotype threat

The phenomenon of stereotype threat impedes both achievement and aspirations in those who anticipate that others will have a negative view of them, because they belong to a particular group (Spencer, Logel & Davies, 2016). It is characterised by increasing anxiety and decreasing performance (Harackiewicz et al., 2014; Walton,

Logel, Peach, Spencer & Zanna, 2015); individuals respond by effectively confirming deficit stereotypes. Conversely, where stereotypes are not in play, the same individuals perform and aspire to a higher educational standard. Stereotype threat affects individuals even if they disagree, question the premise of, or believe that they do not conform to the stereotype (Yeager & Walton, 2011; Aronson, Fried, & Good, 2002). This is attributed to the cognitive and emotional load associated with actively defying a stereotype in addition to responding to the challenge that learning something new brings.

The educational disadvantage of Aboriginal students is demonstrated through the annual government campaign to "close the gap" in outcomes between Indigenous and non-Indigenous Australians (Commonwealth of Australia, 2018). Only 1.7 per cent of Aboriginal and Torres Strait Islander people hold university qualifications (Commonwealth of Australia, 2018), compared to 31.4 per cent of Australians overall (Australian Bureau of Statistics, 2018). While a crucial issue, the focus on resolving Indigenous disadvantage provides fertile ground for stereotype threat to occur – especially as the stories of disadvantage are rarely balanced with stories of Indigenous strength, innovation, resilience and success.

Dandy, Durkin, Barber, and Houghton (2015) evince the impact stereotype threat can have on the capacity of Aboriginal students. They captured the educational expectations of teachers and students regarding Aboriginals with respect to a range of factors including talent, effort and current performance. The results consistently pointed to Aboriginal students being least likely to achieve across all elements. Aboriginal students rated their own capacity as lowest across all five factors. This study suggested that Aboriginal students as young as eight believed they were lazier and less able than their non-Aboriginal peers. Given that all participant cohorts expressed the lowest expectations for the Aboriginal students, across all markers, the risk of stereotype threat affecting Indigenous students as they transition to higher education is high.

A deficit focus can lead to stereotypes suggesting Aboriginal students are not intellectually or culturally equipped for academic success. Indigenous doctors, lawyers, entrepreneurs, and academics are rarely acknowledged in Australian public discourse; their absence suggests that Aboriginal people are unsuited to such positions. The focus on statistical differences between Aboriginal and non-Aboriginal student capacity positions 'Aboriginality' as a barrier to university, instead of identifying obstacles which result from structural inequality and a history of institutionalised racism. In *Big Ideas*, we turned to intersectionality as a way to re-position Aboriginal identity as an enabler in the pursuit of academic success.

Developing an intersectional pedagogy

The *Big Ideas* curriculum shows Aboriginal students that they can contribute to, and direct, wider discussions about diversity, power and inequality. We contend that the basis of this participation is best achieved by highlighting commonalities of experience relevant to other university students, as opposed to differentiating Aboriginal students' university experience from a perceived student norm. An intersectional approach encourages students to view the self through multiple lenses, including those of gender, class, family, race, and citizenship, that intersect with the experiences of university students who are not Aboriginal. This mechanism means Indigenous students can identify strategic and supportive alliances with others who share aspects of their identity, rather than persist as outsiders.

Intersectionality acknowledges connections between marginalised identities, highlighting structural similarities in the oppression of different social groups. Hahn Tapper (2013, p. 421) explains:

> Intersectionality posits that oppression in one place is intricately linked to oppression everywhere else. Because oppression primarily exists in terms of structures, and because these structures are linked to social identities (e.g., white, black, gay, straight, and so on) and their relation to power, oppression is the by-product of unequal structures built around power and identity.

Drawing upon case studies of programs designed to promote mutual understanding between Palestinian and Jewish identifying Americans, Hahn Tapper (2013) advises to pull focus away from myopic understandings of cultural identity, faith, and ideology. Instead, students are encouraged to explore multiple social identities and to learn about other students' multiple social identities simultaneously.

For Aboriginal students, the transition into university is generally perceived as challenging. Students have reported family members accusing them of being a 'coconut'[2] because they are pursuing tertiary study (Hill, Winmar, & Woods, 2018). The cultural interface transitioning Indigenous students experience is characterised by competing epistemologies, where 'home' and 'university' are understood as mutually exclusive 'Black' and 'White' contexts, respectively (Nakata, 2007). The result of this can be the perception that attending university means rejecting, or temporarily suspending, one's Aboriginality.

An intersectional approach highlights discriminatory structures that affect non-Aboriginal and Aboriginal students alike, underscoring the idea that university learning can be both challenging and rewarding irrespective of cultural heritage. In political terms, an intersectional approach "aims to generate coalitions between different groups with the aim of resisting and changing the status quo" (Gillborn, 2015, p. 279). These coalitions de-exceptionalise the challenges that Indigenous students can face at university, suggesting Aboriginality is not the problem; rather, structures of power and inequality, based on limiting stereotypes, create obstacles that *many* university students face.

Big Ideas' pedagogical dividends

To explain our pedagogy in practice, we offer three curriculum exemplars, in light of data collected from student journals that indicates developing confidence, self-efficacy, and a sense of belonging. While most weeks of the 14-week course explore a new issue, these topics address core aspects of identity – race, gender, and class – often associated with negative stereotypes. Each creates a conceptual base upon which students can build detailed, inter-related understandings of their experiences.

Exemplar 1: Educating Rita – first steps in undermining a deficit model

The first topic in *Big Ideas* introduces the film *Educating Rita* (Gilbert, 1983). The movie, about a mature-aged, working class woman struggling to adjust to university culture, helps students visualise the systemic nature of stereotypes involving class, age and gender. Like the majority of our students, Rita begins as an outsider at university. The campus she attends is populated with students and academics from the middle and upper-classes. Rita worries she is not as intelligent as the traditional students, and that staff and students will judge her accordingly. Close members of Rita's working-class family are also antagonistic toward her studies, contributing to the negative stereotypes confronting Rita.

In *Big Ideas*, Indigenous students often attribute anxiety about university to their cultural identity, viewing "Aboriginality as an expression of disadvantage" (Carlson, 2016, p. 240). The story of Rita demonstrates that obstacles to study are not always race related; class and gender are factors too. Tutorial discussions explore class differences, family expectations, spouse/partner demands, gender, and age as challenges many overcome in their study journey. Identification with Rita's experience is evidenced in the following journal excerpt:

> Sounds silly, but I feel like I'm Rita (from *Educating Rita*) and I'm off to change my stars. I truly feel like I'm slowly becoming not so much of a stranger in the academic world … if I can break the mould and become mobile in my social class then [my children] will follow.
>
> *(Participant 27).*

Establishing non-racialised reasons for discomfort adapting to university appears to generate positive learning outcomes. For example, the following student excerpts suggest this approach has led to increased motivation to persist, in spite of barriers:

> I've learned that I am resilient. I faced an obstacle that many other people have come up against … I chose not to be affected by it and move on.
>
> *(Participant 23)*

> I realised that I can't keep sacrificing the things I love because my parents don't like them … I needs to start doing things for me and I hope that they will soon understand this and see that the things I do make me happy and they make me feel whole.
>
> *(Participant 14)*

Exemplar 2: Some Aboriginals are more Aboriginal than others – challenging the 'purity narrative'

> [I am] learning to love my Aboriginal side, which is something I have never done.
>
> *(Participant 8)*

This exemplar explores the complexities of Aboriginal identity. The topic 'Some Aboriginal people are more Aboriginal than Others' references ongoing debate in Australia regarding racial purity and what constitutes Aboriginality. Students discuss a Federal Court case against journalist, Andrew Bolt (2009), for his article suggesting fair-skinned Aboriginals are not really 'Aboriginal'. This case sparked intensive public debate about 'real Aboriginal people', including a return to caste-based, essentialist race frameworks. Responses to the Bolt court case included some support for his premise from within Aboriginal communities.

It is important to acknowledge that Australian Indigenous people grow up in a society soaked in negative stereotypes about Aboriginality. Thus, stereotypes are not imposed from the outside, but are part of the fabric of Aboriginal existence in Australia. Many negative stereotypes have been internalised and reified by Aboriginal people themselves and even been reimagined as defining traits (Gorringe, Ross, & Fforde, 2011). In these circumstances, a form of lateral violence is evinced where failure to comply with stereotypes is interpreted as failure to be Aboriginal. A noted Aboriginal educator, Sarra, observes, "other Aboriginal people have tried at times to suggest I am not Aboriginal because I … choose not to get drunk with them" (Sarra, 2005, p. 139). The absorption of negative stereotyping is clear in early student reflections:

> I am glad I met a couple of other students, ones that are determined like me. I didn't think I would see other Aboriginal people who were motivated and responsible. It's finally great to see.
>
> *(Participant 8)*

> [I am worried that] people might treat me different because I'm Aboriginal. They might think I came into university the easy way.
>
> *(Participant 25)*

To debunk essentialist narratives about what Aboriginal people should be and do, students share stories about self and family. Tutorial conversations are carefully curated as the issue of skin colour arises; lighter skinned students reveal experiences of discrimination for not being 'black enough', while darker skinned students share stories of racism on the basis of aligning with the stereotypical 'Aboriginal appearance'. The impact of these discussions is illustrated in the following student journal entry:

> When we looked at Aboriginality and what it means to be Aboriginal, I found that interesting. I found that the … ideas and perspectives people portrayed were

all different and shows that everyone sees and experiences things differently. This had an impact on me as it made me see things from other people's point of view.

(Participant 16)

Most of our students, often for reasons associated with governmental interference in Aboriginal communities, have fragile or limited kinship networks and traditional cultural knowledge. Through this topic, we resist privileging any one perspective of Aboriginality as being representative of a larger whole, as this risks excluding students whose experience does not align with the image presented.

Exemplar 3: Stop the boats! – the racial lens refocused

Once limiting notions of Aboriginal identity are challenged, it is important to acknowledge that race still matters and racism is a 'big issue' in Australian society. Students analyse potentially racist narratives about refugees coming to Australia by boat. They also hear stories of recently arrived asylum seekers, including reasons they fled their home nations, dangers of the boat trip over, prolonged anxiety and trauma of detention, and the subsequent difficulties as temporary residents who often face a long wait to establish permanent citizenship. These stories often come as a revelation to students, who had not previously considered the refugee situation, as the following excerpt illustrates:

Monday was an interesting day, listening to people's lives about how they got into Australia. There was [much] stuff that happened to them behind the scenes, without me even knowing.

(Participant 24)

Details about the struggle to find acceptance, in a nation where refugees arriving through unofficial channels are often referred to as 'illegals' or 'queue jumpers', often resonates with Aboriginal students' experience of ostracism in everyday life and racially prejudiced depictions in the media. However, tutorial discussions can also expose racism within the class, which can be confronting for some, as this journal entry explains:

… we had 3 guest speakers who spoke to the class about refugees … with great enthusiasm I sat and listened as all three discussed the importance of having a quicker process of letting people into the country. I know this issue of refugees stirs different emotions amongst people, but one of the class members felt it was necessary to voice their opinion which came across as quite rude and intimidating. It made me extremely angry … this comment also made a few other members angry and we later discussed how it made us feel … and came to the conclusion that the comment was just pure ignorance.

(Participant 14)

The exposure to racial bias within Aboriginal communities can be revelatory for students. While they rarely come to a consensus on whether asylum seekers should be embraced in Australia, students become aware of their own biases and some seek to change them:

> I've been trying to change my implicit biases, which I have reluctantly accepted. I've since realised they are not anything intentional and not ... the way I consciously choose to react to people.
>
> *(Participant 11)*

Through the experience of refugees, students are encouraged to view racism as a structural issue embedded into Australian national ideology. The negative media attention, hardship, and racism refugees experience echoes the experience of our Aboriginal students. This topic not only de-exceptionalises racial prejudice as being focused only on Indigenous people in Australia; it also exposes racial biases held by Aboriginal people. Both outcomes position Aboriginal subjectivity in a way that can confound stereotype threat.

Conclusion – overcoming stereotype threat

Big Ideas aims to show Aboriginal students some of the ways in which they can contribute to, and direct, wider discussions about diversity, power and inequality. Anxiety attached to an Aboriginal ontology is distributed over several facets of identity and repositioned as part of the expected spectrum of student experience. We have offered three curriculum exemplars to explain how we apply an educational philosophy, based on intersectionality, to dismantle the deficit model that normalises educational under-achievement for Aboriginal people. We posit that intersectional understandings of identity create space to build Indigenous students' confidence, aspirations and academic skills, in tandem with the growing number of Indigenous graduates, postgraduates and academics. In this space, students not only embrace their own cultural identity, but those of others, as is illustrated in the following student excerpt towards the end of the enabling course:

> I think differently about so much and there are so many controversial topics we have been discussing ... I love learning about the world and how everyone is different. I have been finding myself watching YouTube videos at home. They are about individuals and their journeys or struggles to become the people they want to be, for example transsexual people or vegan people.
>
> *(Participant 8)*

The efficacy of *Big Ideas* is not attributable to the subject alone, as it is situated within a four-subject Indigenous enabling course with a holistic objective to disrupt limiting stereotypes about Aboriginal people (see Bennett, Strehlow & Hill, in press). However, the impact of the subject resonates in the unsolicited references to *Big Ideas* topics in student journals, where students are simply encouraged to reflect on their overall learning week-by-week, throughout the course. As teachers in *Big Ideas*, we view every semester as a learning experience. We respect that students bring pre-existing, legitimate knowledge to the classroom, especially that which concerns Aboriginal culture and identities. Nonetheless, within *Big Ideas* we consider that stereotypes are themselves a barrier and strive to offset them by pointing to an inherently discriminatory and stratified system that privilege some, while prejudicing others.

We conclude this chapter with students' voices. The value of an Aboriginal enabling program curriculum working against stereotype threat is reflected in their journal excerpts, which suggest "a more optimistic account of group differences in performance" (Inzlicht & Schmader, 2012, p. 3) and increasing self-confidence, self-efficacy and sense of belonging as Aboriginal people at university.

> I realised that when I think about what my future looks like nowadays, I imagine myself sitting in a house I own, with my degree, designing games that I love and want other people to love … The way that I view the world has been altered in the way that I realise that my goals aren't as far-fetched as I thought and that if I really put effort into everything I can make it to where I want to be.
>
> *(Participant 12)*

Notes

1   The terms, 'Indigenous', 'Aboriginal and Torres Strait Islander' and 'Aboriginal' will be used interchangeably. 'Aboriginal and Torres Strait Islander' or 'Indigenous' are generally considered more inclusive of all First Australians. However, in Western Australia, where this study took place, most Indigenous people identify as 'Aboriginal'. Thus, the term 'Aboriginal' is included to acknowledge the prevalence of this identification in the region and in the enabling course in question.
2   Used this way, the term 'coconut' is a slur implying that someone is 'black on the outside; white on the inside'.

References

Aronson, J., Fried, C. B., & Good, C. (2002). Reducing the effects of stereotype threat on African American college students by shaping theories of intelligence. *Journal of Experimental Social Psychology*, 38(2), 113–125. https://doi.org/10.1006/jesp.2001.1491.

Australian Bureau of Statistics. (2018, May). 6227.0 Education and Work, Australia, May 2018. Retrieved from http://www.abs.gov.au/AUSSTATS/abs@.nsf/mf/6227.0/.

Behrendt, L., Larkin, S., Griew, R., & Kelly, P. (2012). *Review of higher education access and outcomes for Aboriginal and Torres Strait Islander people: Final report*. Canberra: DIISRTE. Retrieved from https://docs.education.gov.au/documents/review-higher-education-access-and-outcomes-aboriginal-and-torres-strait-islander-people-1.

Bennett, R., Strehlow, K., & Hill, B. (in press). Myth busting in an Aboriginal pre-university enabling program: Embedding transformative learning pedagogy . *Journal of Curriculum and Pedagogy*.

Bolt, A. (2009, April 15). It's so hip to be black. *Herald Sun*.

Carlson, B. (2016). *The politics of identity: Who counts as Aboriginal today?* Canberra, ACT: Aboriginal Studies Press.

Commonwealth of Australia. (2018). *Closing the gap: Prime Minister's report 2018*. Department of Prime Minister and Cabinet.

Dandy, J., Durkin, K., Barber, B. L., & Houghton, S. (2015). Academic expectations of Australian students from Aboriginal, Asian and Anglo backgrounds: Perspectives of teachers, trainee-teachers and students. *International Journal of Disability, Development and Education*, 62(1), 60–82. https://doi.org/10.1080/1034912X.2014.984591.

Day, A., Nakata, V., Nakata, M., & Martin, G. (2015). Indigenous students' persistence in higher education in Australia: contextualising models of change from psychology to understand and aid students' practices at a cultural interface. *Higher Education Research & Development*, 34(3), 501–512. https://doi.org/10.1080/07294360.2014.973379.

Gilbert, L. (Producer & Director). (1983). *Educating Rita* [Motion picture]. UK: Acorn Pictures.

Gillborn, D. (2015). Intersectionality, critical race theory, and the primacy of racism: Race, class, gender, and disability in education. *Qualitative Inquiry*, 21(3), 277–287. https://doi.org/10.1177/1077800414557827.

Gorringe, S., Ross, J., & Fforde, C. (2011). *'Will the real Aborigine please stand up': Strategies for breaking the stereotypes and changing the conversation* (Research Discussion Paper No. 28). Canberra, ACT: Australian Institute of Aboriginal and Torres Strait Islander Studies.

Hahn Tapper, A. J. (2013). A pedagogy of social justice education: Social identity theory, intersectionality, and empowerment. *Conflict Resolution Quarterly*, 30(4), 411–445. https://doi.org/10.1002/crq.21072.

Harackiewicz, J. M., Canning, E. A., Tibbetts, Y., Giffen, C. J., Blair, S. S., Rouse, D. I., & Hyde, J. S. (2014). Closing the social class achievement gap for first-generation students in undergraduate biology. *Journal of Educational Psychology*, 106(2), 375–389. http://dx.doi.org.libproxy.murdoch.edu.au/10.1037/a0034679.

Hill, B., Winmar, G., & Woods, J. (2018). Exploring transformative learning at the cultural interface: Insights from successful Aboriginal university students. *The Australian Journal of Indigenous Education*, 1–12. doi:10.1017/jie.2018.11.

Hodges, B., Bedford, T., Hartley, J., Klinger, C., Murray, N., O'Rourke, J., & Schofield, N. (2013). *Enabling retention: Processes and strategies for improving student retention in university-based enabling programs: Final report 2013*. Australian Government Office for Learning and Teaching. Retrieved from http://eprints.usq.edu.au/26824.

Inzlicht, M., & Schmader, T. (Eds). (2012). *Stereotype threat: Theory, process, and application*. New York: Oxford University Press.

Nakata, M. (2007). The cultural interface. *The Australian Journal of Indigenous Education*, 36 (S1), 7–14.

Pitman, T., Harvey, A., McKay, J., Devlin, M., Trinidad, S., & Brett, M. (2017). The impact of enabling programs on Indigenous participation, success and retention in Australian higher education. In: J. Frawley, S. Larkin, J. Smith (Eds), *Indigenous pathways, transitions and participation in higher education*. Singapore: Springer. doi: http://www.dx.doi.org/10.1007/978-981-10-4062-7_14.

Sarra, C. (2005). *Strong and smart: Reinforcing Aboriginal perceptions of being Aboriginal at Cherbourg State School* (PhD). Murdoch University, Perth, WA.

Spencer, S. J., Logel, C., & Davies, P. G. (2016). Stereotype threat. *Annual Review of Psychology*, 67(1), 415–437. https://doi.org/10.1146/annurev-psych-073115-103235.

Walton, G. M., Logel, C., Peach, J. M., Spencer, S. J., & Zanna, M. P. (2015). Two brief interventions to mitigate a 'chilly climate' transform women's experience, relationships, and achievement in engineering. *Journal of Educational Psychology*, 107(2), 468–485. http://dx.doi.org.libproxy.murdoch.edu.au/10.1037/a0037461.

Wilks, J., & Wilson, K. (2014). *'Can't be what you can't see': The transition of Aboriginal and Torres Strait Islander students into higher education.* Sydney, Australia: Australian Government Office for Learning and Teaching.

Wilks, J., & Wilson, K. (2015). A profile of the Aboriginal and Torres Strait Islander higher education student population. *The Australian Universities' Review,* 57(2), 17–30.

Yeager, D. S., & Walton, G. M. (2011). Social-psychological interventions in education: They're not magic. *Review of Educational Research,* 81(2), 267–301. https://doi-org.libp roxy.murdoch.edu.au/10.3102/0034654311405999.

8

FINDING THE SPACE FOR CONNECTION

Embedding a Pasifika philosophy into pedagogical practices

Dr Fiona Beals and Arden Perrot

> Oceania is vast, Oceania is expanding, Oceania is hospitable and generous, Oceania is humanity rising from the depths of brine and regions of fire deeper still, Oceania is us. We are the sea, we are the ocean, we must wake up to this ancient truth and together use it to overturn all hegemonic views that aim ultimately to confine us again, physically and psychologically, in the tiny spaces which we have resisted accepting as our sole appointed place, and from which we have recently liberated ourselves. We must not allow anyone to belittle us again, and take away our freedom.
>
> *(Hau'ofa, 1994, p. 5)*

Famous eighteenth-century ocean explorer Louis Antoine de Bougainville spoke of the Pacific peoples with admiration. He was inspired by their ability to navigate the vast southern seas with precision and intelligence. He gave the name Navigator Islands to Samoa to acknowledge the people and their ability. Today, in countries like Aotearoa New Zealand (NZ), our Pacific students struggle to navigate their way through life when so many negative stereotypes surround them at every bend. For many Pacific students, simply choosing to do degree study is a challenge, especially if they have had experiences of brokenness in their early schooling. They come to us broken, wounded, and needing to start a journey of healing.

In this chapter, we explore how one programme of study, the Bachelor of Youth Development (BYD), navigated the pedagogical space of learning and healing by embedding its teaching into a Pasifika worldview and philosophy. This required an epistemological shift where elements of space, relationship and dialogue became central pedagogical tools rather than the teacher at the front of the lecture theatre or classroom. In this way, we interpret the concept of philosophy through an epistemological worldview. Rather than taking a western approach which centres on the individual journey to one's own enlightenment, we emphasise the relational and the importance of nurturing this space that occurs within Pasifika contexts. We use two key terms to capture this concept of relational, *va* and *talanoa*. While we will expand on these philosophical concepts later in the chapter, the *va* can be recognised as the spiritual space between people (including people and things) while *talanoa* is the act of conversation, storytelling and story-creating occurring between people. Through framing this chapter as a conversation, illustrated with vignettes between ourselves and these concepts, we will explore how acknowledging the *va* between ourselves, others and our physical environment, enabled a space in our classroom for rich *talanoa*. Through practices of *talanoa,* we could scaffold students from a story of who they were to a story to who they could become. In a classical Freirean (1972) approach, *talanoa* within the *va* enabled us as teachers, and our students, to read our world and rewrite our worlds together.

Entering into the BYD family or #BYD4life

As in other post-industrial countries, where university education is, inadvertently, recognised as the pillar of higher education, Industry Training Provider (ITP/Poly-technic) applied degrees are perceived as somewhat 'easier'. In effect, students enter applied degrees thinking that they are much more attainable than an equivalent university one. There are students, as well, who enter into ITP study as 'wounded learners' (Lange, Chovanec, Cardinal, Kajner, & Smith Acuna, 2015). They have had a negative experience in the schooling system and do not see themselves as 'good enough' for higher education. In Aotearoa New Zealand, these students are disproportionately from our Māori and Pasifika population. An ITP degree education for these students must embrace a vision of transformative learning, where the learning stories of students are re-written from ideas of failure to concepts of success.

The BYD has attracted both youth workers and young people leaving school not wanting to pursue university education. Many students in the BYD have struggled with the mainstream system and may have even failed school. Choosing a career that involves making a difference in the lives of young people has been a key motivation for study; however, underneath this motivation is a desire to experience success and a second chance in education. As teaching staff in the degree, we have actively worked to create a BYD family. Tutors and students learn together, support each other and live life together. It is commonplace to see shared lunches, study sessions, and the odd pizza study group occurring. The active use of closed social media groups has enabled connection outside of the classroom as well; stories are shared and reshared, encouragement is actively given. The saying #BYD4life is said daily; belief in the degree with a fist to the heart, enables belief in oneself. All these actions recognise the healing that must occur in the rewriting of stories. As a team, we have always started with the social. This has enabled the *va* to open in the classroom environment.

Understanding the va

In a Pasifika context, *va* refers to the space and relationship between people and between objects/things over space and time. What is central to the *va* is the notion of relational self. Rather than a western worldview of the individual as the point of reference, in the *va* the relational self is the epistemological centre (Anae, 2016). The *va,* the space between, is central to an understanding of self and a positioning of oneself in the world. It is a deeply spiritual space where all relations are ultimately connecting to a creator God. The *va* can be nurtured and it can also be damaged. When damage has occurred, it is essential that one works to restore that damage as soon as possible.

Anae (2016) describes the *va* in the practice of policymaking and research as an important space. In the *va,* parties can come together in the pursuit of wisdom; they can connect and journey together. Anae argues that the space of *va* calls for relational ethics where our connections to others, the things around us, the past, the future, the present and all aspects of space are nurtured. We, like others, would like to argue, that this same reasoning can be given in the educational context. The space between the teacher and the student can be damaged quickly through a misalignment of culture, misunderstanding and practices of shaming.

In his doctoral research Reynolds (2017) examined how success in Pasifika education was interpreted and understood by Pasifika students. Like Anae (2016), Reynolds found that the concept of the *va* was central to the success of Pasifika students; students described greater success when teachers focused on the relationship between themselves and their students, and between the students as a class. In his conclusions, he encouraged secondary school teachers to be mindful of the relational and to re-vision their practice to take account of the connections that they create, maintain and nurture in their classroom. While our students are in a tertiary setting, we were each keen to centralise the relational aspects of our pedagogy. But as our first conversation indicates, this first had to involve a decentring of self and an understanding of the relational for one of us.

FIONA: It was just a tag along experience, myself as the Palagi (non-Samoan and of European origin) academic with my Samoan colleague entering an Indigenous setting. As Palagi and female I did what came naturally and stood back. Then I watched Arden push forward, not only did he shake hands with each person and introduce himself, he appeared to enter the person's space, something that was culturally wrong in my own context. For the rest of the day Arden created something which was deeper than relationship. By the end of the day, it was as if the life and family of Arden was now a part of the life and families of all he connected with. I challenged myself, was I prepared to take the first step with my students and deeply connect with them in their space?

ARDEN: As I read the above paragraph from Fiona it brought back memories from this day. What was clear and evident was how different philosophies and worldviews can shape our experiences, our thought process and our actions. When Fiona saw the circle of Pasifika people gathered for the lesson, her unique lens started to supplant onto this experience ideas of 'space', protocol and what her normal course of action should be. She saw space as individual, boarded with boundaries which should not be encroached. I saw it totally differently, I saw a connected space, I saw a circle as a function of connection and collectivism. I saw the circle as *tapu* (sacred) and for me to walk into space and not acknowledge its existence, not acknowledge each person within it that created this scared space, and to just start teaching would be a massive sign of disrespect. Acknowledging the people and the space first with *alofa* (love) and respect, sharing stories of family and ancestral ties, and common friends we may know within our shared communities, allowed me to build deep connection. They begin to position me not as an expert to deliver knowledge but as a friend to share some stories and from this authentic and rich learning platform great learning could take place.

FIONA: First day of class after the tag along experience and I found myself with my Auckland students. Most of my students were Pasifika (although NZ born) and as I had flown up from Wellington, I expected the usual pattern of students arriving late to class and walking in with what seemed a cloak of shame. Today was going to be different. I decided it was time for a new word and concept – the Pākehā (non-Māori and of European origin) stare. Too often in lecture theatres and classrooms, both students and teachers would join forces to shame the late students. But after the encounter with my colleague, things were going to be different. I instructed the students that arrived early that we will going to engage in another practice. We were no longer using 'the Pākehā stare'. We would replace it with a welcome; we had to create an opening for the *va*. Rows of desks were replaced with circles and groups with always a space chair. As students arrived, we welcomed them and invited them to sit. As the morning progressed, I noticed something, when the students were warmly welcomed and invited into the space, the student would then come to the front of the room and hug me, or greet me, with a friendly kiss of welcome. Both actions that are normal in Pasifika contexts to show honour.

Talanoa

Essentially *talanoa* is about the relationship between people (within the *va*) and the conversation itself (Perrot, 2015). The conversation can only go as deep as the connection between the people. In that sense, the *va* has to be nurtured as people share. Participants need to go as deep as they want but within a space of safety and respect. A teacher using, and engaging with *talanoa,* needs to understand that this type of conversation is not about talking a lot. It is about talking deeply. In this sense, the teacher needs to talk with, not at, their students. Just as a researcher has to go deep with their own story in the research process, the teacher needs to go deep and share with students. It is this type of relationship created through *talanoa* in the *va* that allows for co-constructed, inter-related and authentic knowledge to emerge. It acknowledges the real lives of people present and encourages empathic listening. It is through this engagement that hopes and struggles can be identified, explored and addressed.

Using the space of the *va* for teaching our staff and students to share their lived reality through *talanoa* allowed students and teachers to bring into the learning space their complete self and life history; their own epistemological and ontological understanding and their unique worldview (Gegeo, 2008). *Talanoa* created a bridge into the academic world for our students because it started with their stories rather than a set of Learning Outcomes to be achieved. As the following conversation demonstrates, through practices of research and learning, we have journeyed with others and learnt to read our world and the information of our world, then rewrite that world to reflect ourselves, our dreams and shared destinations.

ARDEN: Pasifika for thousands of years kept records through oral tradition, through ancestral links and stories. When undertaking my Masters research (Perrot, 2015) I wanted to use the power of sharing stories to understand more deeply the issue of failure but more importantly the power of resilience in education for Pasifika. More recently Pasifika scholars have used traditional forms of sharing, such as *talanoa*, as a qualitative approach to unearth deeper and richer understandings of situations or events. In my research, I shared a similar education story to the people I was researching and rather than approach it with a mindset of a researcher, I argued that through *talanoa* and sharing our collective experience together I could journey with my research participants to go deeper into understanding the impact of our shared experiences.

Once I shared my education story with my participants, I could feel the connection go deeper through our collective experience of similar hardship and struggle. Our *talanoa* was deeper, more insightful from that point because it changed from the participant feeling 'researched' to understanding that we are together on a shared journey not just about our past but a new journey, one of discovery and that our united experience could help future generations of Pasifika in education.

FIONA: The cards laid scattered on the floor. While academic learning is a part of the learning journey for our students, the classroom is set up to be welcoming and hospitable. It is set up to engage with the whole of the student and the stories they bring. I have decided to use *Cars'R'Us* (Jones, 2006), a collection of cards with cars in various states of being and places. The students select a card that represents their 'school' story and stand in a circle. I have chosen my own card that represents the first day of high school for me. We take turns to tell our story. It seems, for most students, the stories are the same, stories of being labelled, being shamed and failing school; one or two students have shared positive stories, but they talk into the factors that made their story different. It is only the first day of class, but already we have gone deeper than imagined and we know that we are family, together we can do this.

The stories are told, and we all leave the classroom and re-enter. As we re-enter, I have us all physically leaving the story card outside of the classroom door. I then tell the students that there is a reason for leaving our story outside; today is a new beginning of their education story. The key lesson that they need to take from this moment is the brutal reality of failure. I then intentionally speak loudly and slowly, students always can be seen writing this down "It is not you that failed school, it is school that failed you".

ARDEN: For several years in the BYD I would have students set goals. While goals in and of themselves are beneficial, the real magic 'juice' or the energy of any goals resides in the 'why' or purpose for you wanting to achieve it. From my experience with students in the BYD, once they knew and shared their real reason for why they wanted to succeed on the BYD, and I knew it as well, it was almost impossible for them to fail. If students started to experience failure, we would sit down together and *talanoa* about life, but our conversation would always steer back to that space about their 'deeper' purpose for them completing the BYD. Their purpose, or deeper, goal would bring them back into re-writing their learning journey as one of success.

I called the process of digging for our deeper purpose for achievement 'seven levels deep'. This is done by asking the question why? Why you are here, why is it important to you to get this degree and with every subsequent answer they gave me I would reframe their answer and again ask why that is answer important to them? This would be done a total of seven times which I felt went deeper into a real reflection as to their real purpose for being there. Students moved from thinking with their 'head' (i.e. superficial answers such as gaining a degree) to thinking with their 'heart' (i.e. deeper answers around difference and purpose). Through the process of sharing student's answers at each level they were able to clarify for themselves their true purpose and connect to their learning at far greater depths. When your reason for being on a degree is about making a massive difference in the lives of young people it holds more motivation and inspiration to be a better learner in the present.

Climbing the staircase of learning

The idea of a learner achieving their potential through journeying with others sits well within both Māori and Pasifika pedagogies. In the 1990s, Tangaere (1996) described this journey through the Māori legend of Tāne ascending to the heavens to acquire three baskets of knowledge; each step was scaffolded to the next and, through learning, each step is accompanied by another person. This is not dissimilar to earlier educational philosophers such as Vygotsky who once said "through others, we become ourselves" (cited in Murphy, Doherty, & Kerr, 2016, p. 129). Vygotsky argued that teachers were facilitators of learning, rather than the providers of knowledge and content. Out of his thinking came the concept of the "zone of proximal development" or the potential of learning when working with others (Vygotsky, 2008). Brunner (1997) would later take this concept and come up with a concept of scaffolding or providing small steps so that teachers and learners could journey together.

In a Pasifika context, the notion that the *va* is a space where we journey together is important. This is symbolised in understanding what the ocean/sea means to different cultural groups. In Aotearoa New Zealand, Pākehā typically see the sea and the ocean as points of division. This comes from the mindset that the vast seas have separated our Pākehā ancestors from their traditional homelands. In Pasifika worldviews, the ocean does not divide, it connects. It epitomises the *va* and the vessels that travel it resonate with the concept of space (e.g. *vaka, waka, va'a*). This final example demonstrates scaffolding in the *va* through both *talanoa* and connection.

FIONA: It's two classes now. Both in the final year. The students and I have journeyed together for three years. We have gone from questioning the reality of where our stories have come from that have created our own stumbling blocks to doing learning together. But now I am back in Auckland, and I have noticed that in the three years, my students have struggled to understand some of the basic rules of referencing. For the students, referencing means nothing in the practical world, it means nothing in the cultural worlds in which they live. For myself as an educated academic, referencing means a lot. We have come to a shared lunch, and I have begun to panic. When 1pm hit, I panicked that teaching was not going to occur, especially as a guitar had emerged and singing was occurring. As the songs were sung, I began to see a connection between the academic world and the worlds of the students outside of the classroom. Both songs and academic writing has structure; there are key themes in songs, just as there can be key themes or arguments in academic writing, which must be repeated again and again; and in both genres there is an acknowledgement of those who have come before. We call this referencing in academic writing, in Pasifika and Maori contexts, it is above attributing mana (esteem and honour) to those who have come before. I decided to take a risk and break into the conversation with questions about songs, structure, and academic writing. We never stopped for 'class' again that day. But we did not have to, the whole afternoon was an encounter with learning, as I encountered the rules of song composition in the Pacific and the students, the rules of academic writing in the western world.

Conclusion

Both of us like to challenge Pasifika myths with a little-known fact, the country with the most PhDs per capita is Tonga. When we say this to our students, they look surprised. This is not the Pasifika experience of education here in Aoteraoa NZ. In Aoteroa NZ, Pasifika faces are rugby players not PhD scholars. So, something has happened with our story here, something has disrupted the *va* between the stories of home and the stories of migration. The BYD is a space, a *va* where we actively work to disrupt the story. This is achieved through three key mechanisms: acknowledging the space, and the role of space; going deep with our students, deeper than we have ever gone before; and just as Tane rose to the Heavens to bring down the three baskets of knowledge, we rise with our students.

Success in education needs to be framed in philosophies and paradigms that make sense to the learner. If the paradigm differs to the one seen as correct by the system, then so be it. There is a need in tertiary education to be relational. To understand that if we are in the *va* we have an ethical responsibility to dialogue with students, learn their stories and then enable them to transform their stories. In our own journey, the greatest learning perhaps occurred with Fiona. She had to let go of her 'western' mindset of 'this is how it is done'. She had to connect with students, change her ideas of time and space, understand that learning occurs in the journey and through this journey a story is told. What has happened over time has been less reliance on the materials of a lecturer and more reliance on presence – being fully there – and allowing the conversation to take both teachers and students on a journey. This must have been what Freire (1972) had hoped for when he first talked about challenging the banking concept of education; learning with is simply more powerful than teaching to. Learning with brings transformation to both the teacher and the learner. Learning with enables connection. It is this connection that leads to success.

References

Anae, M. (2016). Teu le va: Samoan relational ethics. *Knowledge Cultures*, 4, 117–130.
Brunner, J. (1997). Celebrating divergence: Piaget and Vygotsky. *Human Development*, 40, 63–73.
Freire, P. (1972). Pedagogy of the oppressed. In B. N. Schwartz (Ed.), *Affirmative education: Radical approaches to education* (pp.65–73). Englewood Cliffs, NJ: Prentice Hall.
Gegeo, D. W. (2008). *Shifting paradigms in Pacific scholarship: Towards island-based methodologies, epistemologies and pedagogies.* Building Pacific Research Capacity and Scholarship Fono, Fale Pasifika, University of Auckland.
Hau'ofa, E. (1994). Our sea of islands. *The Contemporary Pacific*, 6(1), 147–161.
Jones, M. (2006). *Cars'R'Us.* Australia: Innovative Resources.
Lange, E., Chovanec, D. M., Cardinal, T., Kajner, T., & Smith Acuna, N. (2015). Wounded learners: Symbolic violence, educational justice, and re-engagement of low-income adults. *Canadian Journal for the Study of Adult Education*, 27, 83–104.
Murphy, C., Doherty, A., & Kerr, K. (2016). 'It is through others that we become ourselves': A study of Vygotskian play in Russian and Irish schools. *International Journal in Early Childhood Education*, 7, 129–146.
Perrot, A. R. D. (2015). *Overcoming challenges: Pacific students' experiences of being resilient through tertiary education.* (Masters of Arts), Victoria University of Wellington, Wellington.
Reynolds, M. (2017). *Together as brothers: A catalytic examination of Pasifika success as Pasifika to teu le va in boys' secondary education in Aotearoa New Zealand.* (Doctor of Philosophy), Victoria University of Wellington, Wellington.
Tangaere, A. R. (1996). Maori development theory. In B. Webber (Ed.), *He paepae korero: Research perspectives in Maori Education* (pp. 109–122). Wellington: New Zealand Council for Educational Research (NZCER).
Vygotsky, L. S. (2008). Interaction between learning and development. In D. Bergen (Ed.), *Human development: Traditional and contemporary theories* (pp. 331–338).Upper Saddle River: Pearson Prentice Hall.

9

PULLED BY MOTIVATION, PUSHED BY INSPIRATION

Approaches to transitioning high school students to university

Debra Monteith and Dr Peter Geerlings

Cultural demands and social expectations play a significant role in the educational choices of students identified as having low-socioeconomic status. When weighing up the benefits of a university education some additional, negative influences include the young person's own perceptions of their abilities, their worldview, and family expectations. Our educators function as both mentor and facilitator, within our philosophy in practice, central yet peripheral to learning, as crucial players to the success of our young adults undertaking university-style learning. An inherent understanding of adolescence is vital as the educator works to help the learner establish a sense of self, vocational, and future identity. This program aims to 'level the playing field' for university-aspiring young people, bridging the sociocultural divide to higher education by maintaining the connection with education for marginalised students, moving beyond motivation to reengage and inspire the development of a strong, resilient learner identity.

> Don't judge. Teach. It's a learning process.
>
> *(Carol S. Dweck)*

Introduction

For over a decade the Australian Tertiary Admissions Rank (ATAR) has been adopted as the principal, national entry standard in Australia for young people completing secondary school who want to go to university; a system that tends to work quite well in communities with accumulated social capital. But due to socio–cultural and other factors, Year 12 completion rates in our region remain much lower, making educational prospects more blurred. Interestingly, young people still remain hopeful of attaining a university education, even though the prospects are dim via the ATAR pathway. As a result we see capable, young people wanting a university education, but not necessarily being able to demonstrate their cognitive capacity via traditional means. With a philosophy shared from institutional level through to our tutors, we run a unique enabling program with Year 12 non-ATAR students. As described by Hall and Ponton (2005), our pedagogy aims to motivate and build aspirations without judgment, acknowledges our student's individuality through a wide lens of world exploration, and helps them reshape their belief in their ability to succeed. Building on the students' past educational and social experiences we support second chances, learning from failure, and developing passion for learning in preparation for a future in a rapidly changing world. A university that values diversity, equity, and social justice creates a solid foundation for the development and operation of this unique enabling program.

Here we argue how a common philosophy embedding Vygotskian theory, where teachers should not be in the classroom to act simply as instructors, but should adopt the role of facilitator and guide, gives students the opportunities to discover for themselves and develop as active and independent learners (Dewey, 2011). This chapter argues that while the enabling curriculum should be engaging for the target cohort, the institution, the program itself and the curriculum are passive to some degree; and it is the people within that can bring about change in students. Here we see the academic teaching staff facilitating the development of each student's academic self-efficacy and individual learning identity in the cognitive and emotional realms, alongside the development of academic knowledge and skills to offer greater and equitable chances for higher education.

Background

In 2011 it was reported that in Western Australia (WA) between 30 and 40 per cent of young people were not completing 12 years of secondary education (Down & Choules, 2011). At that time, the WA Secondary Engagement Evaluation Report stated "there is a crisis of motivation as evidenced by a general malaise – low quality work, absenteeism, sullen hostility, waste, alcohol and drug abuse and cognitive illness created by a loss of meaning and purpose in education" (Down & Choules, 2011, p. 9). Adding to this, there is a mounting body of evidence to suggest that "a standardised curriculum gives nonstandard students no place to go" (Down and Choules, 2011, p. 9). Additionally, cultural pressures and social expectations play a significant role in the educational choices of students identified as low-socioeconomic status (SES) (Frigo, Bryce, Anderson, & McKenzie, 2007). To the contrary,

> students from families with higher SES backgrounds, who acquire the values of cultural capital in the form of habitus, attitudes and practices in their everyday interactions with family and associates, are more comfortable in formal educational settings than those from families from lower SES backgrounds.
>
> *(Andres, Adamuti-Trache, Yoon, Pidgeon & Thomsen, 2007, p. 155)*

Quite recently Watson, Vernon, Seddon, Andrews and Wang (2016) clarified that Year 12 students (in our region at least) have experienced disadvantage in accessing a university education via a combination of socio-cultural influences including fear of acceptance, lack of role models, economic pressures and lack of understanding about university life. For many of our students this means that while they may aspire to attend university they may not expect to be able to achieve that goal.

In our locale it became apparent that ATAR might not be the most appropriate measure to determine the capacity of school-leavers potential to undertake under-graduate study. Our university has a main campus near the capital city of Perth, Western Australia, and two regional campuses in the outer, southern suburbs approximately 50 and 70 kilometres from Perth, where the program operates. A lack of opportunity for higher education in the region has been identified with the proportion of people in these communities who hold a university qualification roughly half the national average (Watson et al., 2016). We partner with almost 30 secondary schools in our regional campus catchment and while in some regards our student cohort is homogenous, identified as low SES[1] and non-ATAR Year 12s, they are also very diverse individuals representing a cross section of wealth, employment, education, and social status, cultural heritage and family composition. Our strategic and School Curriculum and Standards Authority (SCSA) endorsed program has a unique parallel goal of high school gradua-tion and university preparation where students, self-identified and endorsed by the school, are simultaneously achieving their Western Australian Certificate of Education (WACE) alongside their ATAR peers, and experientially develop the necessary skills and behaviours to enable a successful pathway to university.

Connecting with students and parents

Our contact with students starts when the unit coordinator visits prospective students at their school towards the end of Year 11. During these information sessions students are encouraged to take the information home to their parents and discuss the potential of entering the course in Year 12. This is for three primary reasons; parents may not be aware of this program that provides a pathway for capable students, class finishes at 6 pm so there will be a time commitment, and lastly but most importantly, it encourages a family conversation around the prospects of a university education. The Australian Council on Educational Research (ACER) report contends that "parental support plays a significant role in adolescents' career development" (Frigo et al., 2007, p. 9). Our connection aims to support individuals in overcoming the significant impact that their circumstances can have on their sense of self-esteem, abilities and achievements.

Because our students come from such varied, often troubled, backgrounds, we start the course by asking them to situate themselves and others in the world. For many, this is confronting and difficult as they challenge their own, often inherited worldview. In our experience, we have made similar observations to Tindall (2017, para 3) who believes "if you have grown up in a home where you were influenced strongly by adults who hold very liberal worldviews on life, you'll likely hold onto liberal values", creating a trap that divides our youth as they become voting adults.

Additionally, many students are first in their family (FiF) to consider university, which often means that the parents either really want their children to have the education that they did not have or, alternatively, do not see the value in a university education. Even if parents aspire for their child to obtain a university education they are not always aware that achieving this might also shift their child's 'thinking', creating a conflict with their inherent worldview.

A shared philosophy

In providing an alternative pathway to ATAR, it is necessary for shared philosophies to coexist. A common philosophy starts at the institutional level where equity and social justice must be embraced by managers and teachers because this filters across the university and into classroom practice; it is the foundation for everything we do. Tinto (2003, pp. 4–5) believes that "effective learning communities require their faculty to collaborate on both the content and pedagogy ... to provide a coherent shared learning experience". It is crucial to create a working team that is cohesive and motivated with like-minded teaching staff. For us, this means having people who demonstrate a fundamental understanding of the educational challenges faced by our students, believing that: All learners are entitled to a quality education, and possess academic entelechy to become independent learners. Our teachers understand these factors, sharing a common philosophy to deliver an appropriate and motivational curriculum, demonstrating a strong understanding of the high emotional stakes and the need for additional student support for effective reengagement with learning.

We understand that a successful learning community does not simply acculturate the student but also causes a cultural shift in their feelings towards education and a reshaping of their 'identity'; a view shared by Lane and Sharp (2014), and Jones, Olds and Lisciandro (2016). What we do in the class reflects a Vygotskian (Zone of Proximal Development or ZPD) philosophy where structured learning opportunities with graduated support identify and develop the academic capabilities of students to become university ready (Goggin, Rankin, Geerlings & Taggart, 2016). Working within the students' ZPD, where they are pushed but not overwhelmed, is a major key to building self-efficacy and eventual student agency, described by Silver and Stafford (2017). Importantly, the development of student agency may be as critical to the outcomes of schooling as academic skills (Ferguson, Phillips, Rowley, & Friedlander, 2015). We use the evidence of Elias and Arnold (2006), which shows that when students feel cared about, are welcomed, valued and seen as active resources and not passive learners, the climate of classrooms and schools change for the better. Thrupp and Lupton (2006) attest that educational institutions appear to be particularly influential in the formation of positive attitudes and behaviours, building a sense of self-efficacy in young people. Our program aims to build student agency through individualized learning opportunities by giving students a voice and empowering them to make informed decisions about their education and future.

Philosophy in practice

We aim to firmly position students in the driver's seat of their own education, and destiny, deliberately making their experience in our program unlike school. It can be difficult for a young person to embrace education and see it as potentially life-changing when their educational experience to date has not been enjoyable or rewarding. For many and varied reasons, towards the end of secondary school, we find students become tired of 'the system' at a time when they need to be focussed, expected to take control, and navigate their path into a career, employment, or higher education. From the time children start school they are socially conditioned to look to the teacher for direction, information, and the answers to their questions; seeing the teacher as the expert. Student-centred university learning means attending a campus, addressing their tutor by first name and working in small groups. We expect to hear students talking and discussing the content as their tutor moves between groups, listening to opinions and viewpoints and explicitly provoking the students as they explore and justify their beliefs and views. In practice, this builds on social constructivism pedagogy where "learning occurs by means of peer interaction (collaboration), student ownership of the curriculum and educational experiences that are authentic to the students" (Jones et al., 2016, p. 26). In our experience, the innate inquisitiveness and desire to learn we see in very young pre-school students as they play tends to become eradicated by some of the constraints and monotony of the large education system that mills out society-ready young adults. We motivate our students by making the content relevant, often fun, and embrace the noise and passion that comes with student engagement. Certainly, some of the feedback on our program points to this format as something students really enjoy. From this we hope, in the very least, students start to question what is happening in the world and begin to think critically, research, and challenge the status quo. They tend to respond positively to this awakening regarding education as they gain some control over their learning.

Part of relinquishing control over learning requires the tutor to share their successes and failures. Students can arrive at university with a preconception that staff are different to themselves. It is vitally important that they connect and relate to their tutor, so early in the unit we share our learning journeys and experiences to illustrate that there are multiple ways to achieving a university education, modelling reflection on the many hurdles to success. Indeed, we challenge the false perception that the successful transition to adulthood is smooth and linear. It is true that young adults may not always be interested in the lives of older people although we believe that there is value in sharing experience. We have found that not only are students interested, they are hungry for information that illustrates we are fallible, persistent and resilient. In sharing we create trust, honesty and what is referred to as having 'skin in the game'. Our educators aim to build social capital with the students to create trust, build a relationship and create new attitudes toward receiving feedback. In creating a bond between the students' and the tutor, messages conveying belonging which tie the individual to the group with a sense of commitment, as described by Tinto (2003), can both motivate and inspire learning to perhaps mitigate some of the challenging personal, social and educational circumstances.

Tutors create a democratic playing field for learning and most importantly, have a history of academic success, demonstrating a love of learning and reflective self-growth, strong work ethic and a dedication to accepting change.

Structured support is essential when re-engaging a learner-identity. Remembering that our students are not on the traditional pathway to university, they must demonstrate considerable determination to complete both their Year 12 study to obtain a WACE, plus our course, concurrently. This is a big commitment and challenge, and students usually arrive on the first day, understandably anxious. Of course, what it is like to be at the university is still a little mysterious. We rely on Bandura's approach to building self-efficacy in the design and delivery of the program through mastery of learning experiences, verbal persuasion, and building emotional intelligence and resilience (Bandura, 1986). In so doing, students attend campus afterschool, start identifying their intrinsic motivational factors and develop their work ethic and time management. Over the course of 30 weeks their experiences on campus involve lectures, followed by university-style tutorial sessions with a strong focus on discussions and sharing of ideas for the construction of knowledge. Students continuously revisit learning experiences to encourage academic growth with the inclusion of skills such as mindfulness, to build self-belief and emotional resilience. To forge a sense of belonging, students receive a university identification card and full online access and privileges afforded to undergraduate students including after-hours access to the library and computer laboratories. They are supported to become familiar with the university's policies, academic expectations, learning platforms, and gain confidence and capability. By attending the campus and having academics as their guide, students develop a strong working knowledge to take into their undergraduate studies and an understanding of what university will be like.

To make learning relevant and motivational, our curriculum connects classroom learning to the students' experiences in society. Described by Herrington and Herrington (2006) as authentic learning, we start by building knowledge around their pre-existing understandings and allow a dynamic flow within the classroom. One challenge for our students is that they are often conditioned to expect a right or wrong answer to any question. The controversial nature of our topics sometimes leaves the matter unresolved, which can be unsettling. We choose topics that young people can relate to which question values and the status quo and are particularly relevant to their age such as driving, drinking, politics, gender, and educational choices. Discussions reach far beyond what is normal in the high school classroom as students explore content within the world context; often considered 'taboo' in the school setting. Topics that are often magnets for student interest include: legalisation of marijuana, abortion, drug testing at festivals, gun rights, and world terrorism. Using the famous Milgram Experiment (Milgram, 1963) we look at how people can be controlled and provoked to behave contrary to their normal beliefs and values by exploring 'mob mentality' and deindividuation. Indeed, moving students from an opinion to a position and viewing alternate perspectives is both challenging and revealing, especially in controversial issues, where their view tends to be fixed. Placing value in what students think and carefully selecting the issues they are asked to consider aims to attach learning in the classroom into life in general. Research surrounding authentic learning suggests "each learner's personal quest for meaning at the heart of curricular and pedagogical decisions, is one most likely to generate the resilient communities needed to face a future of unimaginable challenge and change" (Barnes & Shirley, 2007, p. 163). We place an emphasis on the importance of researching a topic of deep, personal interest to find evidence to substantiate their position, and in some cases we see the beginning of a transformation as they uncover evidence in support of a view alternate to their own inherent beliefs.

We remind ourselves constantly that developmental psychology plays a significant role in how our young people learn by acknowledging that the teenage brain is very responsive to the immediate environment and change. Operating primarily on dopamine reward, the teenage brain is impulsive and often lacks emotional maturity resulting in poor decision-making (Casey, Jones & Somerville, 2011) and may be more vulnerable to risk taking because of limitations in the ability to effectively regulate heightened reward and loss signals (Ernst & Mueller, 2008).We aim to turn around negative attitudes regarding learning by showing that education is not a separate endeavour, but it is preparation for and part of life (Dewey, 2011). We explicitly situate them as the largest stakeholder in their educational journey, making decisions now that benefit them later. External and internal motivation is required to engage the learner, as constructivist theory implicates motivation as a necessary prerequisite and co-requisite for learning (Palmer, 2005). We want our students to enter university demonstrating self-discipline for open discussion and resilience in facing their academic challenges in a safe and encouraging environment. To help build resilience and foster intellectual growth we explicitly introduce and rely on strategies described by Dweck (2007); where a growth mindset recognises failure as an opportunity for improvement and development, and reflection is vitally important.

Reflection is a major component of the curriculum. We start the course asking students to reflect on their educational journey to date, and reflection re-emerges, periodically. This is because, in the tradition of Freire (1974), we view the practice of reflection as ideologically transformative. This is a difficult task and students who demonstrate limited skills and abilities in reflection often require guidance and mentoring; especially in challenging their established worldview. Importantly, students must be explicitly taught how to reflect using tools such as Gibbs' Reflective Cycle (Gibbs, 1981) and how to develop the skills so as to use reflection as a tool for academic growth. Asking students to reflect on important moments in their past educational journey functions to re-capture, re-live, make sense of, think about, contextualize, and evaluate an experience in order to make decisions and choices about what they have experienced, how they have experienced the event, and what they will or won't do next (Goggin, Rankin, Geerlings, & Taggart, 2016). Self-reflection is encouraged on significant issues of social, economic or cultural importance employing a process of social construction and attachment of meaning (Vygotsky & Cole, 1978). Sinatra and Pintrich (2002, p. 2) emphasized the "metacognitive, motivational and affective processes that can be brought under the learner's conscious control may determine the likelihood of change". In our program, this is best-understood where students are asked to reflect upon their educational journey and propose strategies for greater academic success, reflecting pre-and post-course on their progress. It is here we affect behaviour, pulling them from the edge of capability to increased knowledge and from unsure to empowered.

Conclusion

In concluding this chapter, we must acknowledge that the ATAR education system is effective university-preparation for the majority of senior secondary school students aiming to enter university. But we also recognise that it excludes many capable young people who live on the socio-cultural fringes in areas similar to where our course operates. This distinctive enabling program supports students to prepare for university with concurrent attainment of high school graduation, alongside their peers who are completing ATAR studies. Acknowledging adolescence as a time of physical, cognitive, and emotional growth, the enabling educator must demonstrate a formidable understanding of this important transitional period from child to adult, enlisting strategies that facilitate engaging, dynamic student-centred learning situated in a real-world context. Working with students who are establishing their learner and vocational identity means we need to gently push students to work towards the upper edge of their capability. Whilst supporting the active acquisition of the necessary skills for academic growth we provide scaffolded learning opportunities to prepare them to make wise choices in a changing, and often uncertain future. In acknowledging the needs of this at-risk cohort and often disengaged learners, we embed tools in the curriculum such as reflective practice and strategies for developing a growth mindset to build confidence and self-belief alongside resilience; in preparation for the impending successes and failures of university life, and life itself. It starts with sharing the learning experiences of our staff, modelling and mentoring, then goes beyond external motivation, focusing upon the creation of a learning community to collaboratively develop self-belief and take control of their learning where they might otherwise have been lost in the system. In determining what students truly need in this educational journey, and ultimately preparing them for a challenging world, the effective enabling educator should not judge, but rise to support each individual in their journey of self-discovery, pushing them beyond motivation and pulling them towards inspiration as passionate, successful independent learners.

Note

1   SES according to the Socio-Economic Indexes for Areas (SEIFA).

References

Andres, L., Adamuti-Trache, M., Yoon, E., Pidgeon, M., & Thomsen, J. (2007). Educational expectations, parental social class, gender, and post-secondary attainment: A 10-year perspective. *Youth Society*, 39(2), 135–163. doi:10.1177/0044118X06296704.

Bandura, A. (1986). *Social foundations of thought and action: A social cognitive theory*. Englewood Cliffs, NJ: Prentice-Hall.

Barnes, J., & Shirley, I. (2007). Strangely familiar: Cross-curricular and creative thinking in teacher education. *Improving Schools*, 10(2), 162–179. doi:10.1177/1365480207078580.

Casey, B., Jones, R. M., & Somerville, L. H. (2011). Braking and accelerating of the adolescent brain. *Journal of Research on Adolescence*, 21(1), 21–33.doi:10.1111/j.1532-7795.2010.00712.x.

Dewey, J. (2011). *Democracy and education: An introduction to the philosophy of education.* Hollywood, USA: Simon and Brown.

Down, B., & Choules, K. (2011). *The secondary engagement evaluation project in low SES schools.* Murdoch, Western Australia: Centre for Learning Change and Development, Murdoch University. Retrieved from https://researchrepository.murdoch.edu.au/id/eprint/11839/1/seep_report_lr.pdf.

Dweck, C. S. (2007). The secret to raising smart kids. *Scientific American Mind*, 18(6), 36–43. doi:10.1038/scientificamericanmind1207–36.

Elias, M. J., & Arnold, H. (2006). *The educator's guide to emotional intelligence and academic achievement: Social-emotional learning in the classroom.* Thousand Oaks, CA: Corwin Press.

Ernst, M., & Mueller, S. C. (2008), The adolescent brain: Insights from functional neuroimaging research. *Developmental Neurobiology*, 68(6):729–743. doi:10.1002/dneu.20615.

Ferguson, R. F., Phillips, S. F., Rowley, J. F., & Friedlander, J. W. (2015). *The influence of teaching beyond standardized test scores: Engagement, mindsets, and agency.* Retrieved from The Achievement Gap Initiative at Harvard University website: http://www.agi.harvard.edu/publications.php.

Freire, P. (1974). *Pedagogy of the oppressed.* Harmondsworth: Penguin.

Frigo, T., Bryce, J., Anderson, M., & McKenzie, P. (2007). *Australian young people, their families and postschool plans: A research review.* Retrieved from Australian Council Educational Research (ACER) website: https://research.acer.edu.au/transitions_misc/1.

Gibbs, G. (1981). *Teaching students to learn: A student-centred approach.* Milton Keynes: Open University Press.

Goggin, T., Rankin, S., Geerlings, P., & Taggart, A. (2016). Catching them before they fall: A Vygotskian approach to transitioning students from high school to university. *Higher Education Research & Development*, 35(4), 698–711.doi:10.1080/07294360.2015.1137879.

Hall, J. M., & Ponton, M. K. (2005). Mathematics self-efficacy of college freshman. *Journal of Developmental Education*, 28(3),26–32.

Herrington, T., & Herrington, J. (2006). *Authentic learning environments in higher education.* London: Information Science Publishing. doi:10.4018/978-1-59140-594-8.

Jones, A., Olds, A., & Lisciandro, J. (2016). Understanding the learner: Effective course design in the changing higher education space. *International Studies in Widening Participation*, 3(1), 19–35.

Lane, J., & Sharp, S. (2014). Pathways to success: evaluating the use of "enabling pedagogies" in a university transition course. *International Journal on Education*, 2(1) 66–73.

Milgram, S. (1963). Behavioral study of obedience . *Journal of Abnormal and Social Psychology*, 67(4), 371–378. doi:10.1037/h0040525.

Palmer, D. (2005). A motivational view of constructivist-informed teaching. *International Journal of Science Education*, 27(15), 1853–1881. doi:10.1080/09500690500339654.

Silver, D., & Stafford, D. (2017). *Teaching kids to thrive: essential skills for success.* Thousand Oaks, CA: Corwin Press.doi:10.4135/9781506374413.

Sinatra, G. M., & Pintrich, P. R. (2002). *Intentional conceptual change.* Retrieved from https://ebookcentral-proquest-com.libproxy.murdoch.edu.au.

Tindall, A. (2017). *Inherited worldview trap.* Retrieved from http://www.theburgergazette.com/4039/features/politicalcommentary/inherited-worldview-trap/.

Tinto, V. (2003). *Learning better together: The impact of learning communities on student success.* Higher Education Monograph Series. Higher Education Program, Syracuse University, New York, USA. Retrieved from http://www.nhcuc.org/pdfs/Learning_Better_Together.pdf.

Thrupp, M., & Lupton, R. (2006). Taking school contexts more seriously: The social justice challenge. *British Journal of Educational Studies,* 54(3), 308–328. doi:10.1111/j.1467–8527.2006.00348.x.

Vygotsky, L. S. & Cole, M. (1978). *Mind in society: The development of higher psychological processes.* Cambridge, MA:Harvard University Press.

Watson, S., Vernon, L., Seddon, S., Andrews, Y., & Wang, A. (2016). Parents influencing secondary students' university aspirations: A multilevel approach using school-SES. *Issues in Educational Research,* 26(4), 673–693.

10

UNCOMFORTABLE SPACES

Philosophy, pedagogy and practice in online enabling education

Evonne Irwin and Dr Emma Hamilton

Introduction

The Open Foundation enabling program commenced at the University of Newcastle, Australia in 1974, its inception being described as a "ground-breaking experiment in adult education within the Australian university sector" (May & Bunn, 2015, p. 136). Initially inspired by corresponding programs in the United Kingdom and Europe, this, and other enabling education schemes, aimed to provide mature-aged adult learners with the opportunity to gain access to learning at the tertiary level. Like all programs or courses of education, enabling education in Australia has developed – and is experienced, evaluated, and modified – in conversation with its social, historical, and political contexts (Bunn, 2018). These Western higher education contexts are multi-layered; informed by histories of civic duty and public good yet integrated with contemporary market ideologies underpinned by the logics of neoliberalism (Ball, 2003; Davies, Gottsche & Bansel, 2006; Giroux, 2002). Correspondingly, how enabling programs operate throughout the country is, and always has been, diverse and responsive for a variety of reasons, including ideological shifts regarding what the purpose of higher education is and should be (Baker & Irwin, 2016). Technological shifts have added another layer of complexity to these contemporary debates; higher education providers, including those providing enabling education, have increasingly opened up online learning opportunities to students, and analysis of these programs illustrates the tensions and contradictions that sit within discourses surrounding higher education.

We argue in this chapter that the terrain for online enabling programs situated in higher education institutions is particularly complex, occupying as they do, the nexus between higher education's neoliberal/economic rationalist project and the social justice project of equity and access to education, often referred to as 'widening participation'. Online enabling education can be perceived as *both* the instrument of corporatised "technological quick fixes" (Giroux, 2002, p. 442) promising reduced teaching costs and increased "efficiencies" for institutions (Tynan, Ryan & Lamont-Mills, 2015, p. 5), *as well as* a method through which previously excluded or marginalised students can gain access to higher education. Online enabling education programs occupy an 'uncomfortable' space, therefore, suspended between many of the competing impulses and pressures of the current higher education landscape. They present distinct philosophical ambiguities, situated between the seemingly oppositional rhetorical discourses of, on the one hand, widening participation agendas, whereby online platforms provide access to higher education for those who may be otherwise excluded from educational opportunity and, on the other, online education conceptualised as part of the neoliberal educational agenda. While enabling programs are by their nature liminal spaces that operationalise transition or enabling pedagogies to assist students in adjusting to tertiary-level education practices and move into undergraduate pathways (Bennett et al., 2016), they are also transitional spaces in that they operationalise multiple competing discourses surrounding the purposes, pedagogies and practices of higher education.

The philosophies, pedagogies, and practices in this uncomfortable space, therefore, demand critical and empirical examination. There exists a disjunction between the neoliberal promises posited by online education (and the higher education landscape more broadly) and the realities of the needs, experiences, and expectations of students – enabling online students in particular – who require not simply content-based educative experiences but grounding in the skills, practices, cultural capital, and hidden curricula of higher education. For online enabling students and practitioners, then, the tension between neoliberal ideologies and widening participation imperatives can be keenly felt. This chapter will bring together literature regarding the 'neoliberal promises' of online education with the realities of enabling philosophies, pedagogies and practices in the online enabling space in order to illuminate these ambiguities and discomforts. To do this, we first provide a sketch of this complex landscape, taking into account policy, social and historical perspectives. We then present an in-depth view of enabling education in Australia against this complex backdrop, focusing on its philosophies, pedagogies and practices, drawing upon data gathered via a small-scale pilot research project conducted within one online program and analysing that data against identified widening participation policy subject positions. This original study sought to interrogate the attitudes and experiences of students enrolled in an online enabling program using survey and semi-structured interview techniques as investigative tools (Hamilton, Irwin, Djenidi & Sciffer, 2018) in order to better understand the ways in which these 'uncomfortable spaces' are felt and operationalised for students. We found that students themselves were able to articulate – sometimes explicitly, at other times inherently – this uncomfortable space. Indeed, students' views reflected almost uniformly both an acceptance and internalisation of neoliberal discourses about what it is to study in an online enabling program, while at the same time reflecting the program's place within social justice discourses that aim to provide transformative learning experiences for students.

Equity or EFTSL?[1] Philosophy, purpose and policy in higher education

Following World War II Australia has seen the introduction of a variety of measures aimed at increasing participation in higher education (Pitman, 2017). Indeed, equity in and access to higher education have been significant discourses in Australian higher education since. In the 1970s, then prime minister Gough Whitlam's education reform package sought to democratise access to higher education and increase representation amongst previously marginalised groups such as women and working-class people. In more recent decades, equity in and access to higher education have driven policy-making due largely to influential government-initiated reviews and discussion papers: in 1990, *A Fair Chance for All* (DEET, 1990), and, in 2008, *The Bradley Review* (Bradley, Noonan, Nugent & Scales, 2008). In *A Fair Chance for All*, six equity groups were identified and targets set for participation of these groups. These groups continue to provide a framework informing equity policy in higher education (Gale & Tranter, 2011). Over a decade later, *The Bradley Review* recommended targeted funding for these equity groups and as a result the Higher Education Participation and Partnership Programme (HEPPP) was initiated in 2010 (Bennett, et al., 2013). While enabling education has existed in Australia since the early 1970s (May & Bunn, 2015), the introduction of schemes over the years such as the HEPPP initiative has proven a catalyst for the proliferation of programs and Commonwealth supported student places across Australia. In 2015, 27 Australian universities (or entities associated with universities) offered 48 enabling programs (Pitman et al., 2015) and this number continues to grow.

However, across the same period that there has been a push towards the democratisation of higher education and increased representation of those previously marginalised from higher degrees, neoliberal market ideologies have also profoundly impacted the philosophies and practices of higher education. We understand 'neoliberalism', often referred to as economic rationalism in Australia, to indicate a form of governance privileging individual autonomy and choice-making, economic privatisation, minimal State intervention and where markets and governments are intertwined. From the mid-1980s, as part of the neoliberal project, Australian universities have increasingly become integrated into the 'market': a move that has given rise to greater competition for funding and for students (Davies et al., 2006). Many contemporary academics argue that this 'neoliberal turn' has resulted in an inevitable reorientation in underlying philosophy and purpose for higher education; from serving the interests of the public to serving the interests of corporations and other economic drivers (Ball, 2003; Giroux, 2002). Here, we understand 'philosophy' to refer to the principles that guide practices and shape purpose. Arguably, therefore, where once universities were guided by the principle of providing public good to their communities by educating socially conscious citizens, they are now guided by the forces of the market and the 'knowledge economy', with a focus on training their students to compete in the employment market (Giroux, 2002; Chau, 2010).

This shifting purpose has meant corresponding shifts in the ways universities operate both internally and as part of the 'market'. Internally, changes have occurred to the make-up of university staffing and to the role of the academic, with more administrative and managerial staff employed to meet new demands (Giroux, 2002; Macfarlane, 2011; Whitchurch, 2013); academic staff are now measured, valued and rewarded for their work in ways that are often oriented to economic, rather than social outcomes (Ball, 2003; Blackmore, 2002; Davies et al., 2006). Across the sector, universities are under increasing pressure to 'compete' as part of the 'market' for government and industry funding, part of which relies on the number of students they can attract (Marginson, 2006).

With developing technological advances and infrastructure, online education has emerged as an increasingly viable 'solution' to competing in the 'education marketplace' for universities. Chau (2010) argues that the

> online learning movement is motivated by capitalistic ideals in an increasingly knowledge-based economy whereby education is transformed into a com- modity, students into consumers, faculty into entrepreneurs, and institutions of higher learning into storefronts.
>
> *(p. 178)*

Further, "[i]t would appear that the motivation [for institutions] for pursuing online learning may be heavily based on fiscal concerns more than providing an alternative space for learning" (Chau, 2010, p. 184). Online education can, there- fore, be perceived by institutions as both a cost saving – fewer resources needed for staffing and development (Tynan et al., 2015) – and a revenue producer, as it has the potential to attract a broader cohort of students beyond the traditional geographic footprint of a university campus (Chau, 2010).

Multi-layered tensions and overlaps exist between higher education's pervasive neoliberal obligations and widening participation strategies in universities. Indeed, these are not necessarily competing impulses: the 'massification' of higher educa- tion potentially has, at its heart, both market imperatives *and* equity principles (Waller, Holford, Jarvis, Milana, & Webb, 2014). Gale and Tranter (2011) argue that Australia's widening participation discourses are informed by both neoliberal demands, such as future national economic prosperity, *and* social justice motives to improve the entrenched educational disadvantage experienced by many members of the population. They trouble the policy history of Australian universities through a social justice lens, problematising the seemingly 'good intentions' of distributive justice agendas and pointing out that social justice:

> has never been enough (in a policy sense) to justify higher education's expansion. Economic justifications have also been required and, for the most part, they have been positioned as the more substantive element of any argu- ment for expansion.
>
> *(Gale & Tranter, 2011, p. 41)*

Yet, the complex relationship between discourses of social justice and their interplay with neoliberal logics remains a cause for unease for many researchers and has implications for how online enabling educators conceptualise their own roles and the subjectivities of their students. Concerns centre on how social justice and economic rationalist imperatives such as measurement and productivity are operationalised in a widening participation policy context. For example, Pitman (2017) identifies the inherent potential to obscure student disadvantage in the quantitative measurement and reporting of 'equity' initiatives in order to sustain higher education funding; while the 'employability' promises of universities potentially mask classed, gendered and raced misrecognitions (Threadgold, Burke & Bunn, 2018). Of particular interest for online enabling education are the competing, yet overlapping, discourses of 'recruitment' and 'access' as university equity practitioners negotiate their "longer-term concern to bolster capacity for educational achievement in low-SES schools and a shorter-term mandate to recruit high-achieving low-SES and Indigenous students to specific universities" in order to achieve particular reporting goals (Peacock, Sellar & Lingard, 2014, p. 392). More broadly, there are concerns that when social justice discourses such as 'fairness', 'equity' and 'diversity' are co-opted into the rhetoric of neoliberalism, they are reconfigured, and even subverted, to meet economic rationalist objectives, rendering them ineffective in the project of social change (Archer, 2007). It is clear, then, that there is an uneasy marriage between the social justice project of widening participation and the measurement, accountability and competitive demands of neoliberalism.

Enabling education: A quiet revolution

Enabling education in Australia has 'lived through' this turbulent time as higher education's purpose has reoriented under neoliberal aims. For example, community interests formed the basis of the establishment of Australia's first and largest enabling program, the Open Foundation Program, at the University of Newcastle (May & Bunn, 2015). Since then, the Open Foundation Program, its students, and staff, have evolved in response to the changing higher education landscape, while seeking to remain true to what are now termed 'Enabling Philosophies and Pedagogies'. Practitioners guided by an 'enabling philosophy' value students' existing knowledges; they take a personalised and 'care-full' approach to dialogical relationships with their students; and they see that engagement in education can result in a diversity of outcomes, which are never conceptualised as 'failure' (Bennett et al., 2016). Pedagogies and practices that stem from this philosophy privilege contextualised academic practices; see assessment as a tool for developing students rather than ranking them; and encourage students to draw connections between their own lives and academic concepts (Bennett et al., 2016).

These philosophies and pedagogies form the rationale imbued in the Open Foundation Program from its genesis; they emphasise the empowerment of mature-aged learners and the public good associated with widening access to higher education for individuals, families, communities and the nation (Bennett et al., 2016). As Bunn (2018) asserts, "while enabling programs can be viewed as fields of consumption as universities strive for market share and to access equity funding, they are important sites of transformative learning for mature age students" (p. 11). In enacting transformative learning, enabling programs have been quietly revolutionary in their aims, while also providing undergraduate degree programs with between 20–25 per cent of their student cohort.

Almost from its inception, the Open Foundation Program has sought to provide options for 'distance learners'. In 1978, radio delivery of course content in combination with one Saturday per month of face-to-face contact with their academic course staff was piloted as an innovative way to enact enabling pedagogies and demonstrate commitment to addressing the educational needs of students residing at a distance from a university campus, or who were unable to attend regularly due to other commitments. Although discontinued after a year, this initiative "was typical of the adaptions sought to accommodate student needs … it was superseded by more attention to promoting distance education", which included the development of residential weekends, paper-based distance learning, and the development of fully online units of study (Bunn, 2018, p. 112). The history of distance enabling education, then, reflects these parallel discourses; originating from community outreach initiatives, fully online enabling programs are now provided by at least 11 university providers (Pitman et al., 2015) to continue offering transformative learning experiences for students while meeting neoliberal agendas regarding higher education.

Capable, aspirant and so much more

We have made the point in this chapter that programs of education, such as online enabling programs, are products of their historical, social, cultural, and policy contexts, and similar may be said about the students who participate in them. In their 'excavation' of Australia's widening participation policies, Southgate and Bennett (2014) identify two embedded imagined student subject positions: *the cap(able) individual* and *the proper aspirant*. The cap(able) individual is reserved for people from under-represented groups who simply possess 'capability' for higher education where 'capability' is not explained, nor the means to obtain it. One of the effects of this discourse of 'capability' is to deliver the onus for access, participation and 'success' in higher education on the individual since the possession or otherwise of capability is conceptualised as an individual matter (Southgate & Bennett, 2014). The proper aspirant subject position articulated in policy demonstrates "an ability to rationally calculate pathways to and through HE [higher education] (and their subsequent career) for maximum benefit" (Southgate & Bennett, 2014, p. 35). This subject position valorises rational choice-making – in the process masking the social, cultural and affective – and consigns those who are ambivalent about higher education as lesser or 'other'. Both of these subject positions, argue Southgate and Bennett (2014), align closely with neoliberal ideologies.

The findings from our pilot study reflect an internalisation by students of the subject positions identified by Southgate and Bennett (2014), but also offer more complex renderings of student subjectivities, illuminating the interwoven philosophies driving neoliberal and enabling education. We found that students recognise and occupy the liminal space of online education as both socially-just *and* neoliberal in underpinnings and ideology. This is reflected in student motivations for enrolment, perceptions of the program and measures of success (see Hamilton et al., 2018 for full findings, discussion and quantitative data). Student–participants enrolled in this online enabling program reflected in survey responses and via interview almost uniformly upon motivations for their enrolment and measures of success that align with neoliberal philosophies surrounding online education. That is, they overwhelmingly conceptualised their initial reasons for enrolment around rational 'aspirational' industry and employment goals; students enrolled in enabling programs online to embark on the pathway to their 'dream job', to exit unfulfilling or perceived undesirable employment, or to upskill or regain confidence to enter the workforce. Correspondingly, they also largely measured their success in quantitative terms, via achievement of grades and admission into their desired undergraduate degree pathway, thereby demonstrating their 'capability' for higher education. Yet, alongside this internalisation of cap(ability) and aspiration driven by neoliberal philosophies, were a myriad of more complex reasonings that reflect enabling philosophies. That is, participants demonstrated an awareness of the holistic impacts of educational access, especially for those who had experienced marginalisation from educational programs in the past. For example, Rebecca[2] found meaning in her study through its potential to model positive behaviours for her children:

> I think being able to show my kids that if you work hard you can do sort of whatever you want with your life within reason ... I'm the first person in my immediate family to have their HSC[3] and sort of go on to further study, so I'd like to motivate my children that they would want to continue with their studies after school as well.

Student–participants also acknowledged that their motivation for enrolment related strongly to their self-identity and self-esteem, to improve the socioeconomic circumstances of their family into the future and inter-generationally, and as part of a larger process to improve physical and mental health. Grades, and entry into a desired degree program as a result, carried symbolic value in these discussions too; rather than simply being a token for admission, they are potent signifiers of feelings of achievement, acquisition of academic capital, of time spent, and of self-revelation.

Likewise, participants largely endorsed neoliberal discourses that online education is a mechanism of flexibility, which can be fit readily – and capably – around their pre-existing lifestyle and commitments. They explicitly utilised the wording prominent in marketing materials surrounding online learning, suggesting that online study is 'accessible', 'flexible', 'convenient' and available in their own time. Yet, these participants were also largely undertaking paid and/or unpaid work and, while they discussed the virtues of flexibility in online modes of learning, they also acknowledged many strategies designed to make their own lives more flexible and adaptable to this new challenge. For example, Anna cut down her paid work hours:

> I cut down a day at work which has helped a lot with workloads, fitting everything in. ... Like I get up at 5:30 to go to work and I'm just too fatigued by the time I get home at six o'clock to actually put in any solid effort. So I would rather just get up on a Wednesday and commit my whole day to doing it then, rather than doing bits and pieces after work on other days.
>
> *(Anna)*

Marie relied on family support to manage her study, paid work and caring commitments:

> So you know, it just meant that my husband would juggle his afternoons that he finished early or start late, but you know, as a family we managed to work around those obstacles and make it work.
>
> *(Marie)*

Making adjustments to child care arrangements and cutting down on social events also featured in many participants' narratives surrounding the difficulties of fitting online study into already packed schedules. Students also placed a great emphasis on teacher presence, acknowledging that whilst flexibility in the timings and structures of weekly learning materials and assessments is important, so are responsive and proactive educators and other forms of support services.

Recommendations and conclusions

This chapter has theorised the uncomfortable spaces that online enabling learning occupies, caught between neoliberal imperatives, on the one hand, and equity and widening participation impetuses on the other. This tension has implications for the ways in which institutions operate, staff conceptualise their labour, and students see the value in and meaning of their educational participation. Our preliminary study suggests that students internalise neoliberal subjectivities at the same time that they render them complex, or indeed, contradictory. Such findings reflect that while it is important that universities are industry-facing and are able to articulate clear pathways between undergraduate entry, completion and employability, it is equally important that many of the original features of enabling philosophies, pedagogies and practice grounded in community-facing outreach are not lost or sidelined in the process. The student–participants in this project reflected that while employability is important, it is not the sole reason for their engagement in study, nor is it the sole way in which they measure their success. Indeed, the neoliberal imperatives discussed throughout this piece, while evident in their discussion, are not the most profound areas of concern for most student–participants; issues of self-worth, self-identity, family and community were central to their concerns. As researchers and practitioners operating within an individualised, market-driven higher education landscape, we view *enabling* philosophies as central to the ongoing integrity of our work. To serve our students well, therefore, means that institutions (and the policy agendas that drive them) need to take care that online enabling education is, and remains, people-rich, community-facing, and catered to the whole person.

Notes

1 In Australia, EFTSL refers to Equivalent Full-Time Student Load and is a measure used to calculate student numbers, that is, one EFTSL equals one full-time study load for one year.
2 All participants quoted in this chapter have been assigned pseudonyms.
3 HSC refers to the New South Wales Higher School Certificate, which is awarded to students who successfully complete the senior level of secondary school. Other states in Australia have similar credentials, for example, students in Victoria are awarded the VCE (Victorian Certificate of Education).

References

Archer, L. (2007). Diversity, equality and higher education: A critical reflection on the ab/uses of equity discourse within widening participation. *Teaching in Higher Education*, 12(5–6), 635–653. doi:10.1080/13562510701595325.

Baker, S. & Irwin, E. (2016). Core or periphery? The positioning of language and literacies in enabling programs in Australia. *Australian Educational Researcher*, 43, 487–503.

Ball, S. J. (2003). The teacher's soul and the terrors of performativity. *Journal of Education Policy*, 18(2), 215–228. doi:10.1080/0268093022000043065.

Bennett, A., Hodges, B., Kavanagh, K., Fagan, S., Hartley, J. & Schofield, N. (2013). 'Hard' and 'soft' aspects of learning as investment: opening up the neo-liberal view of a programme with 'high' levels of attrition. *Widening Participation and Lifelong Learning*, 14(3), 141–156.

Bennett, A., Motta, S. C., Hamilton, E., Burgess, C., Relf, B., Gray, K., Leroy-Dyer, S., & Albright, J. (2016). *Enabling pedagogies: A participatory conceptual mapping of practices at the University of Newcastle, Australia*. Newcastle, Australia: Centre of Excellence for Equity in Higher Education, University of Newcastle.

Blackmore, J. (2002). Globalisation and the restructuring of higher education for new knowledge economies: New dangers or old habits troubling gender equity work in universities? *Higher Education Quarterly*, 56(4), 419–441.

Bradley, D., Noonan, P., Nugent, H., & Scales, B. (2008). *Review of Australian higher education: Final report*. Canberra: Department of Education, Employment and Workplace Relations.

Bunn, R. (2018). *The history and impacts of the University of Newcastle's Open Foundation Program*. (Unpublished doctoral dissertation). University of Newcastle, Newcastle, NSW, Australia.

Chau, P. (2010). Online higher education commodity. *Journal of Computing in Higher Education*, 22, 177–191. doi:10.1007/s12528–010–9039-y.

Davies, B., Gottsche, M. & Bansel, P. (2006). The rise and fall of the neo-liberal university. *European Journal of Education*, 41(2), 305–319.

Department of Employment, Education and Training (DEET). (1990). *A fair chance for all*. Canberra: Australian Government Printing Service.

Gale. T. & Tranter, D. (2011). Social justice in Australian higher education policy: An historical and conceptual account of student participation. *Critical Studies in Higher Education*, 52(1), 29–46.

Giroux, H. A. (2002). Neoliberalism, corporate culture, and the promise of higher education: The university as a public sphere. *Harvard Educational Review*, 72(4), 425–463.

Hamilton, E. L., Irwin, E., Djenidi, V., & Sciffer, S. (2018). *Reinserting student voices into discourses of retention and attrition in online enabling education*. Retrieved from Enabling Research website: https://docs.wixstatic.com/ugd/eff178_7c91aa136b5141caba343c08581fcf81.pdf.

Macfarlane, B. (2011). The morphing of academic practice: Unbundling and the rise of the para-academic. *Higher Education Quarterly*, 65(1), 59–73.

Marginson, S. (2006). Dynamics of national and global competition in higher education. *Higher Education*, 52(1), 1–39.

May, J. & Bunn, R. J. (2015). 1974–1976: The seeds of longevity in a pathway to tertiary participation at University of Newcastle, NSW. *Australian Journal of Adult Learning*, 55(1), 135–152.

Peacock, D., Sellar, S. & Lingard, B. (2014). The activation, appropriation and practices of student-equity policy in Australian higher education. *Journal of Education Policy*, 29(3), 377–396. doi:10.1080/02680939.2013.839829.

Pitman, T. (2017). Widening participation in higher education: A play in five acts. *Australian Universities' Review*, 59(1), 37–46.

Pitman, T., Trinidad, S., Devlin, M., Harvey, A., Brett, M. & McKay, J. (2015). *Pathways to higher education: The efficacy of enabling and sub-bachelor pathways for disadvantaged students*. Perth, WA: National Centre for Student Equity in Higher Education.

Southgate, E. & Bennett, A. (2014). Excavating widening participation policy in Australian higher education: Subject positions, representational effects, emotion. *Creative Approaches to Research*, 7(1), 21–45.

Threadgold, S., Burke, P. J., & Bunn, M. (2018). *Struggles and strategies: Does social class matter in higher education? Report*. Newcastle, NSW: Centre of Excellence for Equity in Higher Education.

Tynan, B., Ryan, Y., & Lamont-Mills, A. (2015). Examining workload models in online and blended teaching. *British Journal of Educational Technology*, 46(1), 5–15.

Waller, R., Holford, J., Jarvis, P., Milana, M. & Webb, S. (2014). Widening participation, social mobility and the role of universities in a globalized world. *International Journal of Lifelong Education*, 33(6), 701–704. doi:10.1080/02601370.2014.972082.

Whitchurch, C. (2013). *Reconstructing identities in higher education: The rise of third space professionals*. London: Routledge.

11

MANIFESTOS, MUTANTS AND MASH-UPS

Punk and pedagogy in online enabling education

Dr Angela Jones and Anita Olds

Online university enabling programs provide students with learning opportunities to grow their academic literacies and critical thinking whilst still maintaining external commitments. High attrition rates have historically impacted these online learning spaces (Barnes, Gachago & Ivala, 2015) and more so for non-traditional students (Whannell, 2013; Whannell & Whannell 2012). Using the examples of FlexiTrack and FlexiTrack High enabling programs at Murdoch University, this chapter illustrates how online enabling educators can use the philosophy of EduPunk and 'punked' digital resources to meet the student in the "Engagement Zone" (Jones, Olds & Lisciandro 2016). FlexiTrack and FlexiTrack High are two online programs offered as part of a suite of enabling programs at Murdoch for the purposes of meeting widening participation goals. Groom (2009), who originally coined the term, describes Edu-Punk as a playful do-it-yourself (DIY) approach to teaching and learning and a reaction against the "fluorescent lighted space of the Learning Management System (LMS)". We argue that what is born from such a design approach is a new breed of 'mutant' educational programs that can evolve and adapt to changing educational contexts, and an enabling curriculum brimming with resources that have been poached, mashed-up, repurposed and curated specifically for the online enabling learner.

In the last ten years Murdoch University have developed a suite of enabling programs to prepare non-traditional students for university study. Two of these programs, FlexiTrack and FlexiTrack High[1], use the digital space as the central learning platform. When FlexiTrack was first delivered at the beginning of 2017, it had a pass rate of 34.8 per cent and a lack of engagement in the learning management system (LMS) (this was determined through forum use and LMS student tracker). While the interface was clean and navigable, it was not dynamic and required more explicit instructions, "just in time" explanations and connections. A review of Student Surveys from the 2017 pilot iterations, as well as feedback from the FlexiTrack team of experienced online tutors, identified specific "missing" elements in the program such as mini explanations for tasks and assignments that were hindering engagement and retention because students were feeling "lost" or "confused".

Drawing on the DIY philosophy of EduPunk, the designers of FlexiTrack and FlexiTrack High tackled the challenge of engagement and transition for online enabling students. This chapter demonstrates that dynamic and engaging online enabling programs can be created when educators embrace a design manifesto that is informed by transition and digital pedagogies, underpinned by an EduPunk philosophy. The purpose of this chapter is to make explicit the innovative approaches possible when online enabling programs are struggling with retention and to share practical examples of EduPunking a curriculum to foster stronger engagement. Early indicators of online progression and student feedback (Murdoch University, 2018) suggest that this new breed of curriculum is improving learner engagement and retention.

The design manifesto

It is difficult to capture the complex decision making that occurs when creating an online enabling unit, but for the purposes of this chapter the following design manifesto encapsulates the major philosophies that shaped the evolution of the FlexiTrack programs in 2018. The aim of the manifesto was to articulate the values and beliefs integral to Murdoch University enabling programs and to address the issues of engagement and retention affecting the 2017 pilot of FlexiTrack. It was imperative that the programs remained aligned with key educational philosophies of social justice and flourishing that underpin all Murdoch University access programs. We also recognised that we needed to discover a dynamic philosophical approach that provided an edge to the often static space of online learning. EduPunk shone forth as a philosophical nexus between social justice and flourishing.

The philosophy of punk

Punk is more than spiked hair, tartan and safety-pinned pierced noses; it is rooted in resistance, rebellion, resourcefulness and challenging the dominant paradigm. Being a punk or doing punk in the context of the university is not an attempt to de-establish the foundations of the institution. It is an attempt at "taking on the responsibility" (O'Hara, 1995, p. 23) of questioning and challenging dysfunctional modalities; in our case the technological determinism (Jones & Bennett, 2017) that was limiting education – not facilitating it. Of punks, Schofield (2017) observes

> they question and challenge established modes of thought, opening up new questions and finding new perspectives. Cultural expression is relatively unrestricted. Punks can be bold and inventive in their work. Conventions do not hold them back.

(p. 286)

With the knowledge of engagement and retention issues in online learning, when revising FlexiTrack, there was a need to challenge these established modes and look for fresh perspectives within the digital space; as well as to stay true to educational philosophies, strong enabling pedagogical drives and the needs of our learners. The ethos of punk as a counter culture offers curriculum designers a way through what Miller (2018) refers to as the "didactic and authoritarian approaches to pedagogy that promote naive, uncritical engagements with technology" (p. 166). We believed that perhaps our counter cultural enabling students could benefit from the counter cultural education of EduPunk.

In 1964 Richard Hoggart founded the Birmingham Centre for Contemporary Cultural Studies which, like punk, through a mashup of perspectives, challenged disciplinary approaches to culture. The Centre was more than DIY theories researching into areas of popular culture that had previously been deemed "low culture" (University of Birmingham, 2018). Research collaborations, between academics and students who were underrepresented within the university structure, revealed the political, cultural and social importance of popular cultural texts (University of Birmingham, 2018). We recognise that these texts offer a mode of "ideological influence", and can be resistive, but they also hold knowledge systems that our own under-represented students can use to build "new cognitive pegs" (Jones, Olds & Lisciandro, 2016). As Beer remarks, punk "is outward looking and keen to respond, react against and draw upon alternative cultural resources" (Beer, 2014, p. 28). In the online learning space our intention is to, as Schofield remarks, "transcend boundaries and obstacles and erode the lines between performer and audience" (2017, p. 286). This is achieved through the acknowledgement and validation of existing learner knowledge as well as creating digital closeness and movement.

Groom (2008a) coined the term EduPunk in a response to the inferior nature of the LMS and the capitalisation incentives of the educational technology movement:

> I don't believe in technology, I believe in people. And that's why I don't think our struggle is over the future of technology, it is over the struggle for the future of our culture that is assailed from all corners by the vultures of capital. Corporations are selling us back our ideas, innovations, and visions for an exorbitant price. I want them all back, and I want them now!

Groom's word quickly became a movement that was celebrated, unpacked and debated by educators similarly disenfranchised and looking to own their own ideas and politicise the corporatisation of technology in education.

The EduPunk philosophy encourages educators to shake off the shackles of traditional digital learning spaces such as the LMS to meet the needs of their online learners. Brooks (2008) states, "in short, edupunk [sic] is student-centered, resourceful, teacher- or community-created rather than corporate-sourced, and underwritten by a progressive political stance". Groom (2008b) supports the definition and notes that

> if EDUPUNK [sic] is all about people, and some few of us believe that we need to examine what it is we do … then thinking about the intersection of those spaces where our culture and capital come into a very sharp collision, namely gender, race, ethnicity, and class, is of the utmost importance.

This philosophy is possibly why it connects with enabling education, where both non-traditional students and "chimaera" academics (Bennett et al., 2016) are often located as cultural outsiders. EduPunk also resonates with philosophies of social justice and access education. It encourages reflectivity ("an in-depth review of events" (Bolton, 2005, p. 9)) and reflexivity ("finding strategies to question our own attitudes, theories in-use, values, assumptions, prejudices and habitual actions; to understand our complex roles in relation to others" (p. 10)). EduPunk pushes educators to ponder the place where culture and capital meet, and reflect on how *we* use our cultural capital to build students' knowledge and agency, as well as *how* we co-create authentic educationally liberating digital learning communities.

Enabling and digital pedagogies

Though promised to be the new frontier in learning and access, online programs have struggled to achieve the same outcomes as face-to-face teaching. Notably, such programs have historically struggled with retention (Barnes, Gachago & Ivala, 2015; Lee & Choi, 2013) and this problem is noted more so for non-traditional students (Whannell 2013; Whannell & Whannell 2012; Tyler-Smith, 2006). The underlying causes for attrition are complex; while there is less opportunity to change the macro conditions that impact the learner, such as sociocultural factors, many of the micro level conditions of the learning environment, such as content, technology, instructional model and strategy, peer interaction and assessment can be proactively managed (Cho et al., 2015). The historical invisibility of online learning as happening 'out there', an academic workload add-on, an upload of the face-to-face version, or a cheap alternative to face-to-face learning (Jones & Bennett, 2017) has meant that micro level conditions have often been overlooked or lost in digital translation (Cho et al., 2015). Institutional limitations like ineffective course design within the boundaries of the LMS, can be overcome with a cognisance of digital pedagogy.

One digital approach to pedagogy, 'connected learning', emphasises the creation of diverse learning spaces, including student's personal interests, peer cultures and academic environments (Miller, 2018). According to Anderson and McCormick (2005), alignment to outcomes, inclusion and student engagement are the primary principles of e-learning. Hung, Kinshuk, and Chen (2018) suggest that in order to improve learning and retention, a holistic design that incorporates multimedia content such as embodied videos (that simultaneously engage, prompt, provide experiential opportunity, consolidate concepts, model task completion, and invite questions) is required. Similarly, Boling, Hough, Krinsky, Saleem, and Stevens (2012) advise that courses require careful design of interactive technologies. Yet, according to Murphy (2012), the use of the educational technology is often poor, due in part no doubt to limited training in a neoliberal context. Digital pedagogic principles, it could be argued, are of particular import in the online space. The isolation felt by many online students requires more supplementary activities to reduce isolation, create connection and communicate and scaffold outcomes. Uploading the course content into a "neon lit scroll of death" (Groom, 2009) for example, does not make a dynamic learning experience for a student. We need to go beyond e-learning pedagogy and re-vision student learning in the digital age (Brown, 2013).

FlexiTrack and FlexiTrack High not only embrace digital pedagogy but are strongly informed by enabling pedagogy (Jones, Olds & Lisciandro, 2016). The design process, while subject to constant evolution, always remains influenced by the attributes of Tinto's (2011) effective classrooms. He suggests that effective teaching and learning requires clear and appropriate expectations, multiple opportunities for support, frequent feedback, student involvement, and engagement. Faithfulness to these foundational pedagogies are notably evident in the basic structure of the modules, the unit guides, the rubrics, the assessment descriptions, the scaffolding activities, and lectures as well as careful attention to language use and the selection of popular culture references. For example a 'meme of the week' is included at the top of the LMS. The meme is a multi-layered learning text. It has to be humorous to engage the learner, topical to prompt thought regarding the week's concept or skill, and encourage critical reflection on complex ideas (Cho et al., 2015).

Also paramount to the program is a learner-centred approach. Deep consideration of the student cohort is central. Boling et al., (2012) warned that teacher-centred, text-based courses were ineffective when trying to create positive online learning experiences. When scaffolding learning and assessment material to meet the learning outcomes, a filter system was conceived. The filters distilled observances of learner needs in the online enabling learning space. Material needed to pass through the three filters before being deemed fit for inclusion. Filter one became known as the "Two Minute-Noodle" filter. This reminded the designers that material had to be quickly accessed and packaged in a way that appealed to the cohort. The second filter "Tell 'Em Three Times" reinforced the need for the instruction to be communicated in multiple forms thereby providing a variety of learning modalities to reinforce the concepts and the assessments (Glenn, 2016). The third filter applied the theory of "The Engagement Zone" (for an in-depth explanation of The Engagement Zone see Chapter 3) where shared teacher and student passions meet and relationship is the key (Arhin & Wang'eri, 2018).

Swaggerty and Broemmel (2017) advise that course designers need to consider ways to build community. "The Engagement Zone" filter encouraged us to ask, what does online engagement look like? Did the material capture the authenticity of the educators, and appeal to shared interest, thus building relationship and engagement? Glenn further advises that a human touch from instructors "provides students with a deeper sense of care" (2016, p. 386). One example of this is in our weekly aptly named "Two-Minute Noodle: Where We're At" videos recorded on location each week. These two minute videos are full of puns, song lyrics and remind the students of weekly progress goals. The videos foster connection and show care for the student's learning experience with a "we are all in this together" attitude. But how does one simultaneously honour all the pedagogies described above?

"Enter stage left – EduPunk" (Groom, 2008a).

EduPunking FlexiTrack: A mutant program

It should be noted that we recognise that some traditions, because we are transitioning students to university with an ingrained set of structures, need to remain. We do not abandon pedagogic principles; rather we raise them, as EduPunk offers a way to enhance engagement and "dismantle the tyranny of textbooks" (Miller, 2018, p. 167). EduPunk could be considered covert and subversive where non-academic texts are snuck through the backdoor of the often staid university. Our conception of EduPunk utilises the resources we have readily on hand such as pens, papers, phones with photo and video recordings, meme generators, the Internet, social media, music, movies, television, fashion, popular cultural texts and an up-to-date knowledge of what is trending/viral to punk our digital learning space day-to-day. For example, when students were struggling to be able to locate and use the library citation guide we created a DIY video of Professor Quackosaurus, a plastic duck wearing a graduate hat, who cannot find the citation guide in a physical library. This two minutes and twenty-seven-second-long video follows Professor Quackosaurus into the library where he meets Yoda the Librarian who sends him online. The video is sound tracked by Green Day's *At The Library*, and narrated using handwritten and digital speech bubbles. This method was chosen as it mimics the style of DIY YouTube videos. It is intentionally amateur – viewers can see the piece of plastic tape that pulls Professor Quackosaurus around – so that it is memorable, engaging and motivating (Jones and Bennett, 2017, p. 200). It is through the sharing of historical and contemporary iconography, as well as authentic and varied DIY digital communications that new students' knowledges outside of academia are validated and celebrated. The goal is to build academic literacy and "digital agency" (Miller, 2018, p.169), moving students beyond these texts to a place of cultural insider and part of the university community.

When EduPunking the activities and resources in FlexiTrack we became bricoleurs (Strauss, 1962), appropriating, inventing, and experimenting. We re-appropriated digital material such as memes, YouTube clips, and blogs. When needing to remind students of essay planning, we created a meme of Captain Holt from Brooklyn 99 extolling the virtues of planning. When we could not find a digital resource to fit purpose, we went analogue, creating a hand drawn, stick figure, silent film called "Don't be like Bob" to warn students against the perils of writing without planning. We challenged the limitations of the LMS and hacked code to create a more seamless and intimate interface removing any technology superfluous to the learning. We then brought in outside resources: Filmed mini lectures "on location", DIY recordings of ourselves filling poster paper to illustrate the formulas for positive social change and rebranded Barney Stinson's salacious Bro Code into Barney Stinson's reflective Grow Code – a student learning journal. Hanley

(2011, pp.11) terms this approach a kind of "mutant semiotics". We have created mutant programs, hybrids of sorts, evolving in response to learner needs in the digital space. But it is not one-way communication that builds community or digital and academic agency in the students.

The forums also offer the opportunities for punking with the first question of 'who are you?' It is here that the tutors reveal their "authentic selves" (Jones, Olds & Lisciandro, 2016), sharing their passions and learning journeys with the students, and the students are encouraged to do the same. An "Engagement Zone" is created where students and tutors share topical memes, emojis, TED talks and puns. Punking occurs through challenging the limitations of the LMS so that students almost do not 'see' the interface, but see their learning community, and desire to keep coming back because it is dynamic and changing. EduPunk as a part of digital pedagogy is useful for successfully transitioning enabling students into the university culture. Educators can become what Wenger, White, and Smith (2009, p. 132) refer to as "tech stewards" and the LMS operates as a "simple" space to move through with communication happening on either side, rather than a one dimensional didactic place, in which students (and educators) can get stuck. Punking the interface in this way helps to also develop "digital agency" (Miller, 2018, p.169), which is particularly needed by online students.

Reflections on the mutant program

Quantitative investigation on the EduPunking initiative is still in infancy as data collection for all modules is not yet complete. However, early data suggests that 'punking' is yielding positive results. While retention (at the Murdoch University census date) has remained at similar levels in Module 1, the pass rate for students has improved substantially (see Table 11.1). In the first post EduPunking iteration in 2018, Module 1 had 80% retention with a pass rate of 56%. The punking then continued for each subsequent iteration.

In addition to early data, anecdotally tutors have recognised a growth in students' application of skills and deep learning in the assessment tasks. All tutors have noted a rise in the quality of engagement in the forums, depth of reflection in the journals and more assignments meeting the task descriptors. While there is ample dialogue between tutors and students, a change in this dialogue has also been recognised from general 'help seeking' questions about the locations of material to critical questions about skills, concepts and theory.

TABLE 11.1 Retention and Pass Rates for Module 1 2017/2018

Module 1	1st Iteration 2017	1st Iteration 2018	2st Iteration 2018
Retention Rate	86%	80%	84%
Pass Rate	29.6%	56%	66%
n=*	125	77	149

n= proportion of students enrolled in the program retained at census date

Conclusion

The online learning space for enabling education can be a layered terrain to navigate, both in design and delivery. Retention and conversion are part of the neoliberalist agenda of universities to get 'bums on seats' and is often a driving force behind creating programs that achieve this. But it does not have to limit a designer's creativity, and neither does the LMS. Enabling educators' philosophies and pedagogies do not need to be lost in the digital design process, but do need to be reflected on and reshaped in a way to meet the needs of the online student. EduPunk offers us a way to paste together these philosophies, challenge our own pedagogies and DIY new ones into our punked-up mutant programs.

Note

1 FlexiTrack is a predominantly online enabling program delivered to adult learners, whereas FlexiTrack High is the blended online enabling offering delivered in partnership with high schools.

References

Anderson, John, & McCormick, Robert. (2005). Ten pedagogic principals of e-learning. *Insight: Observatory for New Technologies and Education.* Retrieved from https://www.resea rchgate.net/profile/Robert_Mccormick6/publication/47343091_Ten_pedagogic_princip les_for_E-learning/links/02e7e536bed9785354000000/Ten-pedagogic-principles-for-E-learning.pdf.

Arhin, V., & Wang'eri, T. (2018). Orientation programs and student retention in distance learning: The case of university of cape coast. *Journal of Educators Online*, 15(1). doi:10.9743/JEO2018.15.1.6

Barnes, V., Gachago, D., & Ivala, E. (2015). Digital storytelling in industrial design. In P. C. Layne & P. Lake (Eds.), *Global innovation of teaching and learning in higher education: Transgressing boundaries.* Cham: Springer International Publishing. doi:10.1007/978-3-319-10482-9

Beer, D. (2014). *Punk sociology.* New York: Palgrave Macmillan.

Bennett, R., Hobson, J., Jones, A., Martin-Lynch, P., Scutt, C., Strehlow, K., & Veitch, S. (2016). Being Chimaera: A monstrous identity for SoTL academics. *Higher Education Research & Development*, 35(2),217–228. doi:10.1080/07294360.2015.1087473.

Bolton, G. (2005). *Reflective practice: Writing and professional development* (2nd ed.). London, Thousand Oaks, CA: SAGE.

Boling, E. C., Hough, M., Krinsky, H., Saleem, H., & Stevens, M. (2012). Cutting the distance in distance education. *The Internet and Higher Education*, 15(2), 118–126. doi:10.1016/j.iheduc.2011.11.006.

Brown, P. G. (2013). Re-envisioning student learning in a digital age. *About Campus*, 18(4), 30–32.doi:10.1002/abc.21129.

Brooks, L. (2008) Introducing EduPunk. *Blogher.* http://www.blogher.com/intro ducing-edupunk.

Cho, Y. H., Choi, H., Shin, J., Yu, H. C., Kim, J. Y., & Kim, Y. K. (2015). Review of research on online learning environments in higher education. *Procedia – Social and Behavioural Sciences*, 191. doi:10.1016/j.sbspro.2015.04.634.

Glenn, C. W. (2016). Adding the human touch to asynchronous online learning. *Journal of College Student Retention: Research, Theory & Practice*, 19(4), 381–393. doi:10.1177/1521025116634104.

Groom, J. (2008a, May 25) Glass bees. *bavatuesdays*https://bavatuesdays.com/the-glass-bees/

Groom, J. (2008b, May 29) BlogHer Nails EduPunk. *bavatuesdays*bavatuesdays.com/blogher-nails-edupunk/.

Groom, J. (October 2009) *Edupunk Battle Royal: Part 1 & 2*.[video file]. Retrieved from https://www.youtube.com/watch?v=f7MxVqe_uRI.

Hanley, L. (2011). Mashing up the institution: Teacher as bricoleur. *The Radical Teacher*, 90, 9–14. doi:10.5406/radicalteacher.90.0009.

Hung, I., Kinshuk, & Chen, N. (2018). Embodied interactive video lectures for improving learning comprehension and retention. *Computers & Education*, 117, 116–131. doi:10.1016/j.compedu.2017.10.00.

Jones, A., & Bennett, R. (2017) Reaching beyond an online/offline divide: Invoking the rhizome in higher education course design. *Technology, Pedagogy and Education*, 26(4). doi:10.1080/1475939X.2016.1201527.

Jones, A., Olds, A., & Lisciandro, J. (2016) Understanding the learner: Effective course design in the changing higher education space. *International Studies in Widening Participation*, 3(1), 19–35.

Lee, Y., & Choi, J. (2013). A structural equation model of predictors of online learning retention. *The Internet and Higher Education*, 16, 36–42. doi:10.1016/j.iheduc.2012.01.005

Miller, Jamieson. (2018) From EDUPUNK to open policy: Critical technology praxis within higher education. *The Professional Geographer*, 70(1), 165–173. doi:10.1080/00330124.2017.1326086.

Murdoch University (2018). OnTrack testimonials. Murdoch University, Retrieved from http://www.murdoch.edu.au/OnTrack/Testimonials/.

Murphy, Jamie. (2012) LMS teaching versus community learning: A call for the latter. *Asia Pacific Journal of Marketing and Logistics*, 24(5), 826–841. doi:10.1108/13555851211278529

O'Hara, C. (1995). *The philosophy of punk: More than noise!* Edinburgh: AK Press.

Patterson, B., & McFadden, C. (2009). Attrition in online and campus degree programs. *Online Journal of Distance Learning Administration*, 12(2), 1–8.

Schofield, John. (2017). Deviants, punks and pink fairies: Counter archaeologies for unreasonable people. *World Archaeology*, 49(3), 281–290. doi:10.1080/00438243.2017.1383182

Strauss, Claude, Levi. (1962). *The savage mind*. Chicago: University of Chicago Press.

Swaggerty, E. A., & Broemmel, A. D. (2017). Authenticity, relevance, and connectedness: Graduate students' learning preferences and experiences in an online reading education course. *The Internet and Higher Education*, 32, 80–86. doi:10.1016/j.iheduc.2016.10.002.

Tinto, V. (2011). *Taking student success seriously in the college classroom*. Retrieved Sep, 16, 2014. https://www.sdbor.edu/administrative-offices/student-affairs/sac/Documents/Tinto-TakingStudentSuccessSeriouslyintheCollegeClassroom.pdf.

Tyler-Smith, K. (2006). Early attrition among first time elearners: A review of factors that contribute to drop-out, withdrawal and non-completion rates of adult learners undertaking elearning programmes. *Journal of Online Learning and Teaching*, 2(2), 73–85.

University of Birmingham. (2018). About CCCS: History and project. University of Birmingham. https://www.birmingham.ac.uk/schools/historycultures/departments/history/research/projects/cccs/about.aspx.

Wenger, E., White, N., & Smith, J. D. (2009). *Digital habitats: Stewarding technology for communities*. Portland, OR: CP square.

Whannell, R. (2013). Predictors of attrition and achievement in a tertiary bridging program. *Australian Journal of Adult Learning*, 53(2), 280–300.

Whannell, P., & Whannell, R. (2012). *Reducing the attrition of tertiary bridging students studying by distance: A Practice Report*. Paper presented at the FABENZ Conference, Auckland, New Zealand.

THE EDUCATORS' TIPS FOR TRANSITIONING DIVERSE COHORTS (PART II)

Planning learning first requires knowing your student and the learning context. Diverse approaches suit diverse cohorts and contexts.

(Lisciandro, Jones, & Olds)

In our experience working in the enabling space, particularly with Indigenous learners, success in engagement and retention is based on relationships, which take time to develop and are ongoing. As one elder said, "it is a thousand cups of coffee" or as Dr Ober calls it, *kapati* (cup of tea) time – taking time to create space for sharing. On a practical note, celebrations and shared meals are a great way to draw both students and educators together, through planned time to dissolve anxiety barriers; time to develop relationships and the trust bonds necessary for bridging cultures.

(Forrest & Hogue)

Indigenous students are often intimidated by university, struggle with bridging cultures, feel shy and embarrassed by what they don't know and are afraid to ask questions for fear of being judged negatively. It is critical to meet the students where they are at academically, show them where they need to go and take them on a learning journey. Co-create expectations in the learning process and space and work from a strengths-based inquiry for creative and collaborative problem-solving. Choose issues with real world and cultural relevance through which to demonstrate academic skill development, critical engagement and community building.

(Forrest & Hogue)

It can be isolating to work in the enabling space, so it is critical to connect with other educators/colleagues or educator group with like minds and focus; to share best practice, ask the hard questions, trial pedagogical practices and reflect on the journey.

(Forrest & Hogue)

Practice, and model, self-awareness: we need to identify our own biases and actively combat them.

(Bennett & Bennett)

Avoid assumptions: Encourage safe disclosure from each cohort and work with their particularities.

(Bennett & Bennett)

Always remember to create a space for your students. They want to feel acknowledged, supported and a part of the bigger story you are creating with your students.

(Beals & Arden)

Be prepared to go deep, teach through stories and allow the stories of your students to permeate the classroom.

(Beals & Arden)

Teaching staff need to possess a genuine belief in the program and its objectives.

(Monteith & Geerlings)

Teaching staff need to empower students so they take possession of their own learning and make it FUN and INTERESTING!

(Monteith & Geerlings)

Understanding that enabling students' experiences, identities and motivations are multi-dimensional is imperative for educators grappling with one-dimensional institutional concepts of quantifiable 'success' – student wellbeing should always take precedence over measurable institutional targets.

(Irwin & Hamilton)

Online education is not just a financially 'viable solution' for institutions to increase their student numbers. When properly resourced, online educators can play a significant role in facilitating the successful participation of students from diverse backgrounds who might not otherwise have the opportunity to access higher education.

(Irwin & Hamilton)

Consciousness of transition and digital pedagogies can inform the design of online units and provide a better chance of engaging enabling students.

(Jones & Olds)

Go DIY. Don't be afraid to re-appropriate, invent and repurpose any digital and non-digital resource to enhance the learning environment. Sneak non-academic texts through the backdoor of the often staid university and shake off the shackles of traditional digital learning spaces to meet the needs of online learners. Be a punk.

(Jones & Olds)

PART III

Challenges for educators

INTRODUCTION

Dr Joanne G. Lisciandro

As we have discussed so far throughout this book, our ultimate aim as educators is to set up the right conditions for the flourishing of our students as they transition into higher education. We have seen that there are, of course, diverse ways to achieve this, depending on the educational context and the student cohort. In the final section of this book, our authors delve into some of the challenges that exist for educators in navigating this space of transition.

So, what challenges exist? In my first couple of years of working in a pre-university enabling program as a tutor, then later as unit coordinator, and on both regional and metropolitan campuses, I found that the experience was in stark contrast to any sort of teaching that I had done before. I spent more time with these students than other cohorts. While it was my most rewarding experience as an educator, it was, at times, also my most difficult. Growth didn't come without struggle for many of these students; they struggled with coming to terms with their past educational experiences, they struggled with their self-efficacy and confidence, and, more than anything, they struggled with their personal circumstances. Financial, health, and family issues were prevalent but the number of students attempting to navigate this transitional space while dealing with depression, anxiety, and other mental health issues shocked me. I have walked more students to counselling than I can count. I know I'm not alone in my experience. Then come other concerns. There are the worries regarding student growth in academic literacies and the development of their resilience in order to independently weather the transition into a Bachelor degree once we set them free … no one wants to set their students up for failure. Moreover, tensions exist, as we and others try to do justice to the pedagogies and practices that empower students to flourish within a neoliberal university that is constantly pressuring us to do more with less. Things fall by the wayside, like spending time pausing, reflecting and explicitly considering one's philosophy of teaching/education, yet this is so important as it underpins everything we do as educators.

Within these challenges also lay opportunities, and in this section of the book our authors offer solution-oriented approaches to addressing such obstacles or difficulties, often by considering philosophies, pedagogies, and/or practices that may be useful and effective. Wanner and Wanner discuss some of the challenges that have arisen for educators as universities have increasingly operated within a global marketplace. They argue that neoliberal philosophies disempower both students and educators, impacting on their academic identities; and advocate for educators to challenge these dominant ideologies and continue to seek to make critical thinkers of their students. Ardzejewsha and Gorzanelli argue that effective transition of students ideally occurs where academic skill development can be directly embedded in discipline content and show us one model where this has been implemented successfully. Bunn addresses the idea that enabling educators tend not to be conscious of their explicit philosophy of teaching and education, yet opportunities exist to reflect and draw on the collective wisdom of experienced educators within one's community of practice. Lastly, Crawford, Kift, and Jarvis suggest that in order to be proactive about enhancing student academic outcomes, particularly during the stressful phase of transitioning to university, the responsibility for addressing student mental wellbeing has become everyone's business, and not just that of centralised university Counselling services. They discuss how student wellbeing can be supported by academics from within the student curriculum by embedding a philosophy of care into the pedagogies and practices of enabling programs. At the conclusion of this section you will find some top tips for responding to the tensions often encountered in transitional tertiary spaces.

12

THE TENSIONS BETWEEN PHILOSOPHIES OF EDUCATION AND CRITICAL PEDAGOGIES IN NEOLIBERAL HIGHER EDUCATION

Implications for learning and teaching practices

Dr Thomas Wanner and Dr Sarah Wanner

Introduction

Transitioning students into new educational spaces in the university environment – the subject of this book – requires an account of *how* these educational spaces and associated educational philosophies and pedagogies are framed in the neoliberal university. This chapter focusses on the ideological climate in which student transitions happen. Neoliberalism is viewed as a hegemonic ideology that shapes the philosophies and practices of teaching and learning in higher education, and with it ideas about student engagement, student graduate attributes and student empowerment. The aim of *flourishing of students* in higher education is a very recent concept. It can mean to maintain or increase student well-being during their learning experiences, or it could mean more self-actualisation in the sense of engaging and involving students more in their learning experiences (Kahn, 2017). We see flourishing during their education as synonymous with *empowering students* to be critical thinkers and be critically engaged with their own learning; at any stage, whether they are transitioning *into* higher education or transitioning when they are *in* higher education (e.g. between courses or degrees). For us, the focus of *flourishing of students* is about giving them their own transformative and critical agency so that they can flourish *after* their higher education is finished.

There are, we argue, three major tensions between pedagogies and philosophies shaped by neoliberalism and *flourishing* in the sense of empowerment: (i) the increasing focus on student-centred learning leads to the gradual erosion of academics/educators-centred learning and with it neglects the important role of the educator/academic as the 'empowering agent' for the students; (ii) the devaluation of the academic educator as gate-keeper, and guide for students of critical knowledge thinking; and (iii) the pedagogies and practices of learning in the neoliberal university reshape knowledge and student identities with a focus on work skills rather than critical thinking skills. These tensions are interlinked and work together so that students and academics/educators become less, not more empowered as individuals and transformative agents in society.

It is our contention that awareness of these tensions is a critical first step for educators to integrate critical pedagogies into their teaching and learning philosophies and practices. Educators need to become empowering academic educators who provide the opportunities for their students to flourish in the sense of becoming empowered students (learning to think and act for themselves) and to become critical thinkers (learning to think critically about society and their own place in it). The challenge here, we argue, is for the educator to incorporate *critical pedagogy* into their teaching and learning activities because such critical pedagogies and teaching practices are needed to challenge neoliberal education philosophies and overcome the identified tensions. This chapter highlights the crucial role of the academic educator in critical pedagogies and teaching practices, which have the goal of empowerment of the student.

This is increasingly becoming a difficult educational challenge for educators as the neoliberal university sets conditions that inhibit critical pedagogy and thinking despite having critical thinking as a graduate attribute. It is, however, not impossible to integrate critical pedagogies into teaching and learning activities.

Our critical reflections on the links and disconnects between philosophy, pedagogy and practice in higher education in Australia are based on our own views and experiences of teaching face-to-face, blended and online university courses, including the design and implementation of flexible and personalised courses (see Wanner & Palmer, 2015). The chapter starts with a brief overview of the pedagogies and practices of teaching and learning in neoliberal universities, then proceeds to delineate the meanings of 'empowerment', the 'academic' and 'critical thinking'. This is followed by our discussion about the mentioned tensions between neoliberal philosophies, pedagogies and practices and the *flourishing* of students.

Philosophies and pedagogies of education: The neoliberal university

The impacts of neoliberalism on education, in particular higher education, has received much attention in the literature. As Connell (2013, p. 100) states, "neoliberalism [which emerged in Australia and elsewhere in the early 1990s] broadly means the agenda of economic and social transformation under the sign of the free market". Neoliberalism has led to the privatisation, deregulation and marketization of higher education (John & Fanghanel, 2016). The changes to philosophies, pedagogies and practices of teaching and learning through education driven by the logic of the market have been wide-ranging. Some of them include: the intensification of academic work, exposure to increased competition between academics and more accountability measures for them (Davies & Bansel 2007, p. 254); the commodification of knowledge and education (Poon, 2006;

Ball, 2012; Connell, 2013); students have become consumers and 'clients' in a neoliberal marketised university (John & Fanghanel, 2016); heightened insecurity and alienation of the academic workforce (Connell, 2013, p. 106; Poon, 2006); and the progressive dismantling of critical pedagogies and the authority and power of the academic educators vis-à-vis their students (Poon, 2006; Davies & Bansel, 2007; Connell, 2013).

Universities are now seen as producers of knowledge that serve the neoliberal knowledge economy and achieve economic growth and development. The results are that universities "are no longer considered primarily as 'cultural spaces' that can enable individual students and academic educators to engage in critique and discussion" and higher education is considered a commodity rather than a social good (Patrick, 2013, pp. 3–4; see also Connell, 2013). The reshaping of higher education by neoliberal ideology "has acquired a level of dominance in the university, [that] although contested, is increasingly difficult to challenge" (Stirling & McGloin, 2015, p. 3).

Flourishing of students: Student empowerment and critical thinking

Student empowerment

Student or learner empowerment is one of the six new pedagogical ideas of higher education, and is defined as "actively involving students in learning development and processes of 'co-creation' that challenge learning relationships and the power frames that underpin them, as part of the revitalisation of the academic project itself" (Ryan & Tilbury, 2013, p. 5). Our contention is that the focus on flexible pedagogies has the danger of undermining its central component – student empowerment – because it neglects the critical role of the 'empowering educator'. This is not an argument against flexible pedagogies and flexible teaching and learning practices, but to be alert to the implications such pedagogies have on student and academic educators' empowerment. The central focus of 'flexible pedagogies' in higher education in Australia and elsewhere is to enable learners "to anticipate, prepare for and respond to conditions of complexity, uncertainty and change" (Ryan &Tilbury, 2013, p. 13).

Empowerment is a process of increasing the level of self-determination and autonomy of specific agents; and decreasing the level of dependency and discrimination of the agent. In regards to the empowerment of learners, the state of 'being empowered' is a result of intrinsic characteristics of the agent (here the learner), such as self-esteem, motivation, and competence, and external factors that enable empowerment (or empowering factors) such as empowering academic educators (Houser & Frymier, 2009). As discussed below, we see the 'empowering academic educator' as playing the central role for ensuring the flourishing of students in the sense of more student empowerment.

Critical thinking

Like most universities, our university includes 'critical thinking' and 'problem-solving' as graduate attributes because they are seen as required skills graduates need to have in twenty-first-century workplaces. In one of our university's Graduate Attributes it is stated that critical thinking is about "evaluating and challenging current knowledge and thinking". Hunter (2009, p. 2) defines critical thinking as "reasonable and reflective thinking aimed at deciding what to believe and what to do". So critical thinking includes a reflective thinking part and an action part in the sense that the critical thinkers first question ideas, concepts, ideologies which shape social reality and then also do something about it.

Critical pedagogy: Empowerment and liberation

Education can either be an instrument to reproduce the dominant ideologies in societies, which in current times means the reproduction of neoliberal educational philosophies and practices, or it can be a means to challenge dominant ideologies. For Freire, the ultimate function of learning was to overcome oppression. Through a process of *conscientisation*, the learner becomes more conscious of their social reality and of how to transform it (Freire, 1972). We agree with Espinoza (2017, p. 444) who sees it as "urgent and necessary to rescue and apply Freire's ideas" and include critical pedagogies into teaching and learning so that students are able to understand the implications of a neoliberal university and knowledge economy, and can become critical agents to make transformative changes for their own lives and for others.

However, critical pedagogy is "typically messy, difficult and problematic to enact" (Gregory, 2017, p. 2) in the neoliberal environment. But as we argue one of the crucial first steps to enacting a critical pedagogy is to be aware of the tensions that prevent it. In other words, the discursive formations that characterise the neoliberal educational environment need to be exposed.

Tension I: Student-centred vs academic educator centred-learning and empowerment

In Australia's higher education, as elsewhere in the world, there has been a growing trend towards more student-centred, self-directed and personalised learning (Keamy, Nicholas, Mahar, & Herrick, 2007; McLoughlin & Lee, 2010). This trend is linked to higher education philosophies and practices that are shaped by neoliberalism (Patrick, 2013; Olssen & Peters, 2005). Teaching and learning is gradually moving from academic educator-centred pedagogies and practices to flexible and personalised learning where students demand more flexibility in delivery through online and blended university courses (McLoughlin & Lee, 2010; Wanner & Palmer, 2015). The increasing use of social media, 'flipped classrooms', and Massive Open Online Courses (MOOCs) for teaching and learning are some indications of the trends towards more flexibility in delivery and more student-centred learning (Sharples et al., 2014). These kinds of "flexible pedagogies" are perceived as *positive* shifts towards student empowerment and student involvement in shaping educational philosophies and teaching and learning practices (Gordon, 2014; Ryan & Tilbury, 2013). In contrast, we argue that the neoliberal university actually leads to *dis*empowerment of academic educators and students; so the context of the neoliberal university works *against* the flourishing of academic educator and learner, and the flourishing of critical pedagogies and thinking. It is the educator's challenge to resist and transform these constraints and become an empowering academic educator for their students.

In a recent study about personalised learning, it was found that university students want more personalised and flexible teaching and learning but they also like a strong academic educator-centred model of teaching as they require structure and guidance with their learning (Wanner & Palmer 2015). Similarly, Vassalio (2013) found that self-regulated learning is not as it is proclaimed about increasing student empowerment, agency and democratic participation in assessment and curriculum design, but instead is about instilling compliance and obedience in students.

Every learning activity can include real-life examples for problem-solving and to think critically about the information presented. One method used in our courses is the Socratic Method where students learn to question through dialogue. It is important for students to question their own assumptions and biases, and to challenge the particular lenses that they bring to an issue or problem in order for them to develop a deeper understanding. In one of the courses, this is especially important as it concerns the investigation of accidents, which by its very nature requires absolute objectivity, reliance on facts and a critical analysis of causal and contributing factors to an accident in order to prevent reoccurrence. An academic schooled in the Socratic Method is an imperative to this process and the experience of the Socratic enquiry is empowering for both student and the academic. For example, in a case study about an accident or a reconstructed accident scene the academic educator needs to guide the student to a conclusion based on the evidence collected. As such, we ask questions "what do you think has caused the accident", "what conclusions have you drawn from the evidence" and "are there alternative ways to think about the causes of the accident"?

In another course, students have 'flexible assessment' with choices and involvement about the types of assignments, their assessment weightings (within limits: 10 per cent up or down as set by the academic educator) and individual submission dates. This provides students with a more personalised form of assessment instead of academic educator set assignments as they are involved from the start but the academic educator is central in setting the learning outcomes, and implementing the flexible assessment process.

Tension II: The disempowerment of the academic educator

Academic educators must be brave enough to call truth to power and lay bare the discursive formation of neoliberalism as the dominant structuring principle that determines and constitutes the dominant socio-economic experience of themselves and their students. This discursive practice establishes the objective and material existence of inexorable rules to which they and their students are subjected to through a neoliberal education (Lecourt, 1975, p. 196). According to Louis Althusser (1971, pp. 136–137), educators or the education system, in general, are historically complicit in helping to embed the dominant ideology whether they are conscious of it or not.

Critical thinking, questioning ideologies, social norms and own assumptions, and understanding and self-expression in the advent of commercialism and corporatisation are now even less a part of the neoliberal education system. Many tertiary institutions in the western world come to resemble private corporations where education is delivered as a business which means that the broad-based liberal education that traditionally imbued students with the critical and analytical skills to foster self-expression and confidence, has been eroded (Wanner (née Munn), 2004, pp. 161–162). The core disciplines, arguably once the heart of the university, are on the verge of becoming an endangered species. Disciplines within the humanities and social sciences that have critical thinking as their primary learning outcomes (to use the current jargon), are perceived as no longer relevant (Wanner (née Munn), 2004, p. 162; see also Patrick, 2013). Thus, one needs to question the current focus on critical thinking in Graduate Attributes.

In the Foucauldian sense, however, where nothing functions at an optimal level in a system of generalised domination, academic educators must first seek to empower themselves and call truth to power (Foucault, 1980). This is even more so for those academics that profess a critical pedagogy. By not making a stand and prising apart the discursive formation of neoliberalism, the hypocrisy of their calls for empowerment, emancipation and flourishing through critical thinking, is laid bare. As Shahjahan (2014, p. 220) argues, "transformational resistance entails first recognizing both one's complicity and agency with the oppressive logics of neoliberalism, and then experimenting with different ways of knowing and being in line with a future vision" or alternative to neoliberal higher education. Academic educators have the critical roles to challenge their own complicity and that of their students in neoliberal education.

One of the central tenets of critical pedagogy, the desire to introduce a different set of norms to challenge the current marketization and commodification of education as encapsulated in the neoliberal agenda (Serrano, O'Brien, Roberts, & Whyte, 2017, p. 100), may rest on a return to the traditional lecture format. Those who espouse a critical pedagogical point of view have typically led the charge against the lecture format arguing, along Freirian lines, that in higher education in particular it is an obsolete delivery format akin to the banking of knowledge (Morgan & Bojesen, 2018, p. 933). Whereby, the academic lecturer "stands at the front of the class and delivers a monologue on a particular topic, often presenting the information as immutable facts, with little to no participation from the students" (Clark, 2018, p. 986).

The push for flexible learning in neoliberal universities includes a push to disband the lecture as a valuable form of teaching and student engagement. This means that an opportunity is missed to re-think the format as a platform for inspirational and motivational empowerment of both the student and the academic educator. As academic educators are forced to endure the cost cutting business models of neoliberal education, such as large class sizes and fewer financial resources, they should make the lecture work for them in true critical pedagogical style and make it a truly transformative experience. According to Poirier,

> The ideal lecture should stimulate students to evaluate and think. It should challenge and cause interruptions, the so-called "art of thinking." ... This is where students are challenging the truth, critically thinking, reflecting and questioning. When students are listening, they are not just vessels but consist of attitudes, values, biases, experiences, feeling and thoughts. ... Thus, there should not only be a focus on innovative active learning and student-centered teaching approaches, but also a focus on the art of transformative lecturing.
>
> *(Poirier, 2017, p. 2)*

In a style much akin to a TED (Technology, Education, Design) talk, academic educators through transformative lecturing can challenge the current neoliberal discourse. A lecture can be a format to fire the imagination, to inspire, to motivate and to empower.

In one of our courses, interactive face-to-face lectures are used where we watch accident reconstructions and then debate the findings. Have the investigators done a thorough investigation? Have they collected all the evidence to inform their findings? Have they made assumptions that might have influenced the outcome, and how would we have done it differently and why? In another example from our teaching, students create, in small groups of three students, questions about the content material presented in the lecture, which stimulates their own thinking about the presented material. These questions are later used in Reflective Quizzes for the course, which are part of the assessment.

Tension III: Shaping teaching and learning for the knowledge economy

As stated in the introduction, the transitioning *from* the university environment into the work place requires students to be empowered, self-actualising and adaptive individuals who can cope with the multitude of challenges and uncertainties of a globalising neoliberal economy and society.

The neoliberal university claims that it produces critical thinkers and problem-solvers, as stated in the Graduate Attributes, as discussed above, but paradoxically it churns out graduates with mechanistic skills but no habit of independent critical thought (Wanner (née Munn), 2004, p. 162). There is an urgent need of critical thinkers in a neoliberal world and knowledge economy, and the actual production of students transitioning into the workforce with these vital skills. However, the current focus and pedagogies of 'work-integrated learning' and 'student employability and readiness' for the knowledge economy are counter-productive to the integration of critical pedagogies and associated critical knowledge (Connell, 2013). The focus is on 'employable skills' not critical thinking.

The dominant ideology requires that students be job ready for the work force and that they can function effectively in a globalising knowledge economy and social world. Though this sounds like an admirable goal it neglects that students need to learn to question *how* the world is functioning and *why* and with what kind of implications rather than simply accepting dominant ideologies that shape how the knowledge economy and world functions.

Critical thinking through critical pedagogies is vital for all university courses, as we have argued throughout this chapter, including courses which have work-integrated components such as internships. Some of our courses have internships but before students embark on their internship the same critical methodology applies in that they think critically about the internship. Sessions are conducted and quizzes held to assess student knowledge about the organisation they are going into. How much do they know about the organisation? What do they expect to achieve through the internship? In particular, we aim to engage them to think critically about the organisation's objectives and the internship itself.

Conclusion

When transitioning students *into* the Australian higher education, we need to be aware about the context of the higher education system and how pedagogies and practices of teaching and learning in current universities are shaped by neoliberalism. This chapter has highlighted how neoliberal educational philosophies have created major tensions between critical pedagogies and practices which overall have the effect of *dis*empowerment rather than the claimed empowerment of academic educators and students. To counteract the oppressive and disempowering impacts of neoliberal universities, we as educators need to create critical thinkers who have a sense and understanding of their own agency to challenge and transform dominant ideologies. Implementing critical pedagogies is a journey of empowerment for both students and academic educators. It is not easy, takes time and the courage to fail and learn from new teaching approaches which incorporate critical pedagogies.

References

Althusser, L. (1971). *Lenin and philosophy and other essays*. Translated by B. Brewster. London: New Left Books.

Ball, S. J. (2012). Performativity, commodification and commitment: An I-spy guide to the neoliberal university. *British Journal of Educational Studies*, 60(1), 17–28.

Clark, L. B. (2018). Critical pedagogy in the university: Can a lecture be critical pedagogy? *Policy Futures in Education*, 16(8) (Special Issue: Critical Pedagogies and Philosophies of Education),985–999.

Connell, R. (2013). The neoliberal cascade and education: An essay on the market agenda and its consequences. *Critical Studies in Education*, 54(2),99–112.

Davies, B. & Bansel, P. (2007) Neoliberalism and education. *International Journal of Qualitative Studies in Education*, 20(3), 247–259.

Espinoza, O. (2017). Paulo Freire's ideas as an alternative to higher education neo-liberal reforms in Latin America. *Journal of Moral Education*, 46(4), 435–448.

Foucault, M. (1980). *Power/knowledge: Selected interviews and other writings, 1972–1977*. Translated by C. Gordon (ed.). Brighton: Harvester Wheatsheaf Press.

Freire, P. (1972). *Pedagogy of the oppressed*. Translated by Myra Bergman Ramos. New York: Penguin.

Gordon, N. (2014). *Flexible pedagogies: Technology-enhanced learning*. London: Higher Education Academy.

Gregory, M. (2017). Scaling critical pedagogy in higher education. *Critical Studies in Education*, 58(1), 1–18.

Houser, M. L. & Frymier, A. B. (2009). The role of student characteristics and academics/educators behaviors in students' learner empowerment. *Communication Education*, 58(1), 35–53.

Hunter, D. A. (2009), *Practical guide to critical thinking deciding what to do and believe*. Hoboken, NJ: John Wiley & Sons.

John, P. & Fanghanel, J. (eds.) (2016). *Dimensions of marketisation in higher education*. Abingdon: Routledge.

Kahn, P. E. (2017). The flourishing and dehumanization of students in higher education. *Journal of Critical Realism*, 16(4), 368–382.

Keamy, K., Nicholas, H., Mahar, S., & Herrick, C. (2007). *Personalising education: From research to policy and practice*. Melbourne: Office for Education Policy and Innovation, Department of Education and Early Childhood Development.

Lecourt, D. (1975). *Marxism and epistemology: Bachelard, Canguilhelm and Foucault*. Translated by B. Brewster. London: New Left Books.

McLoughlin, C. & Lee, M. J. W. (2010). Personalised and self-regulated learning in the Web 2.0 era: International exemplars of innovative pedagogy using social software. *Australian Journal of Educational Technology*, 26(1),28–43.

Morgan, M. & Bojesen, E. (2018). Editorial: Critical pedagogies and philosophies of education. *Policy Futures in Education*, 16(8), 931–935.

Olssen, M. & Peters, M. A. (2005). Neoliberalism, higher education and the knowledge economy: From the free market to knowledge capitalism. *Journal of Education Policy*, 20(3), 313–345.

Patrick, F. (2013). *Neoliberalism, the knowledge economy, and the learner: Challenging the inevitability of the commodified self as an outcome of education*. ISRN Publication. Available at https://www.hindawi.com/journals/isrn/2013/108705/ [accessed 17 February 2019].

Poirier, T. (2017). Is lecturing obsolete? Advocating for high value transformative lecturing. *American Journal of Pharmaceutical Education*, 81(5), 1–2.

Poon, T. S. (2006). The commodification of higher education: Implications for academic work and employment. *International Journal of Employment Studies*, 14(1),81–104.

Ryan, A., & Tilbury, D. (2013). *Flexible pedagogies: New pedagogical ideas*. London: Higher Education Academy.

Serrano, M. M., O'Brien, M., Roberts, K., & Whyte, D. (2017). Critical pedagogy and assessment in higher education: The ideal of 'authenticity' in learning. *Active Learning in Higher Education*, 19(1), 9–21.

Shahjahan, R. A. (2014). From 'no' to 'yes': Postcolonial perspectives on resistance to neoliberal higher education. *Discourse: Studies in the Cultural Politics of Education*, 35(2), 219–232.

Sharples, M., Adams, A., Ferguson, R., Gaved, M., McAndrew, P., Rienties, B., et al. (2014). *Innovating pedagogy 2014: Open University Innovation Report 3*. Milton Keynes: The Open University.

Stirling, J. & McGloin, C. (2015). Critical pedagogy and social inclusion policy in Australian higher education: identifying the disjunctions. *Radical pedagogy*, 12(2), 1–20.

Vassalio, S. (2013). Critical pedagogy and neoliberalism: Concerns with teaching self-regulated learning. *Studies in Philosophy and Education*, 32, 563–580.

Wanner (née Munn), S. (2004). *Exploring governance: Myths, lies and realities*, Doctoral dissertation, Flinders University of South Australia, Bedford Park.

Wanner, T., & Palmer, E. (2015). Personalising learning: Exploring student and academics/educators perceptions about flexible learning and assessment in a flipped university course. *Computers & Education*, 88, 354–369.

13

ON-BOARDING DISCIPLINE EXPERTS TO ADOPT THE ACADEMIC LITERACIES FRAMEWORK

Associate Professor Kathie Ardzejewska and Dr Michelle Gorzanelli

Introduction

The benefits of embedding generic academic literacy skills into discipline focused learning activities have been researched since the 1980s (see, for example, Wingate, 2006; 2012 in the UK and Arkoudis, Baik, & Richardson, 2012 in Australia). However, the theory is rarely actualised as sustained programs, nor has it become mainstream. There are many reasons for this, including absent institutional policy (Moore & Harrington, 2016). However, our case studies show that it is also about the way academics view their work. Once academic work was to impart discipline knowledge to students and students generally learnt how to meet expectations through osmosis. Today, however, with a varied student body, many academics are frustrated that osmosis no longer suffices, directing their frustrations at student deficits (Lea & Street, 2006). However, for students to be successful, our experience shows that we as academics need to change our ideas about what our work entails. In particular, we need to reconsider the assumptions that all students acquired the skills for academic success as part of their secondary education and knowing this, challenge our traditional views that it is not our responsibility to explicitly teach these skills (Hermida, 2009). Underpinning this is the philosophy that we are 'enablers' of student success. The aim of this chapter therefore is to take readers on a journey; a journey to on-board a pedagogical framework for course design which represents a version of the academic literacies (or embedded) approach privileged by Lea and Street (2006). This model views discipline academics as well-positioned partners to support students to become successful learners in higher education.

Philosophy: Viewing the work of academics as 'enablers' of student success

Many discipline academics have traditionally viewed weak student academic literacy as something requiring remediation by someone else (Hunter & Tse, 2013). For instance, academics will recognise the refrain: *how did they get in?* often followed by: *we shouldn't have to spoon feed them,* and *someone needs to help these students* (Bennett et al., 2016). Such views have typically expected the remediation of student deficiencies by literacy skills advisors (Frohman, 2012; Stratilas, 2011; Thies, 2012). Frohman (2012) has labelled this type of support as first generation, or what Lea and Street (2006) refer to as 'study skills'. The study skills model approach is often actualised through programs that are external to the curriculum. Generally delivered as workshops and orientation programs, "writing and literacy [are seen] as primarily an individual and cognitive skill ... [which] focuses on surface features of language form and presumes that students can transfer their knowledge of writing and literacy unproblematically from one context to another" (Lea & Street, 2006, p. 368). While the remedial approach does achieve a degree of success, an improvement on this model is known as "academic socialisation". In this model students study the discourses and genres that provide them with the knowledge to operate in the discipline. Academics, unfortunately assume that once students know the "ground rules ... they are able to reproduce [them] unproblematically" (Lea & Street, 2006, p. 369). This form of teaching leaves students on their own to negotiate the shifting rules between disciplines (Lea & Street, 2006).

Therefore, the philosophy driving a change in pedagogy and practice involved academics taking responsibility for enabling student success during their transition to university. This shift in pedagogy and practice that supports academic success during transition to university involved academics moving beyond the two models described above, to understand that writing should not be seen as separate from the "real curriculum" (Buzzi, Grimes, & Rolls, 2012). This position closely reflects a third "academic literacies" model, which incorporates both "epistemological issues and social processes, including power relations among people, institutions and social identities" (Lea & Street, 2006, p. 369). Lea and Street outline the difference between "academic socialisation" and "academic literacies" in designing curriculum. In the former, academics might assist students to take notes and transfer these to a presentation, while the latter is framed as something all students need support in, not just those for which English is a second language. The academic literacies model also includes "institutional requirements (e.g., regarding plagiarism, feedback)" (Lea & Street, 2006, p. 369). The three models are not mutually exclusive, and while Lea and Street do not explicitly posit that all academics should be language experts, academics should be cognisant of their role in academic literacies and student success. While academics should not be abandoned to teach academic literacies on their own, Academic Literacy and Language (ALL) advisors reaching out to academics to work collaboratively, report that academics are often reluctant to take up teaching academic literacy as part of their pedagogy (Jones, 2009). Thies

(2012) found that this often stems from a perceived inability to teach academic writing. Our experience suggests that it is also necessary to convince academics that there is a gap between academic and student expectations for explicit induction into higher education. Rather than rallying against students for their perceived deficits, we argue that it is the responsibility of the academic to bridge the gap/s.

Acknowledging the above, the section that follows outlines how to on-board academics to design and deliver a curriculum that supports students' transition into higher education. It includes some suggested resources in support of this goal. It also outlines the working relationships and the explicit and discrete roles of ALL advisors and discipline academics in developing and delivering the curriculum. The framework adopted in 'foundation discipline bachelor degree subjects' is based on explicit instruction and opportunities where students through repeated practice, learn and apply cognitive, meta-cognitive and affective skills that can transfer from one subject, domain or discipline, to another (Gunn, Hearne, & Sibthorpe, 2011). This model benefits all learners (Hathaway, 2015). As such, instead of seeing students in need of remediation, like that of Goldingay et al. (2014), students are instead inducted into the academic discourse. Chanock (2013) argued that this is important as it allows for a greater reach and offers a solution to the problem of accessing those students who are the most in need of support, but do not seek it.

Framework: An embedded academic literacies approach

The framework consists of a number of intertwined components:

(i) Productive relationships and time

Essentially the success of the framework relies heavily on the position that student academic literacies are "every academic's business" (Gunn, Hearne, & Sibthorpe, 2011). Institutional support therefore is paramount, requiring both an approach from the top (i.e. strategy and funding), as well as from the 'bottom' (academics and professional staff driving curriculum design). It is also important to acknowledge that to effectively adopt the approach takes an appreciation of specific expertise, considerable time and energy, and the early identification of the milestones of such a project. This is the key for the team to remain buoyant. This includes: early discussions to 'sell' the embedded approach and create the team; curriculum re/design; and peer moderation of tasks leading to a calibrated marking team. It is also useful to frame this new approach as a scholarship of teaching and learning project, the results of which could lead to further improvements and increased traction of the pedagogical design. Moreover, productive relationships between ALL advisors, faculties and academics enable ALL advisors to share their expert knowledge of academic literacy strategies with academics in the design of curriculum, corresponding teaching, and development of teaching and learning resources. Therefore, both the ALL advisors and discipline academics are responsible for engaging students with core concepts and outcomes presented as part of the curriculum and constructively aligned and tailored to meet the needs of discipline content and assessment (Gunn, Hearne, & Sibthorpe, 2011).

Collaboration of this kind, while positive, is hard work and there are likely to be tensions around power. One tension may result from ALL advisors and academics both "protecting their respective terrains and autonomy", demonstrated as "resistance to the change of the status quo" (Cattell, 2013, p. 10). Consequently, the framework prescribes the allocation of time to regular staff meetings to develop the relationships and calibration of the team (Frohman, 2012; Macdonald, Scneider, & Giselle, 2013). These weekly or fortnightly team meetings provide an opportunity to minimise concerns over losing control over the teaching and learning process, and reconcile differing perceptions over the curriculum, instruction, and assessment (Walton & Lloyd, 2012). It is the open dialogue and peer review of planned learning strategies and formal and informal continuing professional learning opportunities that diffuses tensions around power. Essentially, in line with Cattell (2013), these productive interactions ensure all team members see that the workload and responsibility for the common goal of student success is shared. That is, ALL advisors are positioned as disciplinary insiders rather than "added-on" outsiders. Discipline academics for their part become increasingly aware of the role of the academic in supporting students to acquire academic literacies in aid of student success. These responsibilities are attainable through both parties explicitly teaching within the realms of their prescribed goals. For example ALL advisors focusing on teaching academic skills using discipline-based stimuli, and discipline academics encouraging students to apply academic literacy skills in subject specific contexts.

(ii) Curriculum design

Lea (2004) cautions against a focus on assessment. However, given the conditions of contemporary higher education where students have substantial competing demands, and the acknowledgment that assessment drives learning, we advocate that the course is largely designed with assessment as a reference point. The course is then structured as a series of modules, introducing students to fundamental academic literacy skills in the context of the discipline knowledge. Each week leads with a content discipline "lecture" primarily reflecting the delivery and exchange of information from the discipline academic. This is followed by an "academic literacy tutorial" delivered by the ALL advisor. The ALL advisor led session is followed by the "discipline tutorial" that aims to deepen content knowledge by assisting students to reapply the strategies learnt in the academic literacy session; directly folding the content back into the work of the earlier session. A detailed overview of suggested tutorial topics is briefly outlined later in this chapter.

The tutorial program structure begins with a focus on reading. This decision is based on evidence that the design of an aligned course that places academic reading at the forefront facilitates students' deep approach to reading and learning (Hermida, 2009). Specifically, this program creates class activities that encourage students to use higher-order cognitive skills to construct meaning from the academic texts (Hermida, 2009). To reduce cognitive overload, students are provided with a subject 'reader' containing all of the content material (Wingate, Andon, Cogo, 2011) and templates. Explained further below in the section on assessment, to support students to read, the initial readings are linked to a number of short, formative assessment writing tasks.

Over time the focus shifts to writing, including ethical scholarship and English language proficiency, especially sentence and paragraph structure. In unpacking the reading and applying the knowledge to a task, Derewianka's (1990) '3-steps of genre-based instruction to writing' is a useful starting point. The first step in this process involves modelling the reading of a relevant discipline text. Step two facilitates the joint (or co-) construction of an understanding of the text by asking students to respond to a focus question. The co-construction of knowledge is an important prelude to a student's independent construction of knowledge and understanding (Derewianka, 1990). The final step is the independent construction of knowledge to address the focus question (i.e. the submission of an assessable writing task). Importantly, the first two steps allow for the deconstruction of the features of the genre so they can be imitated and transferred in the context of subsequent assessment tasks or across subjects. The point of difference in this framework is that the co-construction happens in discipline-based classes as opposed to occurring in ALL led sessions. This means that students are given the opportunity to participate in the community of the academy (Scalone & Street, 2006). The tutorials also encourage students to become reflective learners, and engage students in opportunities to practice cognitive, in addition to emotional responses, that together form part of the feedback (Molloy, Borrell-Carrio, & Epstein, 2013; Aoun, Vatanasakdakul, & Ang, 2016). A range of templates/scaffolds support students to summarise key information relevant to assessment tasks.

Acknowledging that good curriculum design takes assessment into account, recommendations specifically related to assessment are now be explored in more detail.

(iii) Assessment design

There are a number of assessment strategies that support student success. Those that best underpin an embedded approach follow:

Scaffolding

The essential component is an assessment regime that begins with a number of scaffolded low stakes, short writing tasks. Academic literacy scaffolds are helpful in preparing students to engage with authentic assessment tasks. For example, as identified by Waters and Waters (1992), it is useful to expose students to the academic literacy competencies including: searching, selecting, analysing and referencing sources. That is, students learn the processes required to create a response to an assessment task through opportunities to "describe, discuss, compare, model, and practise" (Haggis, 2006, p. 532) discipline content as part of the construction of knowledge rather than "spoon feeding" (Haggis, 2006, p. 532). Another strategy to reduce student fears is to design an assessment regimen where the first task is a small group oral presentation. While not strictly a writing task, the oral presentation allows students to demonstrate basic communicative competence through the assessment of spelling, vocabulary and grammar in the presentation slides, and importantly provides students with opportunities to develop a sense of belonging (Marshall, Zhou, Gervan & Wiebe, 2012).

Feeding forward: Deconstructing rubrics

Rubrics need to reflect and assess both academic literacies and disciplinary content. Another meaningful way to support students is through providing them with the opportunity to review and discuss marking rubrics. The marking rubrics should clearly state expectations and also feedforward to subsequent tasks (McCarthy, 2015). To this end, an analytical marking rubric used by all academics teaching first year subjects, which allows for differences between disciplines, helps students reapply successful strategies and focus on areas that require more work. This strategy should reduce confusion such as described by Goldingay et al. (2014) and boost student confidence because they are seeing and hearing the same messages about the conventions of academic writing (Hénard & Roseveare, 2012). A good format is to divide the rubric into two parts (see Table 13.1 for an example of the rubric for a paraphrasing assessment task). Part one is a hurdle, itemising the criteria and descriptors of the minimum standard students have to meet for communicative competence, i.e. traditional literacy skills such as punctuation, grammar and spelling. Part two itemises criteria and descriptors of the generic academic discourse conventions of structure, format and style as well as the discipline content, or what Hathaway (2015) describes as the conventions of constructing and expressing knowledge and meaning. To qualify for a passing grade in both parts, students' responses need to avoid pervasive errors associated with functional literacy (communicative incompetence) and meet all the minimum requirements of academic discourse.

Feeding forward: Draft assessment

Another strategy is to provide students with the opportunity to submit two drafts of a task; the first draft is submitted to the ALL advisors for feedback regarding literacy and the second draft is to the discipline tutor for feedback on content knowledge. While this is demanding for staff (see Wingate, Andon, & Cogo, 2011 whose pilot also provided extensive scaffolded support), the process creates opportunities for students to respond calmly, and implement feedback more effectively (Wingate, Andon, & Cogo, 2011).

TABLE 13.1 Example of the rubric for a paraphrasing assessment task

Feature of Communicative Competence	Quality of Pass Grade
Sentence Structure	• Consistent use of correct sentence structure (for example : minimal run-on Sentence and minimal sentence fragments)
Vocabulary	• Consistently appropriate word choices
Spelling	• Correct spelling of most common words • Correct spelling of specialist vocabulary
Punctuation	• Predominantly correct use of simple punctuation (full stop, capital letters, commas, question mark, quotations)
Grammar	• Consistent use of tense appropriate for the type of text required • Consistent use of subject-verb agreement and noun-pronoun agreement • Conform to conventions of written English sentence construction
Paragraphing	• Consistent use of tense appropriate for the type of text required • Consistent use of subject-verb agreement and noun-pronoun agreement • Conform to conventions of written English sentence construction
Referencing	• Accurate APA style used throughout the in-text referencing • Accurate APA style used in the reference list

Feature of Academic Discourse	Quality of a PASS grade
Content & Evidence	• Shows an understanding of the content • Presents key points and accurate/relevant evidence from the reading • Communicates elements concisely and clearly • Avoids opinions/interpretation

Organisation & Structure	• Introduction presents a thesis addressing the focus question
	• Introduction lists 2–4 main ideas related to the topic
	• Paragraphs in body are organised using:
	  • supporting sentences
	  • some evidence from the source
	• Body is organised in paragraphs dealing with each main idea listed in introduction
	• Conclusion restates thesis from introduction

Style	• No use of personal anecdote or opinion • Formal and objective tone

(iv) Assessment feedback and wellbeing

There is strong evidence to suggest that feedback is one of the most powerful influences on student learning (Hattie & Timperley, 2007). At the same time, it is acknowledged that tertiary students are increasingly challenged by personal life circumstances that may account for the high prevalence and severity of psychological distress. As such, we academics need to add student welfare to our role (Brooker, Baik, & Larcombe, 2017) and consider how feedback can influence student wellbeing, especially during their first year of university studies. Recent research has shown that one of the major barriers limiting the capacity for feedback to enhance student learning and student wellbeing is that academics and students differ in their perspective of what makes for effective feedback. Academics, for instance, typically viewed effective feedback as reflecting design matters such as timing, volume, and connected tasks whereas students' perceptions focused on the quality of personal, detailed comments that could be transferred. Consequently, students generally reported that feedback from academics is "done poorly in higher education" (Dawson et al., 2019, p. 25). It is important therefore, that academics reposition their feedback practice to align with the shift in the literature where feedback is a process that leads to further learning (Sadler, 2010; Carless et al., 2011; Molloy & Boud, 2013). Another barrier to effective feedback is that students' affective state and emotional reactions to grades may prevent them from using feedback for further learning. Recognising this, evidence suggests that students need to be coached to respond to feedback as they have rarely been provided with explicit instruction or support in how to use or seek feedback (Weaver, 2006).

The focus on student welfare, especially amongst first year university students, means that acknowledged in the framework is the importance of academics investing and building relationships with students as part of the feedback process. First, the framework relies heavily on conclusions drawn by Dawson et al. (2019, p. 25) that effective feedback, from both an academic's and student's perspective involves academics providing comments that are "useable, detailed, considerate of affect and personalised to the student's own work". Assuming academics work towards providing such comments, the framework embodies student welfare as part of the next step by applying Molloy and Boud's (2013) feedback model of feedup (i.e. what were my goals), feedback (i.e. how did I go?), and feedforward (i.e. where to next?). This step encourages academics to return the graded task at the beginning of the ALL tutorial. The benefits of this learning experience are twofold. On one hand, students are provided with a supportive environment to engage in a feedback 'episode' involving the opportunity to participate in a dialogue with academics, a personal reflection, and/or a conversation with a peer focused on the elements of feedup, feedback, and feedforward. On the other hand, this process not only encourages students to build their perceived self-efficacy in completing their studies, it diffuses the likelihood of students rejecting or ignoring comments (i.e. limiting receptiveness and future learning) if they evoke negative affective and emotional responses (Ryan & Henderson, 2018). Instead, students are provided with the opportunity to pose and plan strategies for improvement based on the reflection of their own individual strengths, weaknesses, and future goals. This reflective process is thought to encourage students to translate the feedback, as posed by Dawson et al. (2019), into productive behavioural change and promote students' growth. This fits with Dweck's (2002) growth mindset theory, which attributes students' academic performance to the language used in feedback. Once the tutorials are concluded, the discipline academic can review the reflective responses, and provide students with additional resources that might further encourage development of strategies to reach desired goals (Molloy & Boud, 2013).

(v) Teaching and learning resources

To support the recommended approaches to productive relationships, curriculum and assessment design, and feedback and wellbeing, the framework includes a generic set of modules. Importantly, following the work of others such as Hathaway (2015) and Wingate (2012), the modules reflect a set of accessible resources which can be adapted to fit the specific context of the discipline. The focus and concepts covered by each module are listed in Table 13.2. Given the approach to reading appears to be an idea less well explored, the module on reading, as an example, is unpacked further below.

Exemplar: Reading with a purpose

Possibly even more so than writing, there is an assumption that students arriving at university know how to decode and interpret academic texts. However, reading for academic purposes also has its challenges (Ardzejewska, Campbell, & Gorzanelli, 2015); for example, students commonly found reading difficult, tending to highlight large sections of text rather than reading with a purpose. In response, the resources provide teaching and learning experiences that explicitly step academics through the support students need to focus on for processing and synthesising the information found in a text, first individually and then as part of a joint construction learning activity (Derewianka, 1990). Accordingly, teaching this skill of reading with a purpose promoted a shift in understanding our students, not as deficient, but as active participants involved in the "complex social processes" associated with teaching students academic literacy skills (Lea & Street, 2006, p. 369).

Conclusion

On our journey as discipline academics, we have undergone a pedagogical shift where we now see our role as providing very explicit instruction about academic literacies as well as discipline content to enable the success of students' transitioning to university. Like Thies, we have come to the realisation that we need to broaden our concerns beyond the content to see "writing as a social and contextual practice" (2012, p. 375).

TABLE 13.2 Module's focus and concepts

Module	Content / topics
Reading with a purpose	• Modelling reading
	• Developing questions and reciting answers to support understanding
	• Application of reading strategies to a discipline text
	• Joint and independent construction of meaning
	• Strategies to enhance retainment of information
Note-taking	• Preparing for a lecture
	• Strategies for becoming a better listener
	• Strategies for taking notes during lectures (mind maps vs. Cornell method)
	• Revising notes following a lecture
	• Active construction of knowledge and memory
Summarising and paraphrasing	• Interpreting text
	• Maintaining meaning of the original sources
	• Promoting academic and professional integrity
	• When to and how to paraphrase vs. summarise
Features of academic writing and text types	• Structure of writing tasks
	• Features of an introduction, body paragraph, conclusion
	• Using evidence
	• Tone and style
	• Sentence types
Gathering and evaluating sources	• Key terms
	• Data-base searching
	• Strategies for using evidences
	• Currency, relevance, accuracy of sources
	• Sources of the information
	• Distinguishing between statements, supporting evidence and analytical statements
Using turnitin and teacher feedback	• Academic integrity
	• Interpreting similarity reports as formative feedback
	• Become a reflective student
	• Goal setting

Module	Content / topics
Referencing	• Conventions of in-text and referencing list referencing • Secondary sources • Use of quotations • Evaluating student samples
Deconstructing assignment tasks	• Nature of formative vs. summative assignment • Recognising action verbs, topic areas, and limiting words • Unpacking and making meaning of the marking criteria and rubric • Selecting appropriate evidence • Promoting higher-ordering thinking
Exam preparation	• Revision techniques • Understanding key verbs • Examining the structure of multiple-choice questions • Short answers vs. extended responses • Time management
Student welfare	• 'Checking in before checking out' (i.e. student retention) • 'Are you ok?' (www.rouk.org.au) • Working effectively in groups • Managing and coping with stress • Student services

By allocating time to do this in our tutorials we have, like Scalone and Street (2006), found that an explicit approach to the teaching of academic skills embedded in the discipline allows students to participate in the community of the academy which is formed by students coming together and co-constructing their knowledge. The framework also provides academics and students with a tangible process for thinking about feedback as a tool for learning in a supportive environment and also sends the message to students that academics are concerned for their welfare; which is significant given that students' academic performance is also linked to their attitude towards feedback (for example, see Kohn, 2011; Pulfrey, Buch, & Butera, 2011) as well as their attitudes towards the person who provided the feedback (Tippin, Lafreniere, & Page, 2012).

The success of the framework and our new roles is evidenced by the 201 per cent increase in pass rates in one faculty. In addition, 43 per cent of the cohort recorded an improvement in a standardised writing test. It is also seen in a selection of responses students provided in a survey of their experience at the end of the semester:

Was helpful for transition from high school as experience of tertiary education was quite different from perceptions.

Underlying 'mental' support not just academic was important.

Feedback helped for next assignment.

Extracts from unsolicited emails from students also speak to their increasing confidence and self-regulation:

Why wasn't I told how to write like this before, I always thought I had good writing skills ... but I 'sucked' compared to now.

I never thought the reading part was what was making me struggle.

I feel so much more prepared ... literacy was always scary before.

Clearly the journey is a worthy one for students, academics, and ALL advisors alike.

References

Aoun, C., Vatanasakdakul, S., & Ang, K. (2016). Feedback for thought: Examining the influence of feedback constituents on learning experience. *Studies in Higher Education*, 43(1), 72–95. https://doi-org.ipacez.nd.edu.au/10.1080/03075079.2016.1156665.

Ardzejewska, K., Campbell, W., & Gorzanelli, M. (2015). Learning to think differently before mastering a new way to teach academic literacy skills. *Education Today*, 65(1), 17–24.

Arkoudis, S., Baik, C., & Richardson, S. (2012). *English language in higher education: From entry to exit*. Camberwell: ACER.

Bennett, R., Hobson, J., Jones, A., Martin-Lynch, P. M., Scutt, C., Strehlow, K., & Veitch, S. (2016) Being chimaera: A monstrous identity for SoTL academics. *Higher Education Research & Development*, 35(2),217–228. doi:10.1080/07294360.2015.1087473.

Brooker, A., Baik, C., & Larcombe, W. (2017). Understanding academic educators' work in supporting student wellbeing. In R. G. Walker & S. B. Bedford (Eds.), *Research and Development in Higher Education: Curriculum Transformation* (Vol. 40, pp. 50–60). Sydney, Australia: Higher Education Research and Development Society of Australasia.

Buzzi, O., Grimes, S., & Rolls, A. (2012). Points of departure: Writing for the discipline in the discipline? *Teaching in Higher Education*, 17(4), 479–484. doi:10.1080/13562517.2012.711932.

Carless, D., Salter, D., Yang, M., & Lam, J. (2011). Developing sustainable feedback practices. *Studies in Higher Education*, 36(4), 395–407.

Cattell, K. (2013). 'Fit for change': A preliminary exploration of the relationship between academic literacy practitioners and disciplinary specialists as a complex system. *Perspectives in Education*, 31(4),5–14.

Chanock, K. (2013). Teaching subject literacies through blended learning: Reflections on a collaboration between academic learning staff and teachers in the disciplines. *Journal of Academic Language & Learning*, 7(2), 106–119.

Dawson, P., Henderson, M., Mahoney, P., Phillips, M., Ryan, T., Boud, D., & Molloy, E. (2019). What makes for effective feedback: Staff and student perspectives. *Assessment & Evaluation in Higher Education*, 44(1), 25–36. doi:10.1080/02602938.2018.1467877.

Derewianka, B. (1990). *Exploring how texts work*. Rozelle, NSW: Primary English Teaching Association.

Dweck, C. S. (2002). The development of ability conceptions. In A. Wigfield & J. Eccles (Eds.), *Development of achievement motivation* (pp. 57–88). New York: Academic Press.

Frohman, R. (2012). Collaborative efforts work! Reflection on a two-year relationship between Faculty of Health and International Students Services – Language and Learning Unit. *Journal of Academic Language & Learning*, 6(3), 47–58.

Goldingay, S., Hitch, D., Ryan, J., Farrugia, D., Hosken, N., Lamaro, G., Nihill, C., Macfarlane, S. (2014). 'The university didn't actually tell us this is what you have to do': Social inclusion through embedding of academic skills in first year professional courses. *The International Journal of the First Year in Higher Education*, 5(1),43–53. doi:10.5204/intjfyhe.v5i1.194.

Gunn, C., Hearne, S., & Sibthorpe, J. (2011). Right from the start: A rationale for embedding academic literacy skills in university courses. *Journal of University Teaching & Learning Practice*, 8(1), 1–10. https://ro.uow.edu.au/jutlp/vol8/iss1/6.

Haggis, T. (2006). Pedagogies for diversity: Retaining critical challenge amidst fears of 'dumbing down'. *Studies in Higher Education*, 31(5), 521–535.doi:10.1080/03075070600922709.

Hathaway, J. (2015). Developing that voice: Locating academic writing tuition in the mainstream of higher education. *Teaching in Higher Education*, 20(5), 506–517. doi:10.1080/13562517.1026891.

Hattie, J., & Timperley, H. (2007). The power of feedback. *Review of Educational Research*, 77(1), 81–112. doi:10.3102/003465430298487.

Hénard, F., & Roseveare, D. (2012). Fostering quality teaching in higher education: Policies and practices. *An IMHE Guide for Higher Education Institutions*. Retrieved from http://www.oecd.org/education/imhe/QT%20policies%20and%20practices.pdf.

Hermida, J. (2009). The importance of teaching academic readings skills in first-year university courses. *The International Journal of Research and Review*, 3, 20–30. doi:10.2139/ssrn.1419247.

Hunter, K., & Tse, H. (2013). Making disciplinary writing and thinking practices an integral part of academic content teaching. *Active Learning in Higher Education*, 14(3), 227–239. doi:10.1177/1469787413498037.

Jones, A. (2009). Redisciplining generic attributes: The disciplinary context in focus. *Studies in Higher Education*, 34(1),85–100. doi:10.1080/03075070802602018.

Kohn, A. (2011). The case against grades. *Educational Leadership*, 69(3), 28–33.

Lea, M. R. (2004). Academic literacies: A pedagogy for course design. *Studies in Higher Education*, 29(6),739–756.doi:10.1080/0307507042000287230.

Lea, M. R., & Street, B. (2006). The 'academic literacies' model: Theory and applications. *Theory into Practice*, 45(4), 368–377. https://doi.org/10.1207/s15430421tip4504_11.

Macdonald, S., Scneider, B., & Giselle, K. (2013). Scenarios for collaboration: Idiosyncratic and ad hoc. *Journal of Academic Language & Learning*, 7(2), 11–19.

Marshall, S., Zhou, M., Gervan, T., & Wiebe, S. (2012). Sense of belonging and first-year academic literacy. *Canadian Journal of Higher Education*, 42(3), 116–142.

McCarthy, J. (2015). Evaluating written, audio, and video feedback in higher education summative assessment tasks. *Issues in Educational Research*, 25(2), 153–169.

Molloy, E., Borrell-Carrio, F., & Epstein, R. (2013). The impact of emotions in feedback. In D. Boud and E. Molloy (Eds.), *Feedback in higher and professional education* (pp. 50–71). Oxon: Routledge.

Molloy, E., & Boud, D. (2013). Feedback models for learning, teaching and performance. In J. M. Spector, D. Merrill, J. Elen, and M. J. Bishop (Eds.), *Handbook of research on educational communications and technology* (4th ed., pp. 413–424). New York: Springer.

Moore, P. J., & Harrington, M. (2016). Fractionating English language proficiency: Policy and practice in Australian higher education. *Current Issues in Language Planning*, 17(3–4), 385–404. doi:10.1080/14664208.2016.1212649.

Pulfrey, C., Buch, C., & Butera, F. (2011). Why grades engender performance-avoidance goals: The mediating role of autonomous motivation. *Journal of Educational Psychology*, 103(3), 683–700.

Ryan, T., & Henderson, M. (2018). Feeling feedback: Students' emotional responses to educator feedback. *Assessment & Evaluation*, 43(6),880–892.doi:10.1080/02602938.2017.1416456.

Sadler, D. R. (2010). Beyond feedback: Developing student capability in complex appraisal. *Assessment & Evaluation in Higher Education*, 35(5),535–550.

Scalone, P., & Street, B. (2006). An academic language development programme (widening participation). In C. Leung and J. Jenkins (Eds.), *Reconfiguring Europe: The contribution of applied linguistics* (pp.123–137). London: Equinox.

Stratilas, K. (2011). The evolving nature of support: A new horizon. *Journal of Academic Language & Learning*, 5(2), 44–49.

Thies, L. C. (2012). Increasing student participation and success: Collaborating to embed academic literacies into the curriculum. *Journal of Academic Language & Learning*, 6(1), 15–31.

Tippin, G. K., Lafreniere, K. D., & Page, S. (2012). Student perspectives of grading in physical education. *European Physical Education Review*, 1(21),409–420.

Walton, E., & Lloyd, G. (2012). From clinic to classroom: A model of teacher education for inclusion. *Perspectives in Education*, 30(2), 62–70.

Waters, M., & Waters, A. (1992). Study skills and study competence: Getting the priorities right. *ELT Journal*, 46(3), 264–273. doi:10.1093/elt/46.3.264.

Weaver, M. R. (2006). Do students value feedback? Student perceptions of tutors' written responses. *Assessment & Evaluation in Higher Education*, 31(3), 379–394. doi:10.1080/02602930500353061.

Wingate, U. (2006). Doing away with 'study skills'. *Teaching in Higher Education*, 11(4), 457–569. doi:10.1080/13562510600874268.

Wingate, U. (2012). Using academic literacies and genre-based models for academic writing instruction: A 'literacy journal'. *Journal of English for Academic Purposes*, 11(1), 26–37. doi:10.1016/j.jeap.2011.11.006.

Wingate, U., Andon, N., & Cogo, A. (2011). Embedding academic writing instruction into subject teaching: A case study. *Active Learning in Higher Education*, 12(1), 1–13. doi:10.1177%2F1469787410387814.

14

"WE NEED TO HELP STUDENTS DISCOVER THEMSELVES AND SEE INTO THE LIFE OF THINGS"

Advice from Open Foundation lecturers

Dr Rosalie J. Bunn

The University of Newcastle's (UON) Open Foundation Program (OFP) is the largest and oldest continuously operating tertiary preparation program in Australia. Successful completion of the program allows mature students from the age of 20 years access to undergraduate university studies without the need for any prior educational qualifications. Established in 1974 as a pilot program, OFP continues to thrive and transform the lives of many people in the Hunter and Central Coast regions and more broadly through its Distance offerings. As part of ethics-approved doctoral research into the history and impacts of OFP (Bunn, 2018) 21 experienced lecturers, 12 women and 9 men who taught in arts, social science, science, and mathematics disciplines, were asked about their reflections of teaching into the program in order to explore those impacts on students, UON and the wider community over more than 40 years. Lecturers were questioned about their philosophy of teaching and what teaching strategies they had found useful during their careers to meet the challenges of the space. These questions were posed in order to ascertain what beliefs and values may have influenced the delivery of OFP, how lecturers went about their work and whether there were any particular andragogical strategies they found useful to engage mature age students. The questions invited them to cast back over their long careers to highlight what sometimes may have been unconscious or not well-developed rationales for how they performed their teaching roles and what they believed was essential to effective andragogy.

When interview responses were collated and analysed, it became apparent that these lecturers, who had often been teaching for decades and were well respected by both students and colleagues within the university, recognised that the art of andragogy involved a clear understanding of the reciprocal nature of teaching and learning which placed the mature student's needs as well as the lecturer's professional and well-practiced teaching skills at the centre of their endeavours. Positioning these responses within Mezirow's (1978) Transformative Learning theory, which focuses on the importance of perspective change and confidence building through critical self-reflection during the learning process, this chapter shares lecturers insights into what it means to 'be' an enabling educator as well as how to 'do' enabling education. It highlights the importance of authenticity when teaching in tertiary preparation spaces, the relevance of cultivating a culture of care for these often vulnerable students as well as the need for adaptability and flexibility to respond to a diverse range of learners where "one size does not fit all".

The art of 'being' an enabling educator

Recent research exploring the role of academic staff in enabling programs concluded that a reconceptualization of a solely academic role to one that incorporates and acknowledges the practice of care and support of students is required to meet the holistic needs of students. The researchers argued that an understanding of the diversity and complexity of teaching this particular cohort of students was based on philosophies and ethics of academic staff who acknowledged student health and wellbeing as a teaching and learning issue (Crawford & Johns, 2018, p. 17). Attempting to ascertain more specific components of enabling teaching philosophy was, however, not as simple to compile as not all the lecturers in my research had thought about or articulated what that philosophy might be. One lecturer who later moved into undergraduate teaching commented: "my own philosophy of teaching, it's one of these questions that we ask our first year students to enunciate and we get very cross when they can't, but it's always a difficult thing to enunciate ourselves".

When applying a thematic analysis to their oral history responses it became clear that lecturers' philosophies were informed by intrinsic factors about what they believed one should 'be' as an enabling educator of mature age students as well as how that was enacted. Desirable personal characteristics were often inextricably entwined with what they believed one must 'do' as an effective educator, covered in the second section of this chapter.

Contrary to the idea that teaching is a performance, these lecturers considered being genuine or 'true to yourself', an important attribute to engage mature students. Part of displaying an authentic self was a capacity to be 'open-minded', a quality that has been equated with intellectual virtue, which in turn is linked to wellbeing (Mavropoulou, 2017). One study on authenticity in teaching (Ramezanzadeh, Adel, & Zareian, 2016) found it included a sense of responsibility, authentic relations, and a capacity for deconstructive thinking. The authors based their theoretical understanding of the concept on Heidegger's (1962) notion that education in its proper sense was the formation of authenticity which led to empowerment of students. Lecturers provided further examples of authenticity as being 'a grass roots teacher', explaining things as simply and clearly as possible, and being 'able to stand up and deliver' discipline content confidently while ensuring students understood its relevance to their future academic pursuits.

Role-modelling good learning behaviours was seen as a way of connecting the authentic educator with creating an authentic learning environment. Rather than simply providing relevant content and ensuring effective delivery, lecturers saw a:

> need to search for ways to ensure students understood what they were learn-ing. You must be modelling the behaviours that you want to see. That is, respect for yourself, respect for others, openness to learning, openness to the opinions of others, problem solving, interest in problem solving, reading things.

Another lecturer advised "Always try to be positive. Negativity does not work!" By exhibiting pro-social behaviour this educator was setting a standard for students to follow.

Demonstrating that lecturers genuinely cared about students, another variant of authenticity, was also seen as an important trait of an enabling educator. Cavanagh, Macfarlane, Glynn, and Macfarlane (2012) identify a culture of care as building relationships, exercising holistic caring, building capacity, and trust. Increasingly, lecturers were aware of the importance of student mental health and wellbeing to student success. Collaborative research on how best to implement initiatives that promote student mental health and wellbeing within the field is gaining increasing attention in Australian universities (Crawford et al., 2016). Enhancing tolerance and understanding of society more broadly was mentioned as part of creating a healthy teaching environment. This position is supported by Noddings' (1984) work on caring, which argues for a feminine approach to ethics and moral educa-tion. Comments such as "look after your students and show an interest in them" and "demonstrate commitment to students and to the course" indicated that lec-turers understood the significance of pastoral care when connecting with students. An enabling counsellor with many years' experience observed that lecturers she had worked with provided a nurturing and safe learning environment:

> Well I think it [OFP] provides a very nurturing response from the academic staff, that's always the feedback that the students give me on just how sup-ported they feel. The feedback they get is comprehensive, it's encouraging. That others have faith in them when they might be doubting themselves. And it's that kind of attitudinal response to their learning, and assuming they have the capability. It's just about tailoring it, yeah, and there's things they need to learn and that they are capable of that learning. And just that really safe learning environment, safe and supportive. And I think that's what they love and that's what I think has made it such a positive program is the safety and the security. And yet, they're challenged, you know, and they're educated, and they're informed of what will be required of them. But it's done in such a paced way and a gentle way that it's not too threatening or overwhelming or scary, you know. It's that lovely, just pacing it well and getting them up to the mark so they are ready for undergraduate [studies].

As observed, this caring attitude also translated into lecturers' approach to marking student work, an area in which students were particularly vulnerable to criticism. The art of being a good enabling educator was to manage this aspect of the lecturer-student relationship with sensitivity.

One lecturer commented that education can also be therapeutic due to the personal growth and development potential that results from students' learning experience. Having empathy with student ambitions and sensitivity for the emotional commitment they were making when returning to mature age study were deemed essential to building positive classroom relationships. In turn, good relationships were deemed important to a productive learning space. This involved creating a learning environment that "makes for relaxed and happy students", and breaking down barriers that positioned the lecturer as authority by providing spaces for student voices and listening to and respecting student views. However, one lecturer advised: "You need to tailor the experience so that they are comfortable coming, they are not immediately threatened, but not so comfortable that they settle into a comfort zone and don't go beyond it".

With this in mind, lecturers recognised the importance of creating a non-threatening environment in which fun and humour could contribute to teaching effectiveness. This view is supported by Kher, Molstad, and Donaghue (1999) who argue that humour fosters openness and respect in the classroom and can be especially useful when teaching more difficult or 'dreaded' subjects. However, the fun was to be tempered by the need for hard work, and students were to expect the humorous and joyful times along with the challenges.

These lecturers regarded the capacity to be flexible in one's approach to students and also within the learning environment. First, it was recognised that students' lives were incredibly complex and competing familial and work responsibilities could hamper their educational commitments. A flexible attitude to matters such as assignment deadlines which took this into account was considered necessary. Yoo, Schallert, and Svinicki (2015) argue that when effective teachers are also flexible, student learning improves. Second, lecturers expressed the need to be flexible in teaching delivery to ensure that as many learner types could benefit from a variety of delivery modes. Like Bigum and Rowan (2004) who argued that the concept of flexible learning, while well intentioned, must also be subject to critique, one lecturer commented: "the old fashioned chalk and talk still works". Another lecturer remarked on the need to reconcile traditional and progressive education methods to ensure that outcomes for students were tailored to a range of andragogical strategies.

Many lecturers held the view that students were on a journey where what they learned along the way was often more important than what students sometimes regarded as the ultimate goal of passing the course or transitioning into undergraduate programs. Lecturers were conscious that self-development was occurring alongside the acquisition of knowledge and skills. Sometimes this resulted in students deconstructing their former identity and changing their habitus (Bunn, 2017). Interestingly, having a sensitivity to these changes in students' lives also impacted favourably on the lecturer:

First of all, respect the student. Respect the student, because they come with a bank of knowledge and information, skills and background. You have to be able to take them from where they're at to a new level of learning. That's my core belief. And once you do that your teaching changes and you evolve into a person who is able to connect with the student and then direct their learning. So that's my philosophy.

These lecturers promoted the value of education by showing commitment to life-long learning. They recognised that people from any educational background or of any age could benefit from the enabling experience. In order to make their learning journey easier the lecturers aimed to demystify difficult or previously inaccessible paths to knowledge. They also believed that setting high standards and goals for their students must be accompanied by showing them how to achieve them.

Lecturers also recognised the part they played in assisting students on their personal journey was helping students "discover themselves and see into the life of things". The effects of this transformation are explained by Mezirow (1978, p. 101) as "significant phases of reassessment and growth in which familiar assumptions are challenged and new directions and commitments are charted". OFP lecturers recognised the point at which enabling students differ from other HE students is that they are "beginning again" (Mezirow, 1978, p. 102). It is a process in which learners come to see themselves differently and develop a critical consciousness which Mezirow sees as a prerequisite for liberating personal development. As these students engage in this "structural reorganization of their lives" (Mezirow, 1978, p. 108), self-confidence is built by increased competency as they are introduced to new skills and a supportive social environment, which is generated in large part by the lecturer and their broader educational experience. Dirkx (2012, p. 400) argues that "complex processes of elaborating and remaking ways of understanding the self", require a shift that is fostered through academic study that challenges students and can be a very emotional experience. One lecturer commented "it's not what they get out of it but what they learn along the way" that was important.

Prominent in some philosophies was promoting ideas about social justice and equality, and enhancing tolerance and understanding of society. In fact, OFP itself was regarded as a socially responsible activity that addressed inequality and disadvantage:

> I have a special place in my esteem for teaching in Open Foundation, because there was a sense that you were doing something that was socially useful, and something that put you in touch with adult people, and doing a bit more than just recovering untapped resources.

Comments such as "convince students it doesn't matter what their background is, they can still learn" and "give everyone an equal voice" demonstrated a commitment to principles of social justice and equity. While it was acknowledged that education can be a liberating experience for students, this was seen as dependent upon creating just the right environment in which students could flourish:

My philosophy of teaching is that education, essentially, should be liberating. The best way to make education liberating is to make it non-threatening but challenging; fun but preparatory of hard work; open, so inclusive but funnily that is gradually excluding certain characteristics, that is, capacity not to organize yourself, not to work hard, those sorts of things. So you open it up to everybody early on.

These seemingly contradictory aims, expressed by Dewey (1916) as "the problem of dualisms", were often expressed as part of the balancing act of the enabling educator who needed to be alert to the dangers of taking certain approaches. Cautions such as: finding the right balance which ensured facilitating learning rather than taking a 'jug and mug' approach in which the educator pours all their knowledge into an empty vessel; teaching students how to learn as opposed to just teaching them content; working from the known to the unknown; introducing new material and vocabulary gradually; were offered as tips to teaching effectiveness.

Effective andragogies for teaching in the enabling space

'Doing' enabling education was shown to be multifaceted and the interviews elicited a great amount of advice about how to put enabling education into practice. Lecturers' responses offered advice on how to approach students (see Table 14.1) and on classroom practice (see Table 14.2). One lecturer who was herself an OFP student and had therefore experienced this teaching environment from both teacher and student perspectives commented on her teaching philosophy:

> It's more of a constructionist sort of one I guess if I'm thinking back to terminology. One where, if at all possible, try and work out the best way a student's going to learn and to work with them. So it's the idea that your learning shouldn't be top down but at University it often is, in a sense, top down. But more, very student centred … so that you can work with the student and the groups of students and start where they are starting from, and try and work with them.

Helping students see the value of what they are studying was deemed essential to student engagement. In fact, it was thought that the approach taken by OFP enabling educators was beginning to influence the broader teaching and learning culture at UON. One former program convenor stated:

> There is a slowly growing recognition, I think, that Open Foundation staff … know a lot about teaching and learning for non-traditional, particularly low SES students and that the University needs to get a whole lot better at that at the Undergraduate level. I think there's a slowly increasing awareness of that and I think we have had some impact and I think that is going to increase, slowly.

TABLE 14.1 Tips on approach to students

Help students discover themselves and see into the 'life of things'	Respect, reassure and encourage students	Take students as they are	Make relaxed and happy students
Help students see study takes time and effort	Provide opportunities for growth and development	Teach students how to learn	Train students in educational capital
Connect with students	Work with students	Help students see the value in want we do	Show students what is possible
Place students in a quasi-teaching situation where they teach others	Guide and mentor students rather than instruct or control them	Never override student contribution	Entertain students, but not with jokes
Try not to offend students (but you can send politicians up)	Help students get past that inner voice that tells them they can't do it	Look after your students and show an interest in them	Teach students a love of learning as well as skills
Make students comfortable but not too much!	Provide space for student voices, and listening to them	Teach students to think about their thinking	Recognise that one size does not fit all!

TABLE 14.2 Tips for classroom practice

Classes to be fun but preparation for hard work	Teach problem solving and to be reflective	Provide strategies, like colour coding or baking analogies	Take time to teach basic skills
Use humour as a learning device	Teach skills that are transferrable	Mix up your teaching delivery	Encourage discussions, student views are important
Have clear and specific goals and aims	Open knowledge up but funnel down as well	Provide non-threatening but challenging tasks	Teach values and critique of them
Avoid academic language	The old-fashioned chalk and talk still works	Teachers as tool and facilitators of learning	Work from the known to the unknown
Introduce new ideas and more sophisticated vocabulary gradually	Create independent learners	Use contemporary models to engage eg. Song lyrics rather than poetry	Scaffold knowledge and tasks
Introduce a variety of ways of understanding material and check they do understand it	Reconcile traditional and progressive education	Provide practical examples and translate them to theory	Have a thorough knowledge of your discipline
Show passion and enthusiasm for your topic	Facilitate learning with different experiences & opportunities	Teach from the bottom up	Make things simpler

In order to be an effective teacher lecturers were keen to constantly reflect on their practice in order to provide the most appropriate learning experience for their diverse range of students. This was expressed as "keep asking yourself 'How else can I teach it?' for those who don't get it" and "Remind yourself Uni is a strange lifestyle and environment for our students". Being able to place oneself in the role of the other, a sociological concept coined by Mead (1934) in order to think through how students might be approaching tasks, and thoughtful consideration and questioning of what does and does not work within classrooms were regarded as essential to quality teaching.

Other personal qualities that affected lecturers' approach to their work and which constituted an enabling ethos included commitment to students as well as loyalty to the program. The Director of enabling programs at UON at the time of interview commented:

> So it's the commitment of people. I very rarely have had a staff member from our Enabling Programs coming to me and saying "I want this for myself." It tends to be "Can we get this for the students?" And I think talking to people who come from other areas of the University, I think they are surprised at the amazing commitment. Yes, we are all being paid to do it, but the extra work that is put in is because they believe in it … People will go the extra mile for the student.

The staff themselves recognised this commitment in their own approach, but also in their observations of their colleagues' teaching which was seen as "value-adding" to their paid duties:

> We tend to put an awful lot into our teaching, and do a lot of pastoral care, and a lot of extra work, give students a lot of feedback. So I think the "value adding" that we do is very important, and it's not just academic … it's the whole person.

An enabling ethos that included taking students "as they are"; starting their learning journey "where the student is starting from" and assisting to build their self-confidence were frequently mentioned in lecturers' philosophies. Creating confident students had ramifications far beyond preparing them for university entry. It helped shape their lives in productive and positive ways and impacted their wider relationships (Bunn, 2013). Student surveys included in the wider research project revealed that a greater number of students cited issues relating to self-identity than any other response as their reason for enrolling in OFP (Bunn, 2014). In addition to gaining educational skills, these students often sought to test or prove their intellectual capability and to elevate the esteem in which they were held by others. The delicate balance of juggling these sensitivities formed part of these lecturers teaching philosophies.

The complexity of creating a productive learning space for enabling students was therefore dependant on the lecturer demonstrating passion and enthusiasm for, as well as competence in, delivering course content; in conjunction with a focus on the students' learning needs. This was expressed as:

Helping them to learn to become independent learners and people who enjoy the learning process and have the skills they need in order to learn further, so meta skills in fact, so that they can in fact become not just independent learners but lifelong learners, so that whatever situation they're in they can approach it with a whole suite of problem solving skills and internal review and monitoring skills that allow them to learn from that experience ... You have to challenge them. And doing that to this massively diverse group of students at the same time, is to me the central pedagogical challenge of Open Foundation teaching. And it's one that I think we're pretty good at.

Conclusion

These UON enabling educators were already "pay[ing] attention" to the transformation taking place in their students' lives, long before Dirkx (2012, p. 404) advised to do so. Their collective wisdom has shown that lecturers' attitudes and values coalesce with their classroom approaches such that their choice of curriculum and relationship with students is tailored to ensure productive andragogy takes place. Personal qualities of lecturers directed toward facilitating student empowerment and growth, implementing critical pedagogy in the form of a social justice agenda, establishing positive classroom relationships and learning communities, enhancing logical and conceptual growth of students all formed part of the philosophies and strategies of these enabling educators despite the fact that some had never, prior to interview, explicitly considered or reflected on their philosophy of teaching. These lecturers recognised the many checks and balances required for effective teaching and were aware of the problem of dualisms discussed by Dewey (1916). Their guiding principles were authenticity, care, respect and reassurance.

References

Bigum, C., & Rowan, L. (2004). Flexible learning in teacher education: Myths, muddles and models. *Asia-Pacific Journal of Teacher Education*, 32(3), 213–226.

Bunn, R. J. (2018). *The history and impacts of the University of Newcastle's Open Foundation program*, Unpublished Doctoral Dissertation, University of Newcastle. http://hdl.handle.net/1959.13/1391980.

Bunn, R. J. (2017). 'Rewarding, enlightening, empowering, challenging': The importance of habitus and embodied cultural capital in restructuring student lives following successful completion of a tertiary preparation program. In S. Broadhead, M. Hill, A. Hudson, C. McGlynn, S. McHendry, N. Raven, D. Sims, & T. Ward (eds.) *Widening participation in the context of economic and social change*. Forum for Access and Continuing Education. London: University of East London.

Bunn, R. J. (2013). *I wanted to prove I had a brain and give my life a purpose: Preliminary analysis of survey responses of former Open Foundation students on their lives before, during and after completing the program*. Paper presented at Flexibility: Pathways to Participation 5th National Association of Enabling Educators of Australia Conference, Australian Catholic University, Melbourne, Australia.

Bunn, R. J. (2014). *Reasons people enrol in tertiary preparation courses.* Refereed conference paper presented at Foundation and Bridging Educators New Zealand, Bay of Plenty Institute of Technology, Tauranga, New Zealand.

Cavanagh, T., Macfarlane, A., Glynn, T., & Macfarlane, S. (2012). Creating peaceful and effective schools through a culture of care. *Discourse: Cultural Politics of Education,* 33, 1–13.

Crawford, N., & Johns, S. (2018). An academic's role? Supporting student wellbeing in pre-university enabling programs. *Journal of University Teaching & Learning Practice,* 15(3),1–21.

Crawford, N., Lisciandro, J., Jones, A., Jaceglav, M., McCall, D., Bunn, R., Cameron, H., Westacott, M., & Andersen, S. (2016). *Models of support for student wellbeing in enabling programs: Comparisons, contrasts and commonalities at four Australian universities.* Proceedings of the 2016 FABENZ Conference, UNITEC Auckland, New Zealand. http://fabenz.org. nz/wp-content/uploads/2016/12/Nicole-Crawford.pdf.

Dewey, J. (1916). *Democracy and education: An introduction to the philosophy of education.* New York: Macmillan.

Dirkx, J. M. (2012). Self-formation and transformative learning: A response to 'calling transformative learning into question: Some mutinous thoughts', by Michael Newman. *Australian Education Quarterly,* 62(4), 399–405.

Heidegger, M. (1962) *Being and time.* Translated by John Macquarrie and Edward Robinson. London: SCM Press.

Kher, N., Molstad, S., & Donahue, R. (1999). Using humor in the college classroom to enhance teaching effectiveness in 'dread courses'. *College Student Journal,* 33(3), 400–407.

Mavropoulou, C. (2017). *Is open-mindedness necessary for intellectual well-being in education?: Bringing together virtue, knowledge and well-being in initial teacher education.* University of Edinburgh. Electronic thesis. http://ethos.bl.uk.ezproxy.newcastle.edu.au/OrderDetails. do?uin=uk.bl-ethos.736009.

Mead, G. H. (1934). *Mind, self and society.* Chicago: University of Chicago Press.

Mezirow, J. (1978). Perspective transformation. *Adult Education Quarterly,* 28(2), 100–110.

Noddings, N. (1984). *Caring: A feminine approach to ethics and moral education.* Berkeley: University of California Press.

Ramezanzadeh, A., Adel, S. M. R., & Zareian, G. (2016). Authenticity in teaching and teachers' emotions: A hermeneutic phenomenological study of the classroom reality. *Teaching in Higher Education,* 21(7), 807–824.

Yoo, J. H., Schallert, D. L., & Svinicki, M. D. (2015). The meaning of flexibility in teaching: Views from college students and exemplary college instructors. *Journal on Excellence in College Teaching,* 26(3), 191–217.

15

SUPPORTING STUDENT MENTAL WELLBEING IN ENABLING EDUCATION

Practices, pedagogies and a philosophy of care

Dr Nicole Crawford, Professor Sally Kift and Dr Lynn Jarvis

Introduction

High rates of mental ill-health amongst students have been a catalyst in recent years for universities to reconsider their attitudes and approaches to supporting student mental wellbeing. At the coalface in Australian university enabling programs (also known as access courses and alternative pathways), educators teach and support diverse student cohorts, including students with mental health difficulties. Acknowledging this additional challenge for students transitioning to university, educators in some programs have implemented proactive initiatives in response to their students' needs. Using enabling education in Australia[1] as a case study of supportive learning environments with intentional curricula, structures, and strategies to support student mental wellbeing, this book chapter explores the practices, pedagogies, and philosophies common to such programs. It describes the strategies evident in enabling education and proposes that the initiatives display interweaving elements of *enabling pedagogy; third generation transition pedagogy*; and *pedagogies of care*. Furthermore, it contends that the practices and pedagogies are underpinned by a philosophy of care, which resists the type of dualistic thinking present in higher education that under-values *caring* work.

Background

In recent decades, research has revealed that university students report higher rates of psychological distress and experience lower mental health status compared to the general population (Cvetkovski, Reavley, & Jorm, 2012; Larcombe et al., 2016; Orygen, 2017; Stallman, 2010), and highlights the negative impact studying at university can have on students' mental health (Slavin, 2016; Storrie, Ahern, & Tuckett, 2010). The latter point acknowledges the negative impact that the *setting* in which students learn (i.e. learning environment and campus culture) can have on their mental health, and thus on their engagement and learning. Internationally, several charters and networks promote an institution-wide settings approach to supporting students' health and wellbeing (Healthy Universities, 2019; JED Campus, 2019; Okanagan Charter, 2015; TWANZ, n.d.; WHO, 2019).

In response to a range of coalescing factors (such as: university student mental health data; settings approaches; general prominence of mental health in the media and in the broader community; and government policy drivers), universities in numerous countries are now actively investigating potential settings that impact on their students' mental wellbeing. They are increasingly considering whole-of-institution approaches, and are examining the culture and environment, the curriculum, and the teaching and learning contexts. In Australian higher education, recent reports and frameworks have propelled the issue of student mental health into the national spotlight (Baik et al., 2016, 2017; Higher Education Standards Panel, 2018; Orygen, 2017).[2] Such approaches and responses are a major shift from viewing students' mental health as the responsibility of the individual student and/or of disability and counselling services at institutions. This attention on mental health as an issue of specific concern for the university sector has taken place in the context of broader public and community advocacy and recognition of the high prevalence of mental illness in the general population, a prevalence hitherto overlooked with mental health being shrouded in stigma and ignorance.

Broader philosophical context

The practices, pedagogies and guiding philosophies in enabling education need to be understood in the broader higher education philosophical context. Some equity researchers in higher education note the existence of problematic dualistic philosophical thinking in neoliberal higher education discourses that empower or value one group (or aspect/characteristic) over another (Burke & Crozier, 2014; Motta & Bennett, 2018). Such hierarchical binaries may include, for example: *Masculinity versus femininity; mind versus body; rational versus irrational; reason versus emotion; human versus nature*; and *competition versus caring*. The first item in each pairing is privileged and the second item is under-valued. Such hierarchical dualistic thinking, which is common in the western philosophical tradition, has been critiqued by feminist and ecological/environmental philosophers for several decades (see, for example, Gatens, 1991, and Plumwood, 1986, 1991). Feminist critiques do not simply reverse the dualism to value the *rejected* side of the dichotomy, but call for an erasure of the binaries and aim to transcend hierarchical dualistic thinking. Simply reversing the hierarchical dualism is said to be inadequate as it descends into the problems of essentialism, such as perceiving qualities and attributes as ahistorical and fixed (Grosz, 1995, p. 49).

An antidote to hierarchical dualistic thinking can be found in care theory. Two key theorists in care-focused philosophy are Nel Noddings and Joan Tronto. In the context of the philosophy of education, Noddings (2002) stresses the importance of *responsiveness*: For example, of listening to students in order to address their needs. Thus, she takes a student-centred approach to caring. For Noddings (2002, 2005), an ethic of caring is relational. Tronto (1993, 2005) also highlights the relational aspect of caring, with a focus on: attentiveness (being attentive to others' needs); responsibility (taking it upon oneself to care); competence (being able to care adequately); and responsiveness (understanding the vulnerability of the care receiver). Central to this relational philosophy of care are trust and reciprocity, relationships, and context (Goralnik, Dobson, & Nelson, 2015; Goralnik, Millenbah, Nelson, & Thorp, 2012). This approach to care, which requires responsiveness to the needs of the participants (e.g. students) has direct application to teaching and learning (Goralnik et al., 2012; Isenbarger & Zembylas, 2006).

Care-focused philosophy has its roots in feminist and environmental philosophies that critique established philosophical traditions (Goralnik et al., 2015) and seeks to erase hierarchical binaries. Viewed in this way, a philosophy of care is an example of non-dualistic thinking. As such, it has the potential to challenge and resist dualistic thinking in academia, and also provide a more supportive philosophical underpinning to the practice of enabling education.

Practices: Supporting student wellbeing

At the program/course/unit level, educators in enabling programs have been responding to students' individual needs for many years by implementing proactive student-learning-centred initiatives to lessen barriers and create engaging, inclusive and supportive learning environments for all students.[3] In an exploration of how student wellbeing is supported in four enabling programs in Australia, the researchers found that at the core of each program was a "culture of care" and a "culture of self-development and growth" (Crawford et al., 2016, p. 13). This section will briefly present initiatives from three university enabling programs.

In Murdoch University's *OnTrack* enabling course, the approach to supporting student wellbeing is multi-faceted, with "program level initiatives, curricula choices and specific pedagogical principles, in addition to the existing wider institutional support" (Crawford et al., 2016, p. 8). At the program level, initiatives are embedded and include a lecture series by the university counselling staff to foster resilience; this series is integrated into the curriculum, rather than being a voluntary extra-curricular option. A focus on socio-emotional learning underpins the core curriculum, with the aim of cultivating "emotional resilience, academic self-efficacy and sustained motivation" (Crawford et al., 2016, p. 9).[4] Dweck's (2008) growth-mindsets learning theory underpins the pedagogy; staff undertake professional development on appropriate growth-mindsets language for the learning environment and for use in assessment feedback rubrics in order to model and promote a growth mindset.

The University of Tasmania's *Pre-degree Programs* is driven by Engstrom and Tinto's (2008) maxim that "access without support is not opportunity"; support is an essential component of the teaching and learning. The support mechanisms are not extra-curricular; they are optimally embedded within the course (Kift, 2009) and staff structures. For example, on each campus a designated lecturer/tutor is a Student Coordinator; this staff member has a holistic view of the students' progress and challenges in all of their units/subjects (Jarvis, 2018).[5] As a lecturer and tutor, they have the opportunity to develop a rapport and trust with students, which enables the students to feel comfortable to ask questions, seek advice and guidance (Crawford & Johns, 2018). Furthermore, every student is enrolled in Supported Studies units in their first and second semesters; these classes have an informal home-room atmosphere in which students are encouraged to ask questions and work together; they develop peer learning groups, connections, a sense of belonging and confidence (Jarvis, 2018). Socio-emotional learning, mental health awareness, strategies to enhance students' self-efficacy, and Dweck's growth mindsets are also embedded in some of the core units.

Quite a different strategy has been implemented in the University of Newcastle's *Open Foundation* enabling programs. For nearly a decade, a counsellor role has been embedded in the enabling programs to improve accessibility, in response to "enabling staff recognising that their students face a variety of personal and social barriers to education and that students and staff would benefit from a co-located model of counselling support" (Crawford et al., 2016, p. 11). Furthermore, an extra layer of support has been provided with the addition of a Student Support Advisor[6] to the counselling team.

Support and care are core to these initiatives. Embedding support illustrates that students' wellbeing is a teaching and learning issue, as does embedding mental health awareness and self-efficacy strategies in teaching and learning activities. The focus on student-to-teacher and student-to-student relationships highlights the intention to foster belonging and connections in these learning communities.[7]

Pedagogies

To gain further insight into the enactment of such supportive practices, this section will explore three relevant pedagogical approaches: enabling pedagogy; third generation transition pedagogy; and pedagogies of care.

The term enabling pedagogy has been used in some recent studies of enabling programs in Australia. For example, in the report *Enabling Retention*, Hodges et al. (2013) stated the need for inclusive and innovative pedagogies in enabling education and recommended that further research be undertaken "to develop a range of appropriate enabling pedagogies" (p. 6). Lane and Sharp (2014) responded to this call and undertook an evaluation of an enabling program with the aim of identifying "exemplary research-based enabling pedagogies" (p. 68). They developed a model of enabling pedagogy with practices and strategies to create a "positive and supportive culture". They stress that the key to enabling pedagogy is community; a supportive learning community provides the conditions for belonging and trust to develop, which is required for self-esteem, self-efficacy and confidence to grow, all prerequisites for academic achievement. Lane and Sharp's (2014, p. 70) model of enabling pedagogy contains four linked quadrants: Leadership; teaching and learning; community; and individual engagement, with open communication between each quadrant (as opposed to a hierarchical structure). Common to each quadrant (implicit if not explicitly stated) is an emphasis on support and relationships, and an overarching "holistic collaborative culture" (p. 70). Bennett et al. (2017) followed a reflexive and participatory approach in their exploration of enabling pedagogies at the University of Newcastle. Some of the key themes identified include: taking a strengths-based approach; acknowledging students' capabilities; and valuing students' existing knowledges. Teachers were found to "embrace the complex relational dynamics involved in teaching" and "follow an iterative reflexive approach" (p. 9). Such enabling pedagogies take a student-centred, supportive and caring approach.

For more than a decade, Sally Kift and colleagues have seen their focus on student engagement in the first year of university evolve from a *first generation*, essentially co-curricular, approach, through a *second generation* in-curricular focus, where learning and success support is explicitly embedded in scaffolded course design, onto an ideal culmination in *third generation* transition pedagogy, in which a student success orientation is holistic and seamlessly integrated across all institutional policies, practices and processes (Kift, 2009, 2015; Kift, Nelson, & Clarke, 2010). Kift and colleagues realised that the framework required for improving the student experience and engagement – for inspiring and supporting students, and for assisting them to gain a sense of belonging – already existed; it was, in fact, the curriculum (Kift, 2009, 2015; Kift et al., 2010). In this conceptualisation, curriculum is posited as the "missing link" and the "organising device" (Kift et al., 2010, p. 4); curriculum is the "glue that holds knowledge and the broader student experience together" (McInnis, 2001, p. 11, in Kift et al., 2010, p. 4). Kift and Field (2009) argue that student engagement is supported by an intentional first-year curriculum that "*motivates* students to learn, provides a positive learning *climate*, and encourages students to be *active* in their learning" (p. 2). Transition pedagogy's curricular focus thus promotes "student learning, success and retention" (Kift & Field, 2009, p. 10). The holistic approach aspired to in third generation transition pedagogy, as Kift et al. (2010, p. 1) note, "provides the optimal vehicle for dealing with the increasingly diverse commencing student cohorts by facilitating a sense of engagement, support and belonging". Such practice is core to supporting students and, thus, to enabling pedagogies.

Pedagogies of care were found to be fundamental in Bennett et al.'s (2017) study of enabling pedagogies. A relational approach to caring, as espoused by Noddings (2002, 2005) and Tronto (1993, 2005), emphasises "receptivity, relatedness and responsiveness" (Isenbarger & Zembylas, 2006, p. 122). For example, in a teaching and learning context, "[c]aring requires teachers to elicit and listen to how students are feeling, to evaluate their purposes, to help them to engage in self-evaluation, and to help them grow as participants in caring relations" (Isenbarger & Zembylas, 2006, p. 122). This caring approach requires time and an "affective and embodied praxis" (Motta & Bennett, 2018, p. 642). It requires a focus on the whole student; that is, an understanding that their academic and non-academic challenges are inseparable (Crawford & Johns, 2018). These elements of care are often associated with tensions and challenges in the broader institutional contexts and neoliberal discourses. The praxis of care is often *under-valued* and *unrecognised*, due to "its feminised and invisibilised nature" (Bennett et al., 2017, p. 17). Here, it sits on the under-valued side of the binary in hierarchical dualistic thinking. Furthermore, as caring in teaching is emotional work (Isenbarger & Zembylas, 2006) and is experienced at the visceral level, another challenge is the physical and emotional impact of the high *emotional labour demands* on educators (Crawford et al., 2018). Crawford et al. (2018) found, however, that enabling educators adopt protective factors to combat this burden, including communities of care and support, and the rewarding experience of bearing witness to students' transformations.

These three pedagogies create the conditions – the teaching and learning environment, the setting, and the community – for students to feel comfortable, to connect, and to belong – essential conditions for engagement, learning and mental wellbeing.

A philosophy of care

At the core of the practices and pedagogies in enabling education that support student wellbeing, we contend, is a relational philosophy of care. Students who undertake enabling programs have frequently had less than satisfactory prior educational experiences, are often positioned as *other* in the formal educational context and are quite vulnerable to being overwhelmed by a lack of academic confidence. To mediate the potential for such factors to work against creating mentally healthy learning environments, a philosophy of care, whether explicitly articulated or intrinsically adopted, is frequently embraced to support student wellbeing and enable individual student success.

This philosophy of care is relational and responsive (Noddings, 2002, 2005; Tronto, 2005); relationships (student-to-teacher; student-to-student) are fundamental to this type of caring. Relationships formed upon trust are required for the proactive practices and pedagogies to be enacted and experienced. Such relationships are the building blocks of the learning environments, communities, and settings that foster belonging and in which students' wellbeing can be supported and learning fostered.

A philosophy of care resists and transcends the type of dualistic thinking present in higher education discourses that values mind over body and other hierarchical dualisms that would (if not resisted) discourage and devalue the foci essential for supporting student wellbeing in enabling education. A philosophy of care underpins a student-centred holistic approach, particularly one that values the importance of relationships and community. In fact, this caring can be seen as a form of resistance per se to neoliberal hierarchical dualistic thinking and continues in the tradition of feminist, ecofeminist, and environmental philosophers' critiques of the western philosophical tradition. Indeed, a philosophy of care is an example of the broader impact of such feminist critiques in academia.

Conclusion

Student mental health and wellbeing is everyone's business. Through the case study of enabling education, this chapter has shown that educators can embed proactive initiatives in their teaching and learning activities and develop supportive learning communities and cultures that enhance student mental wellbeing. Enabling educators explicitly enact pedagogies that are student-centred, with a focus on relationships and responsiveness to students' needs. The underpinning driver and guiding principle for their practice is a relational philosophy of care. Simply put, a philosophy of care can work to support the mental wellbeing and, thus, learning engagement of enabling cohorts.

This chapter has also illustrated how taking a caring approach is a worthwhile endeavour; it challenges hierarchical dualistic thinking that positions caring on the under-valued side of the binary, along with student health, emotions, and other individual circumstances that are frequently considered to be beyond an educator's remit. In taking a holistic – seamless, whole-of-student – inclusive approach that supports student wellbeing and prioritises it as a teaching and learning issue, enabling educators resist discourses in higher education that undervalue *caring* work.

Notes

1 For a detailed explanation of enabling education in Australia, see the Introduction to this edited collection.
2 Recommendation 8 in the *Higher Education Standards Panel Final Report* (2018, p. 9) states: "Every institution should have an institution-wide mental health strategy and implementation plan". The Minister accepted the recommendations in 2018 and Universities Australia commissioned Orygen with the task of developing a framework, which is currently a work-in-progress. Influencing Recommendation 8 is Standard 2.3 (Wellbeing and Safety) in the Higher Education Standards Framework (2015). Standard 2.3.3 (p. 7) explicitly refers to mental health and wellbeing needs in the context of support service provision. Furthermore, Standard 6.1.4 (p. 12) mentions fostering student and staff wellbeing in the context of corporate governance.
3 Such initiatives complement the existing centrally-located university counselling services.
4 For details, see: Lisciandro, Jones, & Strehlow (2016).
5 The enabling program at Central Queensland University has also implemented this model (Seary, Willans & Cook, 2016).
6 A similar role exists in Edith Cowan University's UniPrep enabling course (S. Sharp, personal communication, 9 July, 2018). This staff member focuses on supporting student and staff wellbeing.
7 These features are fundamental to self-determination theory. In particular, the practices enable growth in motivation, belonging, relationships, autonomy and competence – the five factors for wellbeing and growth outlined in Baik et al. (2017). See: http://unistudentwell being.edu.au/wp-content/uploads/2016/08/MCSHE-Student-Wellbeing-MBRAC.pdf.

References

Baik, C., Larcombe, W., Brooker, A., Wyn, J., Allen, L., Brett, M., … James, R. (2016). *A framework for promoting student mental wellbeing in universities.* Retrieved from http://uni studentwellbeing.edu.au/framework/.

Baik, C., Larcombe, W., Brooker, A., Wyn, J., Allen, L., Brett, M., … James, R. (2017). *Enhancing student mental wellbeing: A handbook for academic educators.* Retrieved from http://m elbourne-cshe.unimelb.edu.au/__data/assets/pdf_file/0006/2408604/MCSHE-Student-Wel lbeing-Handbook-FINAL.pdf.

Bennett, A., Motta, S., Hamilton, E., Burgess, C., Relf, B., Gray, K., … Albright, J. (2017). *Enabling pedagogies: A participatory conceptual mapping of practices at the University of Newcastle, Australia.* Retrieved from https://nova.newcastle.edu.au/vital/access/manager/Reposi tory/uon:32947.

Burke, P. J., & Crozier, G. (2014). Higher education pedagogies: Gendered formations, mis-recognition and emotion. *Journal of Research in Gender Studies, 4*(2), 52–67. Retrieved from https://www.researchgate.net/publication/272941068_Higher_Education_Peda gogies_Gendered_Formations_Mis-recognition_and_Emotion.

Crawford, N., & Johns, S. (2018). An academic's role? Supporting student wellbeing in pre-university enabling programs. *Journal of University Teaching & Learning Practice, 15*(3), 2. Retrieved from https://ro.uow.edu.au/jutlp/vol15/iss3/2/.

Crawford, N., Lisciandro, J., Jones, A., Jaceglav, M., McCall, D., Bunn, R., … Andersen, S. (2016, December). *Models of support for student wellbeing in enabling programs: Comparisons, contrasts and commonalities at four Australian universities.* Paper presented at the Foundation and Bridging Educators New Zealand Conference. Auckland, NZ. Retrieved from http://ecite.utas.edu.au/115259.

Crawford, N., Olds, A., Lisciandro, J., Jaceglav, M., Westacott, M., & Osenieks, L. (2018). Emotional labour demands in enabling education: A qualitative exploration of the unique challenges and protective factors. *Student Success, 9*(1), 23–33.doi:10.5204/ssj.v9i1.430.

Cvetkovski, S., Reavley, N. J., & Jorm, A. F. (2012). The prevalence and correlates of psychological distress in Australian tertiary students compared to their community peers. *Australian and New Zealand Journal of Psychiatry, 46*(5), 457–467. doi:10.1177/0004867411435290.

Dweck, C. S. (2008). *Mindset: The new psychology of success.* New York: Random House Digital, Inc.

Engstrom, C., & Tinto, V. (2008). Access without support is not opportunity. *Change: The Magazine of Higher Learning, 40*(1), 46–50. doi:10.3200/CHNG.40.1.46–50.

Gatens, M. (1991). *Feminism and philosophy: Perspectives on difference and equality.* Oxford: Polity Press.

Goralnik, L., Dobson, T., & Nelson, M. P. (2015). Place-based care ethics: A field philo-sophy pedagogy. *Canadian Journal of Environmental Education (CJEE), 19,* 180–196. Retrieved from https://cjee.lakeheadu.ca/article/view/1279.

Goralnik, L., Millenbah, K. F., Nelson, M. P., & Thorp, L. (2012). An environmental peda-gogy of care: Emotion, relationships, and experience in higher education ethics learning. *Journal of Experiential Education, 35*(3), 412–428. doi:10.1177/105382591203500303.

Grosz, E. (1995). *Space, time and perversion: The politics of bodies.* New York: Routledge.

Healthy Universities. (2019). *What is the UK Healthy Universities Network?* Retrieved from https://healthyuniversities.ac.uk/about-the-network/.

Higher Education Standards Framework. (2015). Australian Government, Department of Education and Training. Retrieved from https://www.legislation.gov.au/Details/ F2015L01639/Download.

Higher Education Standards Panel. (2018). *Final report – improving retention, completion and success in higher education.* Retrieved from https://docs.education.gov.au/node/50816.

Hodges, B., Bedford, T., Hartley, J., Klinger, C., Murray, N., O'Rourke, J., & Schofield, N. (2013). *Enabling retention: Processes and strategies for improving student retention in university-based enabling programs: Final report 2013.* Retrieved from http://enablingeducators.org/resources/CG10_1697_Hodges_Report_2013.pdf.

Isenbarger, L., & Zembylas, M. (2006). The emotional labour of caring in teaching. *Teaching and Teacher Education,* 22(1), 120–134. doi:10.1016/j.tate.2005.07.002.

Jarvis, L. (2018). *Risk or opportunity: The journey of students entering university via an enabling program.* Doctoral thesis, University of Wollongong, Wollongong, Australia. Retrieved from https://ro.uow.edu.au/theses1/503/.

JED Campus. (2019). *JED Campus.* Retrieved from https://www.jedcampus.org/.

Kift, S. (2009). *Articulating a transition pedagogy to scaffold and to enhance the first year student learning experience in Australian higher education: Final report for ALTC Senior Fellowship Program.* Strawberry Hills, NSW. Retrieved from http://transitionpedagogy.com/reports-andresources/fellowship-report/.

Kift, S. (2015). A decade of transition pedagogy: A quantum leap in conceptualising the first year experience. *HERDSA Review of Higher Education,* 2, 51–86. Retrieved from www.herdsa.org.au/herdsa-review-higher-education-vol-2/51-86.

Kift, S., & Field, R. (2009, July). *Intentional first year curriculum design as a means of facilitating student engagement: Some exemplars.* Paper presented at the Proceedings of the 12th Pacific Rim First Year in Higher Education Conference. Queensland University of Technology, Townsville, Queensland. Retrieved from https://eprints.qut.edu.au/30044/.

Kift, S., Nelson, K., & Clarke, J. (2010). Transition pedagogy: A third generation approach to FYE: A case study of policy and practice for the higher education sector. *The International Journal of the First Year in Higher Education,* 1(1), 1–20. doi:10.5204/intjfyhe.v1i1.13.

Lane, J., & Sharp, S. (2014). Pathways to success: Evaluating the use of 'enabling pedagogies' in a university transition course. *GSTF Journal on Education,* 2(1), 66–73. doi:10.5176/2345-7163_2.1.45.

Larcombe, W., Finch, S., Sore, R., Murray, C. M., Kentish, S., Mulder, R. A., … Williams, D. A. (2016). Prevalence and socio-demographic correlates of psychological distress among students at an Australian university. *Studies in Higher Education,* 41(6), 1074–1091. doi:10.1080/03075079.2014.966072.

Lisciandro, J., Jones, A., & Strehlow, K. (2016, July). *Addressing social and emotional learning: Fostering resilience and academic self-efficacy in educationally disadvantaged learners transitioning to university.* Paper presented at the Students Transitions Achievement Retention and Success (STARS) conference, Perth, WA. Retrieved from https://researchrepository.murdoch.edu.au/id/eprint/33032/1/09A.pdf.

Motta, S., & Bennett, A. (2018). Pedagogies of care, care-full epistemological practice and 'other' caring subjectivities in enabling education. *Teaching in Higher Education,* 23(5), 631–646. doi:10.1080/13562517.2018.1465911.

Noddings, N. (2002). *Educating moral people.* New York: Teachers College Press, Columbia University.

Noddings, N. (2005). *The challenge to care in schools: An alternative approach to education* (2nd ed.). New York: Teachers College Press, Columbia University.

Okanagan Charter. (2015). *Okanagan Charter: An international charter for health promoting universities and colleges.* Retrieved from http://www.healthpromotingcampuses.ca/okanagancharter/.

Orygen. (2017). *Under the radar: The mental health of Australian university students.* Retrieved from https://www.orygen.org.au/Policy-Advocacy/Policy-Reports/Under-the-radar.

Plumwood, V. (1986). Ecofeminism: An overview and discussion of positions and arguments. *Australasian Journal of Philosophy*, 64(sup1), 120–138. doi:10.1080/00048402.1986.9755430.

Plumwood, V. (1991). Nature, self, and gender: Feminism, environmental philosophy, and the critique of rationalism. *Hypatia*, 6(1), 3–27. doi:10.1111/j.1527–2001.1991.tb00206.x

Seary, K., Willans, J., & Cook, C. (2016). Design for success: Did we get it right? Measuring the success of STEPS as a remodelled CQUniversity enabling offering. *International Studies in Widening Participation*, 3(1),4–18. Retrieved from https://novaojs.newcastle.edu.au/ceehe/index.php/iswp/article/view/41.

Slavin, S. J. (2016). *How can academic educators rethink teaching and learning to better support student wellbeing?* Paper presented at the National symposium: Student wellbeing matters, The University of Melbourne. Retrieved from http://unistudentwellbeing.edu.au/wp-content/uploads/2016/09/Slavin-Presentation-20160909.pdf.

Stallman, H. M. (2010). Psychological distress in university students: A comparison with general population data. *Australian Psychologist*, 45(4),249–257. doi:10.1080/00050067.2010.482109.

Storrie, K., Ahern, K., & Tuckett, A. (2010). A systematic review: Students with mental health problems—a growing problem. *International journal of nursing practice*, 16(1),1–6. doi:10.1111/j.1440–172X.2009.01813.x.

Tronto, J. (1993). *Moral boundaries: A political argument for an ethic of care*. New York: Routledge.

Tronto, J. C. (2005). An ethic of care. In A. Cudd & R. Andreasen (Eds.), *Feminist theory: A philosophical anthology* (pp. 251–263). Oxford: Wiley-Blackwell.

TWANZ. (n.d.). *Tertiary Wellbeing Aotearoa New Zealand*. Retrieved from https://www.twanz.ac.nz/.

WHO. (2019). The Ottawa Charter for Health Promotion: First International Conference on Health Promotion, Ottawa, 21 November 1986. Retrieved from http://www.who.int/healthpromotion/conferences/previous/ottawa/en/.

THE EDUCATORS' TIPS FOR RISING TO THE CHALLENGES OF THE SPACE (PART III)

Reflect on your core beliefs about learning and teaching and develop your own educational philosophy: you need to assess your own assumptions and thinking about the purpose of education and think critically about your role in challenging or reproducing dominant ideologies.

(Wanner & Wanner)

Work with your academic colleagues not against them: critical pedagogues are not created overnight but also need learning, sharing of knowledge and what works in the classroom. This counteracts the pressures of neoliberal education of individualised teaching and academics/educators competing with each other (for student numbers, for teaching resources, grants etc.).

(Wanner & Wanner)

See students as having potential to succeed. Explicitly open the doors to the academy.

(Ardzenjewksa & Gorzanelli)

Adopt the [academic literacies] framework, its habits of thinking and learning and teaching strategies. Specifically: collaborate with ALL advisors; design curriculum which scaffolds success and positive well-being; adopt a communicative competence hurdle and learn to teach academic literacies (reading and writing).

(Ardzenjewksa & Gorzanelli)

Take notice of the collective wisdom of experienced and long-term enabling educators and reflect carefully about your own philosophy of teaching because that underpins what you do and how you do it.

(Bunn)

Embrace a holistic, student-centred approach in your teaching and learning to support and enhance students' wellbeing. Don't be afraid to be human and caring in the learning environment; learning is a profoundly social experience and relationships are important.

(Crawford, Kift, & Jarvis)

Be aware of the challenges associated with caring and emotional work, and be proactive in looking after your wellbeing: know your limits and boundaries; debrief with your trusted colleagues; and incorporate self-care strategies into your daily practice.

(Crawford, Kift, & Jarvis)

Educators should remain cognisant of the tensions existing in the transitional space; we need to honour the needs of the learner whilst retaining the identity of our academic selves.

(Jones, Olds, & Lisciandro)

16

FINAL MUSINGS FOR THE FUTURE OF TRANSITIONAL EDUCATION

Dr Angela Jones, Dr Joanne G. Lisciandro and Anita Olds

As the pages of these chapters fold behind us, we are left to ponder reoccurring themes of the flourishing liberated learner, dynamic curriculum in spaces of diversity, transformation and challenges to learner identity, academic identity and even the "identity" of transitional education. So, what will the future of transitional education look like? Like a goldfish cannot see the water within its fishbowl, so too can the ubiquitousness of neoliberalism that pressurises the space of higher education remain unseen. We note an undertone (and sometimes an overtone) of rebellion within these writings, and these chapters show that educators within the space of transition not only see it, but 'feel it'. There are key themes of 'resistance' and 'radical teaching' in these pages. As Matisse once uttered, "creativity takes courage" (1998, p. 62), and through their philosophical lens each author has offered us their creative pedagogical responses to the diverse challenges and politics of the transitional space. These final musings tether the common threads of philosophy, pedagogy and practice found within the chapters. They offer insight into future implications for transitional education – the space, the student, and the educator.

Perhaps the strongest evidence for rebellion in these pages is the focus given to the philosophy of emancipation. Social justice remains a clear concern for most authors within this text and much care is taken to explain the conditions necessary to enact emancipation. This focus is unsurprising given its alignment with widening participation goals of many countries. Government agendas such as the "A Fair Go for All" (DEET, 1990) in Australia were created due to a commitment to social justice. There is much acknowledgment therefore in the chapters of the difficulties faced by the disadvantaged in gaining equal access to services and opportunities that enhance their lives. There is also an acknowledgement that university institutions are no longer the home of the elite, that the balance is changing. Universities are increasingly serving the educational needs of students from disadvantaged, low socioeconomic, first in family and/or Indigenous backgrounds, as well as students with disabilities or from rural areas.

The message is strong and clear; for an educational experience to truly enhance the lives of the disadvantaged, transition programs need to ensure that the ideals of social justice are upheld. Many in this book drew from the grandfather of emancipatory education, Freire, to support their position. Freire saw the liberating potential of education. He espoused the importance of actively questioning systems with our students, uncovering the systems that marginalise some and privilege others, in order to help our students achieve new sorts of freedoms (Freire, 1973). Freirean principals can be evidenced in the chapters through the cries for a focus on empowerment through critical literacy. Much talk centred too on the importance of developing self and developing autonomy. Wanner and Wanner explained that empowering students enabled flourishing. Emancipation in practice is no easy feat, particularly in the existing neoliberal context. Fortunately, the chapters of this book have offered the critical pedagogies and the practices, such as the right range of supports, in order to move closer to social justice goals.

As the authors in this book considered how their philosophies of, for example, care, social justice, and flourishing filter into their work, a pattern of successful pedagogies and practices core to the space of transition emerged. Teaching and learning in this space is evidently student-centred, inclusive, and focused on development of the whole student. There is unanimous acknowledgement that a focus on academic skill development is simply not enough to support the transition of non-traditional students to university; their success is a function of their social and academic engagement, development of cultural capital and tied up with their socio-emotional learning (such as the building of self-efficacy, resilience, and growth mindsets). Tinto argued that establishing successful learning communities is key to flourishing students in transition, through lifting their engagement, sense of belonging, confidence, and motivation for learning; a sentiment echoed in the approaches to pedagogy and practice explicated in most other chapters of this monograph. Critical pedagogies and opportunities for transformative learning featured heavily as a response to the desire of educators to enact social justice, emancipate their students from past disadvantage and push back against neoliberalist agendas. The way these pedagogies were implemented in practice were diverse and dependent on an understanding of the nature and needs of the cohort, as we saw in chapters by Hattam and Stokes, Monteith and Geerlings, and Bennett and Bennett. The EduPunks also offered creative solutions to the complexities of straddling multiple educational spaces. Lastly, themes around pedagogies of care were pervasive throughout this monograph, described explicitly by Bunn, and Crawford, Kift, and Jarvis, and observed implicitly across most other chapters – a response to ensuring holistic student development and reducing barriers to successful transition such as poor student mental health and wellbeing. Pedagogies of care also deeply align with philosophies of social justice and flourishing, support widening participation agendas and repel neoliberalist agendas that see students as profit rather than people.

We and other contributors to this monograph recognised and drew on Kift, Nelson, and colleagues' third-generation transition pedagogy model as an organising pedagogical framework for inspiring curriculum, processes, and practices. In our chapter on transition and flourishing, we demonstrated how we have adapted this model more specifically to the enabling education context. Our 'enabling transition' pedagogy model aims to holistically capture and package all of the pedagogical strategies that foster *engagement, belonging* and *learning*. We see all of these pedagogical strategies as essential ingredients for creating inclusive teaching and learning environments, opportunities for transformation and flourishing, and for enacting social justice in this transitional space.

Future musings and implications

In the contemporary higher education space, we recognise that tensions remain between supporting and addressing the needs of our learners, and balancing our own needs as educators and scholars. It is acknowledged too that enabling academics and their students, while increasingly represented in mainstream university, are often placed on the fringes of acceptance, and positioned as 'other'. Historically, enabling students have been written about in deficit terms, however, more and more educators are now recognising the transferable power of the diverse capitals that non-traditional students bring with them to the transitional space. We hope that this manuscript has contributed to a reframing of perceptions about enabling students, educators, and programs supporting transition. By challenging dominant paradigms that remain rooted in traditional understandings of universities, students, as well as neoliberal objectives, transitional education is changing the landscape of higher education. The longitudinal impacts of implementing transitional philosophies, pedagogies, and practices are only beginning to be uncovered in research. In the future we hope to see further research in this area. Transitional education is engaging, inclusive, and transforming the lives of students, their families and communities. It is an exciting and dynamic space that can set the tone for teaching and learning more broadly in higher education.

References

DEET (1990). *A fair chance for all: National and institutional planning for equity in higher education*. Canberra: Australian Government Publishing Service.

Freire, P. (1973). *The pedagogy of the oppressed*. New York:Continuum International Publishing Group.

Matisse, H. (1998) in Brown, C. (Ed.) *Artist to artist: Inspiration and advice from artists past and present*. Corvallis: Jackson Creek Press.

INDEX